# THE LUCKY SEVENTH
## VOLUME II

# HISTORY
# OF
# THE
# SEVENTH ARMORED DIVISION
# AND THE
# SEVENTH ARMORED DIVISION ASSOCIATION

### VOLUME II

Copyright 1987, Seventh Armored Division Association

Headquarters: 23218 Springbrook Drive, Farmington Hills, Michigan 48024

All rights reserved. No part of this publication may be reproduced in any form, or by any means, without permission in writing from the publisher.

For information on this publication, contact the Seventh Armored Division Association.

Copyright 2011, Seventh Armored Division Association.

Credits:

| | |
|---|---|
| Neil Chapin | Editor and Chairman, Book Committee |
| Carl K. Mattocks | President, Seventh Armored Division |
| Margaret Kemp | Layout and Design |
| Ted Kemp | Consultant |
| Karen Luna | Production Coordinator |

Trade Paperback 10 Digit ISBN: 1-58218-847-5
13 Digit ISBN: 978-1-58218-847-8

**Published by Digital Scanning Inc. Scituate, MA 02066**
**781-545-2100** http://www.Digitalscanning.com *and*
http://www.PDFLibrary.com

# THE SEVENTH ARMORED DIVISION

## VOLUME II

# DEDICATION

KENNETH RAYMOND DANIELSON
1919-1985

This volume of the Seventh Armored Division History is dedicated to Kenneth R. Danielson (DIVISION ARTILLERY), President of the Seventh Armored Division Association from 1981 to 1984. Ken left an indelible mark wherever he went and those of us who knew him will always miss his deep resonant voice, his genuine courtesy, his attention to detail, his individual love for each of us and his unlimited devotion to anything pertaining to the "LUCKY SEVENTH."

## HISTORY COMMITTEE NOTE

Volume I of the Seventh Armored Division History, which was published in 1982, describes in detail the major battles and campaigns and the accomplishments of the Seventh Armored Division in the European Theater of Operations and covers the Association's activities from its inception in 1946 to 1982. Unlike Volume I, which is more official in its content, this book is primarily a pictorial account of the division's actions and focuses on human interest stories and experiences of the men of the division. It is designed to complement Volume I in both the organization of the photographs and stories and appearance.

In addition to the material the History Committee had on hand, this volume contains biographical sketches and "then and now" photos of old and new members of the Association who missed inclusion in Volume I. It also features recent significant memorialization events in Europe and the United States and covers the Association's activities since 1982. Moreover, we have endeavored to include as much of the new material received since the notification of plans to publish Volume II as space permitted.

Despite our best efforts, there will be names and photos missing in this volume because of late submissions and, again, due to space limitations. To those who are affected by these omissions we humbly ask your understanding.

Neil M. Chapin (B/434), Chairman  
Harry E. (Bud) Edelman (147 Sig)  

Norman G.J. Jones (Div QM)  
John Margreiter (C/23)

**WILLIAM A. KNOWLTON**
General, US Army Retired
C.O. Troop B, 87th Cavalry Reconnaissance Squadron

# PREFACE

In March of 1982 our late battlefield leader, Major General Robert W. Hasbrouck, wrote the preface of what was to become our Division History. For him that book represented the culmination of many years spent, along with General Bruce C. Clarke, ensuring our division an adequate place in history and a formal recognition of sacrifice and service.

He would be pleased to know that this second book has come out, devoted not so much to official history as to an opportunity for sharing our photographs and telling what has happened to our lives. Above all, it is one more bond of remembrance to bring us back together.

From his earliest days, man has always celebrated dedicated service in the face of mortal peril. As Vergil wrote of the battles of Aeneas, he penned "... perhaps some day it will be pleasant to remember even these things." Shakespeare wrote lines for King Henry V which had him proclaim, in the face of larger enemy forces, that whoever shared the battlefield that day would be his brother. He also admonished his soldiers to gather on the anniversary of the battle, show their scars and share their reminiscences.

And so we have done for over forty years. The first volume was official history. This is a more light-hearted remembrance in picture and biography. It still memorializes sacrifice and shared service.

WILLIAM A. KNOWLTON
General, U.S. Army Retired

General Hasbrouck being awarded the French Legion of Honor and Croix De Guerre by General Koeltz, CG, 2nd French Corps at V Corps Hq, March 12, 1945

# CONTENTS

| | |
|---|---|
| 11 | Preface |
| 14 | ACTIVATION AND TRAINING |
| 26 | THE LIBERATION OF FRANCE AND THE CROSSING OF THE MOSELLE RIVER |
| 34 | THE NETHERLANDS CAMPAIGN |
| 40 | GERMANY AND THE ROER RIVER |
| 44 | THE ARDENNES |
| 68 | THE RHINE RIVER PLAIN OPERATIONS |
| 72 | REDUCTION OF THE RUHR POCKET |
| 84 | THE ADVANCE TO THE BALTIC SEA |
| 94 | VICTORY — OCCUPATION — DEACTIVATION |
| 108 | THE SEVENTH ARMORED DIVISION ASSOCIATION: 1982-1986 |
| 125 | MEMORIALIZATION |
| 137 | BIOGRAPHICAL SKETCHES |

"Tank Busters" playing for dance at Fort Benning, Ga., February 1944.

31st Armored Regimental Dance Orchestra, formed from the Regimental Band.

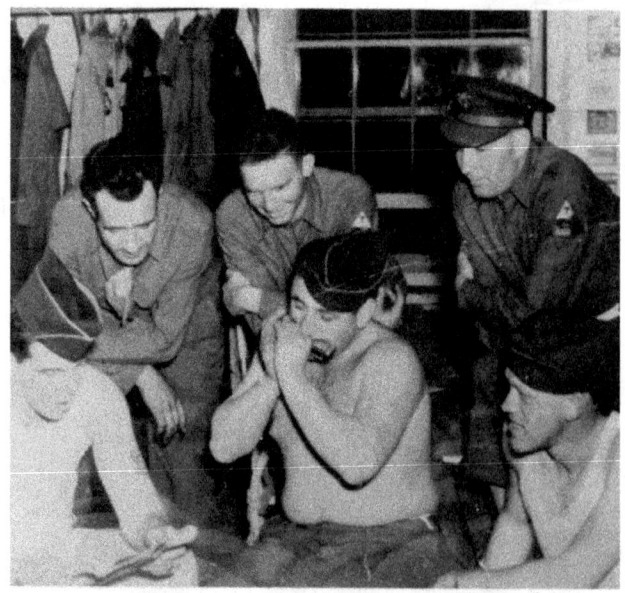
Relaxing in barracks, Co. A, 38th AIB, Fort Benning, Georgia.

# ACTIVATION AND TRAINING
## (March 1, 1942-August 10, 1944)

The Seventh Armored Division was activated March 1, 1942, at Camp Polk, Louisiana, under the command of Brigadier General L. McD. Silvester (who was shortly thereafter promoted to the rank of Major General). At Camp Polk it sweated through training and maneuvers in '42, and grew into a fighting team. It sort of annexed the name "Lucky" at Camp Polk and was referred to as "The Lucky Seventh" when it moved to California for desert training. Here it stayed in and around Camp Coxcomb for five months, learning and perspiring, becoming a fighting outfit. The division went back to the South, arriving at Fort Benning, Georgia, in August, 1943, where it remained until mid-April, 1944, when it staged at Camp Miles Standish, Massachusetts. A week there and then the Seventh went to Camp Shanks, New York, where it stayed until June 6, D-Day in Europe. On that day, the men of the division boarded the Queen Mary in New York Harbor. Debarkation was at Grenock, Scotland, on June 13. Then came Tidworth Barracks, Wiltshire, England, where final preparations were made for entering combat. The call came and on August 7, the Seventh Armored Division rolled to the ports of Southampton and Portsmouth and boarded LCTs and Liberty ships to cross the English Channel. The first boatloads of Seventh Armored Division men and equipment put foot on French soil on August 10, 1944.

31st Armored Regimental Band, Camp Polk, LA.

Sgts. Petty and Cooper, Hq 48th AIB.

Division Field Artillery Air Section, "The Desert Rats." Camp Coxcomb, California, spring of 1943. L-R standing: Carl Clifton, Oscar Vickers, Ned McCord, Regal Leftwich; L-R front row: Mark Miller, Deward Leighton, "Spec Davis."

147th Signal Company Softball Champs. Back row, left to right: Lt. Stidham, Arnold Drewers, Lewis Yuhas, Sim Hardy, Donald Avery, Larry Shaw, Clyde Kumpf, Pat Phalen and Lt. Thompson; Front row: Oscar Hochstein with mascot "Bonnie," John Thackaberry, Ray Winslow, Louis Mellilo, Wally Krass, Robert Uber and Charles Slocum.

The beginning of the 87th Recon Dance Band, Camp Coxcomb, California.

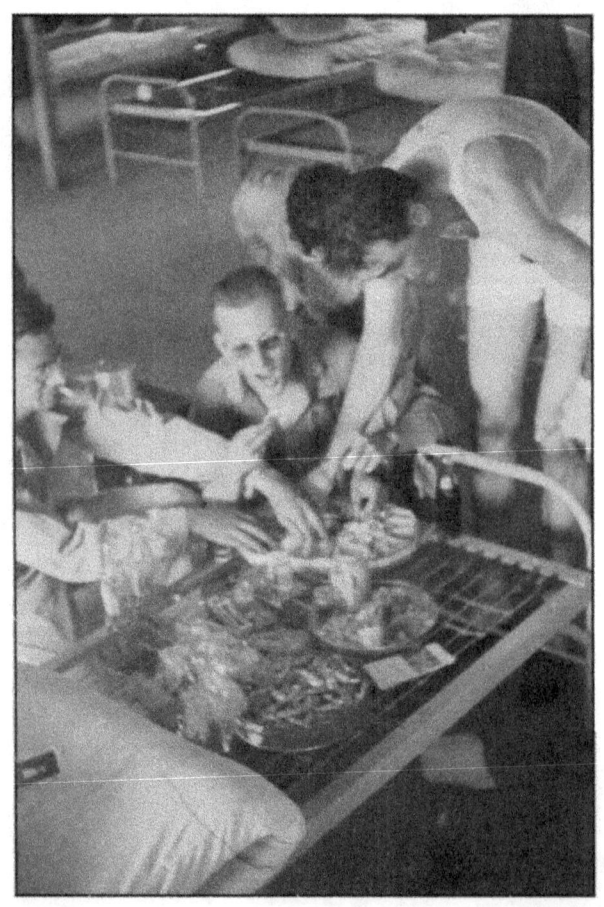

Karl Thies, Harry Edelmann and Henry Choate enjoy "goodies" from home.

Joan Blondell and Susan Hayward with General Silvester. At Camp Coxcomb, CA to entertain troops.

M-8 Assault Gun, Camp Coxcomb.

Division Headquarters Officers at Camp Polk, LA. General Silvester is 5th from left, first row.

Stanley Novak (Hq 31st Tank Bn) in front of M-3 "Grant" tank, Camp Polk, LA, May 1942.

147th Signalmen, L to R: Lewis Yuhas, Robert Hedlund, Don Avery, and Sim Hardy.

Men of Co. B, 48th AIB, Camp Polk, November 1942.

Sgt. Phillips and his Tank Crew.

Halftrack, Desert Maneuvers.

"Care Package" from home.

Mail Call, Louisiana Maneuvers.

William Gleason (Division Hq. Co.) pulling KP, in California Desert

Commando Detachment in full battle dress, Louisiana Maneuvers, 1942

USO Show, Camp Coxcomb.

Assaye Barracks, Tidworth Barracks, England, Lt. Eckstein and Lt. Gwinn.

Artillery Observer Plane, Salisbury Plain England, July, 1944.

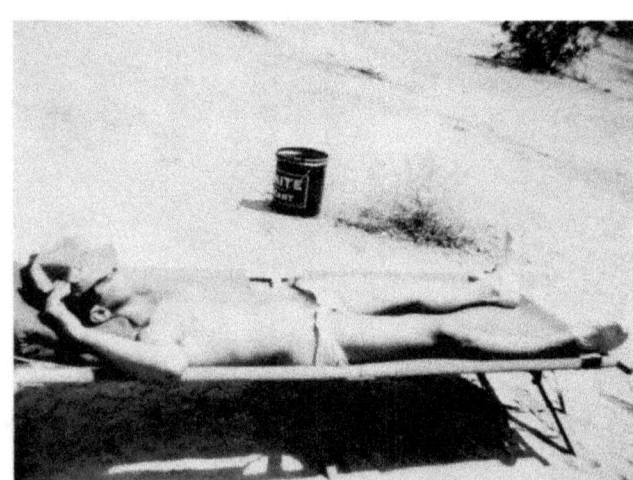
Lt. Laddy Rice tacking a "noon siesta," Camp Coxcomb.

P.X. on a Sunday afternoon, Camp Coxcomb, California.

Pontoon Bridge, Louisiana Maneuvers.

Pvt. Kling loading tank for evacuation, Desert Maneuvers.

Artillery Observer Plane, Salisbury Plain, England, July 1944.

L-R standing: Unknown, Lewiche Picone, Al Plucienski. Kneeling L-R: Bruno Plucienski and Alton Roberts. Probably the only tank crew with two brothers in the Division, Al and Bruno Plucienski. (B-17th Tank Bn.)

Field Exercise, Fort Benning, GA.

Kay Kyser Orchestra performing in California Desert.

Division Artillery Hq. Staff, Tidworth Barracks, England. L-R standing: Col. O. W. Martin, C.O., Maj. Scott, Maj. Rawlings, Maj. Weber, Maj. Safer, Maj. Barardi. L-R front row: Maj. Powers, Capt. Neal, Capt. Barry, Lt. Swan, Lt. Sheehan.

Typical scene, Camp Coxcomb, California.

"Crap Game." Camp Polk, LA.

"Assembly," Camp Polk, LA.

Lt. Joe Tunnell on Field Exercise, Fort Benning, GA.

Outdoor Music Festival on Desert Maneuvers.

Ernest Grattino, 147th Signal Co., on messenger motorcycle.

"Chow Time," Louisiana Maneuvers.

Bus from Camp Polk to Leesville or DeRidder.

"Home away from Home."

Members of B Co., 17th Tank Bn., in Coxcomb Mountains, Desert Training Center, California. L-R: Alton Roberts, Alfred Holt, Unidentified, Edward Ryczak and Sam Lucas.

"MA CHERIE" and her crew on the day she departed Tidworth Barracks, England for Normandy, France, August 1944. (G-2 Section, Hqs. Seventh Armored Division) Major Morris E. Sorenson, Asst. G-2, standing extreme left. Note: Men in this section compiled the statistics and did the art work for "The Box Score" which appears on inside cover of VOL 1 of Division History.

Mass in the Field, Desert Maneuvers.

Co. B, 48th AIB, Camp Coxcomb, California, April, 1943

"Catholic Mass," Camp Coxcomb, California.

Co. B, 48th AIB, detraining at railhead in Needles, California, 1943.

"Stonehenge," Ancient Druid Temple, located near Tidworth Barracks, England. Lucky Seventh units maneuvered around this site prior to embarking for the Normandy Beaches.

"Laundry" in the Field, Camp Coxcomb, California.

Co. C, 38th AIB Living Quarters, Camp Coxcomb, California.

Typical "Warning."

17th Tank Battalion arriving in France on LST.

Lt. Gen. George S. Patton being briefed by Maj. Gen. Silvester at Division Hq. somewhere in France, August 16, 1944.

# LIBERATION OF FRANCE AND CROSSING OF THE MOSELLE RIVER
(August 10, 1944-September 25, 1944)

From August 10 to August 14, units of the division debarked at both Omaha and Utah Beaches and assembled near La Haye du Puits, France. While some of its troops were still at anchor off the beaches of Normandy, other troops of the division were engaged in bitter initial combat 190 miles to the east, spearheading XX Corps, Third US Army, in the breakthrough operations from the costly beachhead.

During the next three weeks, the Seventh Armored Division rolled some 600 miles (65 miles was the record for one day), and during that 21-day period (August 10 to August 31), the Seventh liberated approximately 150 French towns with an aggregate population of over 350,000. The toll on the enemy had been heavy, but the heaviest losses that the German had suffered were the river lines — barriers — that he had hoped to use to delay the advancing Allied armies. The spearheading Seventh Armored had wrecked his plans — from Normandy to Verdun — the World War I famous city was taken by the division's troops.

For six long days the division waited at Verdun for gasoline. Word came down from XX Corps that the division would, when it got gasoline, advance to the east in multiple columns to seize crossings over the Moselle River at Metz, France. There were many things that didn't meet the eye on this planned junket, and there were enough things visible to discourage the doughtiest. The weather was bad; it had rained for days, and the terrain was highly unfavorable to armored operations.

What the troops couldn't see from their areas around Verdun was the minutely-laid-out perimeter defense of the city of Metz. The Metz locale was honeycombed with concrete forts that were so old the earth had almost swallowed them into her makeup, but they had been modernized by the enemy, and interconnecting underground passages were numerous. Moreover, the whole perimeter approach to Metz was dominated by the city's garrison; artillery pieces looked down from every fort and from every high point of ground. The garrison consisted of the students and faculty of a military school located there, and every member had fought school problems over the whole area that had to be conquered. As has been said, there was a lot that didn't meet the eye.

When the Seventh hurled its strength against the renowned fortress city, it was the first American division to batter at the place — the first of several to pour brave men into a bitter, lengthy battle.

Finally, after overcoming all the bitterest of opposition, the troops of the division reached the Moselle south of Metz. Near the French hamlet of Dornot it marked up another distinction for the command by forcing a crossing of the river and establishing a bridgehead and holding it against fanatic Germans in the face of more artillery pounding directed on the bridge site from the nearby heights and from commanding forts. This crossing was made in conjunction with the Fifth Infantry Division, but Seventh Armored men were the first across the muddy Moselle on the night of September 8, 1944.

The heavy fighting and the inch-by-inch progress continued after the Moselle was bridged. The division fought from hill mass to hill mass, from town to town, killing the enemy that barred the way and destroying his machines. Every inch of ground was contested; every inch was fought for and won. Prisoners were few; the battlefields were dotted with enemy dead.

Troops of the division had fought their way to the Seille River, well to the east of the Moselle, when orders arrived on September 24, carrying it to Holland.

Fred H. Johnson, Div. Ammo. Officer, watching off-loading of LST on Omaha Beach, France.

Train Station in Metz, September 1944.

Tanks of the 40th Tank Bn. rumbling through Arpajon, France, 1944.

World War I Memorial at Verdun.

German General Von Gutnecht and Staff captured by "CCA" near Provence, France, September 1944.

One of our tanks has been hit by enemy fire.

Seventh Armored Medic gives first aid to a wounded German Officer, near Chartres, France, August 15, 1944.

## CROSSING OF THE SEINE RIVER
by John E. Kennedy, Jr.

At Melun southeast of Paris, the Germans defended well against our initial attempt to cross the Seine. Having driven straight towards the city versus disorganized resistance, we were abruptly stopped there. Our attempt to force a crossing in the heart of the town, where our approach to the bridge site was restricted to city streets and was hindered by a railroad underpass, was repulsed. At the crossing site the river was unusually wide and was divided by an island in its middle. To my dismay we faced two river crossings. Against determined resistance, small parties of engineers and infantry got to the island. Lt. Brandt, 33rd Armd Engr Bn. was there, wounded. Boats with Red Cross flags to the island were fired upon. General Walton Walker (Corps Comdr) arrived. Pacing the near shore, he ordered an immediate crossing which was simply impossible under the existing conditions.

Unable to do more I returned rearward in despair. At the west of town, wondering what really was needed, and realizing I could never know without being there I turned again towards the river. This time I was blocked by the railroad embankment. The underpass was now under intermittent fire, and the approach to the river seemed effectively blockaded. Our columns were stopped. The traffic jam was bad.

On the second morning I was delegated to reconnoiter elsewhere for an assault crossing site. Aerial photographs were lacking, but we had good maps, from which it was possible to identify four likely locations, all downstream from Melun towards Paris.

It was a beautiful September morning, the 23rd, when I departed along the main highway towards Paris, paralleling the river, to inspect and compare them. Our divisional formations faded away to my rear and no others were in the zone to our left. No friends or enemy or civilians were anywhere to be seen. Kilometer markers indicating my distance from Paris clicked by. Orly Field was less than twenty miles distant. My driver and I wondered if we could motor unopposed into the city to become the first of its liberators there to arrive.

As glorious and appealing as that seemed, it was not to be, for the mission was urgent and time short. The location which from map reconnaissance seemed best was a ferry site surrounded by a settlement of houses and barns about ten miles downstream from Melun.

On arrival there no one was in view. Dismounting at the river bank to examine the texture of the soil and to plan the traffic patterns and the unloading points, we seemed to be in a deserted fairyland from an Engineer Field Manual. It was perfect. Concealed unloading areas for assault boats; concealment for the infantry; ample unloading and turn around space for bridge trucks; double trails to and from the bridge site affording good circulation; even the geography of the river cooperated with its convex curve for converging fire on the opposite bank. Perfect!

Somehow the environment was strange. There seemed to be no enemy anywhere. Yet the civilians were all gone. And where were our troops? CCA, and an Infantry Division of the Corps who were supposed to be closing on the river line from the West were miles away.

As I walked along the river bank I knew this was a school solution. We remounted our jeep and went up the slope about 200 feet to the road along the river. All was peaceful. We were startled out of our wits by a man wearing his FFT brassard who jumped over a small wall calling "par ici" (this way). He led us to the attic of a large two-story house next to our beautiful crossing site and pointed across the river to what I judged was a light infantry battalion or maybe two companies, well dug in, directly in face on the opposite side. To conceal their position they had not shot at us at the river bank.

On my return, my recommendation was accepted: CROSSING AT 1500 HOURS (3 PM). As I observed and helped guide its occurrence, what a fantastic tribute I thought this was to the excellence of American arms. In some six to eight hours from its selection we mounted a coordinated river crossing assault. Knowing the order, and with one eye on my watch, I saw our planes come in to strafe at exactly H hour minus five minutes, and heard our outbound artillery ("outbound mail" we called it) also exactly on time. Whence they came I don't know, but next I saw CCA Infantry behind the hedgerow married with engineer assault boat crewmen and boats. Out of the book!!! The assault was successful. Unhappily a German sniper had a temporary success. He shot through the head a sergeant standing on the river bank in conversation with me and one other. We did not know we were in small arms line of fire.

Next a sad event occurred. There was a small cottage on the river bank, which during my earlier reconnaissance I had ignored. A young woman emerged who shortly after was killed by the sniper. An older man, surely her husband or father, dashed to the river and splashed in to swim across and avenge her death. Some soldiers restrained him.

Someone located the sniper's position. A tank came forward and blasted into the trees on the other side. End of sniper.

Building the bridge should have been a two or three hour job. Unhappily, two occurrences delayed it until the next daylight.

1. Enemy artillery fire, which was not eliminated because of the dug-in infantry who slowed our advance, knocked out engineer truck-mounted air compressors needed to inflate the pneumatic pontoons. Time was lost while replacement compressors came forward.

2. A summer rain squall occurred with thunder and lightning and gusts of wind. At an upstream inflation point one pontoon (or more, I was not there) broke its moorings. One of our sergeants was decorated for holding the hawsers to save a pontoon until help arrived, though the rope slipped through his palms, as he gripped with all his might, and peeled away the skin and muscles of his hands. Clouds obscured all starlight and moonlight. Our bridge crews had to work in total darkness.

Because of these unforeseen complications, enemy artillery fire on the bridge site and adverse weather conditions, the estimated time for completion was advanced repeatedly. Finally near daybreak our first vehicles crossed. One by one they mired in mud on the far shore. It was another problem for the engineers, which further delayed the division's crossing. At last, about sixteen to eighteen hours after the assault, our crossing was affected and the column was again rolling.

*Note: This is the personal account of the Seventh Armored Division, a crossing of the Seine River on August 23-24, 1944, by Captain John E. Kennedy, Jr., Division Engineer Reconnaissance Officer. This is a particularly significant story in view of another division's claim to have crossed the Seine River first in this vicinity.

General Silvester greets General Patton near Melun, France.

Capt. Posey's Combat Liaison Team (129th Ord. Bn.) just before Metz.

One of the many German planes knocked down.

L to R: Platoon Sge. Tom Daily, Platoon Leader Lt. Bill Knowlton and Rifleman Wade Jutchins. (2nd Platoon, Troop E, 87th Recon Sqdn.) France, August 1944.

Crossing the Seine River at Melun, France.

Crew of Halftrack in Verdun.

A "downed" German fighter plane.

French townspeople viewing arrival of the "Lucky Seventh."

One of our medium tanks knocked out on the approach to Verdun.

"Lucky Seventh" column passing through Arpajon, France.

Maintenance and rest time in France. Bob Blake is in the middle (B-87th Recon.).

Knocked-out German "Command Car."

Sgt. John Avila, T/4 Frank Clouse, Pfc. George Dyer, and Pvt. James Byland waiting to cross river at Epernay, France. Clouse was later KIA in January, 1945. (D-87th Recon.)

Pontoon bridge over the Moselle River.

German tank captured by "Lucky Seventh."

Gen. Silvester awarding the "Purple Heart" to Pfc. Thomas A. Rowan, (Co. A, 48th AIB) at Verdun, France.

33rd Armored Engineer Bn. taking prisoners.

An M-7 105mm. Artillery piece of Battery C, 434th Armored Artillery Bn., in action.

French Military Liaison Team with the Seventh Armored Division. 2nd from left, kneeling, Association Member, Nick Daniloff, (B-203 AAA). Standing, on left, Major Marcel Miltat, Chief, 7th Armored Division Military Mission.

L-R: Gen. Silvester, Col. Rosebaum and an English Captain at CCA Hq. located outside of Verdun, early September 1944.

Bridge at Fontainebleau, France, destroyed by the Germans to slow the advance of the "Lucky Seventh."

Gen. Silvester congratulates T/Sgt. Grady H. Blazier, Co. C, 48th AIB, on his receiving a Battlefield Commission near Arnaville, France, September 23, 1944.

Self-propelled Artillery crew at the 434th Armored F.A. Battalion.

Troops of 23rd AIB meet French girls in Chartres, France, (LIFE Magazine photo, August, 44).

Entering Chateau — Thierry, France.

Gen. Silvester (left) outlines the tactical situation north of Overloon, Holland, to British Officers preparing to take over that sector with their units, October 7, 1944.

British Lt. General Sir Richard N. O'Connor, pins 2nd Lt. bars on Sgt. Robert Rummer.

Gen. Silvester watches British engineers working on a dynamited bridge over a canal near Grindtsveen, Holland. The repaired bridge was later used by the "Lucky Seventh."

# THE NETHERLANDS
(September 26-November 7, 1944)

The Seventh Armored Division moved rapidly from the Metz area across Belgium and Luxembourg to Holland. The division became a part of the First US Army and was assigned the mission of clearing the Peel Swamp west of the Maas (Meuse) River. Vortum, Holland, was attacked on September 30, with CCB as the striking force. Along the route to the town, the troops met strong anti-tank gun and enemy bazooka fire and overcame it, wiping out the defenders and rolling on. The leading elements captured Vortum on October 2, and the Seventh had liberated its first Holland town.

Overloon, another small town, was attacked by CCA simultaneously with "B's" attack on Vortum. It was a much more difficult task — the taking of Overloon. It was heavily defended by German paratroops and former German Air Force personnel, fighting from well-prepared positions.

The going was tough. Tanks, canalized as they were on the roads through the swampy area, were held up by carefully sited anti-tank weapons. A lot of the enemy's guns were knocked out, but there seemed always to be others "just around the corner." The infantry, however, battled its way to the outskirts of Overloon during the late afternoon of October 1. The doughboys were under heavy artillery fire, as they had been all the way to the town, and there were a lot of Nebelwerfers ("Screaming Meemies") to contend with, too, but they dug in to defend what they had fought so hard to gain. Elements of the division assaulted the town for the next several days, but enemy fire held the force on the outskirts of Overloon.

On October 8, the division was assigned to another army — this time the British Second, under command of Lt. Gen. Miles C. Dempsey. General Dempsey had a more important mission for the division — that of protecting the vital right flank of the British-Canadian drive to clear the northern and western approaches to the strategically important port of Antwerp. (The Seventh Armored is now officially credited with saving this campaign from possible disaster.)

The division's mission was purely defensive — a new role for this armored force — and it was disposed accordingly. There were a few battles to gain ground more advantageous to the defense, and there were local victories gained by the Seventh, but for the most part the command was spread out fanlike across the canal-laced flatlands — watching, patrolling, keeping alert. The Seventh was spread thin over a 22-mile front, hinged in the center on Meijel, and stretching to both north and south on canal lines. The "line," so called, consisted of a number of outposts of a few men each, sometimes as much as 800 yards apart. German patrols had been active, and the weather had kept Allied air patrols on the ground. Enemy intelligence evidently had become well informed as to the Division's precarious position, for it was at this time that the German launched his now famous counterattack designed to disrupt British operations on Antwerp. The German did not, however, with all his carefully laid plans, give full enough consideration to the fighting spirit of the separated groups of the American Seventh Armored, or their collective potency.

For the next three days the Germans repeatedly struck the Seventh Armored Division positions with numerically superior forces. Enemy artillery support for all of the operations in this counterattack was heavy and the armor was bountiful. Prisoners yielded the information that the forces involved were the crack Ninth Panzer Division and the 15th Panzer Grenadier Division, plus thousands of oddments — mostly engineers and former Luftwaffe personnel.

The defensive positions established by the Seventh were consolidated and were taken over after dusk on the 29th by the reinforcing troops of Gen. Dempsey. The gallant men of the Division had accomplished the assigned mission. At no time during those three days was a superior German force able to crack the will or the lines of the units of the division. There had been withdrawals, granted, but that was with a view to economy of personnel, and the mission in mind. The big thing was that the Germans had not gotten through!

On November 6, the Seventh Armored Division was ordered to the Ninth US Army. Thus ended the Seventh's Holland campaign.

PREPAREDNESS!

A place called home by infantrymen of the "Lucky Seventh."

33rd Engineer Bn soldier using a flamethrower.

Division Headquarters (building to left of church) near Heerlen, Netherlands, November 1944.

Capt. Arthur, left, and Capt. Sorenson, Division Hist. S-2 (right) with German soldiers captured by CCB. Helmond, Netherlands, October 1944.

Demolished bridge over the famous Albert Canal just north of Maastricht, Netherlands, October 1944.

Damaged church in Nederwert, Holland, the Germans kept shelling believing it to be an Observation Post.

Bridge built by 33rd Armored Engineer Bn., over a canal in Holland.

Sherman Tank of the 31st Tank

"Dutch Lassies" in Klimmen, Holland, November 1944: L to R: Mary Meens, Tinie Deckers and Truus Jansfen.

Dutch couple in whose home Hq. Co. CP 23rd AIB was located, Klimmen, Holland, November, 1944.

Canal boat in Holland.

ear Overloon, Holland.

German rocket over Holland.

# 'World War I' Battle Rages In Dutch Town

By Walter Cronkite
United Press Correspondent

WITH AN AMERICAN ARMORED UNIT IN HOLLAND, Oct. 15. — For five days last week, 500 Americans and 800 Germans fought a bloody miniature of World War I in a tiny boot-shaped wood near the crossroads town of Overloon. For 120 nightmarish hours, Americans and Germans with fixed bayonets chased each other from foxhole to foxhole and from tree to tree. They fought without quarter day and night, in sunlight and driving rain.

Finally, the Americans withdrew. They had not taken their objective, but when they left the moans of German wounded filled the air with a chorus of human agony and the stench of the German dead poisoned the pleasant autumn smell of the tiny forest.

The boot-shaped wood had been a trap. Ostensibly, it was held lightly by a German labor battalion and Americans of this armored unit were sent to clean out and solidify Gen. Dempsey's right flank.

### Pillboxes in Dirt Mounds

The 500 infiltrated and met a hail of death. Three mounds of dirt turned out to be pillboxes, and the clearing beside the wood, through which the tanks had planned to roll in a flank movement, turned out to be alive with mines.

The Americans were immobilized on the edge of the wood and then German artillery and "moaning minnies" (huge rocket mortars) blasted their hastily-dug positions. The "labor battalion" turned out to be fanatical German SS troops.

As the initial American thrust spent itself in the face of the murderous fire, the Germans counterattacked and with their light weapons and bayonets the smaller American force stopped them again and again. For five days and nights the battle raged; sometimes the German and American foxholes were only ten feet apart.

### Dawn-Dusk Fighting

At dawn and dusk the Germans went "over the top," charging the nearest American positions. After they were beaten off the German artillery opened up. Following that, the Americans would come hurtling out of their foxholes and the wood resounded with the clatter of steel and the cries of the triumphant and dying. By night, the wood echoed with the constant pop of hand grenades as the Yanks and Jerries tossed them back and forth from foxhole to foxhole.

Finally, the hopelessness of the tank position — nine U.S. tanks had been destroyed by mines and German cross-fire — dictated the withdrawal of the infantry.

As the lieutenant-colonel commanding the battalion ordered the withdrawal over his "walkie-talkie," two Germans appeared out of a bush five feet away and ordered his surrender at gun point. Before the colonel could reply the Germans crumpled under the fire of Americans in the next foxhole. The colonel summed up the battle with "We killed a lot of Germans."

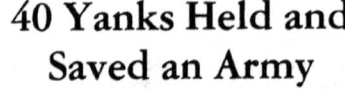

Hq. Squad, 2nd Platoon, Co. B, 48th AIB in Holland, November 1944.

Main intersection in Dutch town of Geldrop. The Lucky Seventh was attached to British 2nd Army at this time, October 1944.

German Commander Hauptman Paul, who lost 80% of his command while defending Overloon against the "Lucky Seventh."

St. Nicholas Church, Meijel, Holland, prior to demolition by the Germans in October 1944.

## 40 Yanks Held and Saved an Army

Fifty yards away, the German Tiger rumbled toward the 40 Yanks of an armored infantry platoon well dug-in in the marshy earth of southern Holland. Quickly a few Americans led by T/Sgt. Harold P. Brown of Dallas, Tex., thrust forward the long snouts of their bazookas and fired. The tank fell back.

For two days and a night, this tank and seven other Tigers had been firing at the small group from point-blank range, never from more than 100 yards away — never nearer than 50.

S/Sgt. Raymond Malionewski, of Detroit, was directing artillery fire on a Nazi position 50 yards from his own — good shooting distance, too. He killed eight Nazis with his rifle fire. Then an 88 came hurling at him, and his leg was broken in three places. T/Sgt. Joe Detchememdy, of St. Louis, took a platoon from Co. A of an armored infantry battalion and wiped out a company of German infantry.

The Americans held.

If they had not, the German counter attack would have swung behind the British-Canadian forces and cut their supply lines, bringing possible disaster to Lt. Gen. Miles C. Dempsey's campaign for Antwerp in late October.

Details of the battle, with official praise from the British for the men of the Seventh Armored Div., have just become known. At the same time, the wraps were down on the strict censorship which has hidden the movements of the "Lucky Seventh" since they ran out of gas after liberating Verdun.

From Verdun, the Seventh, which had spearheaded the Third Army's drive across France, went on to Metz, and forced a bridgehead across the Moselle south of the city. That was in early September. Orders came transferring the division to the U.S. First Army, then storming Aachen.

The division moved up to southern Holland and was clearing the Germans out from west of the Meuse, when it was assigned to protect the right flank of the British Second Army.

In Holland, the division's armor was stretched precariously thin over a 22-mile sector around Meijel. On Oct. 27 the Nazis aimed a counter-attack squarely against the U.S. sector.

The attack was launched against the town of Meijel, held by 43 men in all. Against them came rushing 200 German infantrymen, backed by Tiger and Panther tank formations.

While the Americans were holding there, the Nazis' major offensive developed to the north at Heitsk.

When the Seventh moved away after this engagement Lt. Gen. Dempsey wrote to Maj. Gen. Lindsay M. Sylvester, commander of the division since its activation in March, 1942:

". . . You were heavily outnumbered, but by holding firm as you did, you gave me time to bring up necessary reserves. I appreciate the high fighting qualities which your division showed."

But greater praise came from the German radio. German forces, Berlin said, were engaged in "very heavy fighting with numerically superior forces."

Another view of destroyed St. Nicholas' Church, Meijel, Holland.

## How Yanks Saved British In Holland

WITH THE NORTHERN GROUP OF ARMIES, Nov. 20. — (AP.) — A valorous stand by the American Seventh Armored Division late in October in Southeastern Holland saved the British-Canadian Antwerp campaign from possible disaster, it was announced officially today.

The Seventh delayed and finally helped stop a strong German counterattack against the eastern side of the British Second Army salient into Holland. The Americans were outnumbered three to one.

A spokesman said:

"The Yanks slugged it out toe to toe with the superior enemy forces. Each company fought like a battalion. Each squad fought like a company and each man fought like a lion. Unbelievable heroism was the order of the day."

When the Seventh was moved into Southeastern Holland to protect Lt. Gen. Miles C. Dempsey's right flank during the month-long campaign to clear the northern and western approaches to Antwerp, its armor was stretched precariously thin over a 22-mile section around Meijel.

Knowledge of the situation evidently leaked through to the Germans for on October 27 — when Dempsey's drive was rolling the Germans back toward the Maas in Western Holland and Canadians were liquidating the Nazis along the Scheide — Field Marshall Gerd von Rundstedt aimed a mighty counterattack squarely at the Americans.

For an hour and ten minutes before dawn, German artillery rained shells on the American positions. The town of Miejel was assaulted first.

Forty-three Americans of a cavalry reconnaissance squadron — the Headquarters Platoon of "C" Company and a platoon of assault guns — were pitted against 200 German infantrymen backed by Panther and Tiger tank formations.

An official account related:

"They advanced in three waves, wildly without the caution usually displayed by German troops. In a matter of moments the first two waves had been annihilated."

The Americans were forced to fall back but joined forces with "B" troop of their outfit, counterattacked and kept the Germans busy the rest of the day.

The Ninth German Panzer Division and the 15th Panzer Grenadier Division smashed at the Yanks at Hitak, slightly to the north.

Dempsey ordered reinforcements into the critical battle and told the Americans to hold on.

For two days and a night the Nazi tanks fired at the men, dug in deep in the marshy ground. But when the tanks tried to break through a few Americans popped out of their foxholes and let go with bazookas.

After four days the Germans knew they were licked.

Men of Hq., 38th AIB outside of the house they were billeted in somewhere in Holland, Fall 1944.

British tanks (modified U.S. Shermans) in Holland.

Pfc. D. Halinauskas and Pfc. Corete Maineri, (Co. B, 38th AIB) try on new winter clothing in Holland, October 9, 1944.

This small creamery in Neerkant, Netherlands, was the Command Post for Co. B 17th Tank Battalion. The owner of the creamery is in the picture.

Capt. Tucker looking over the damage to a German village.

Mine field after snow melted.

Road sign outside Aachen, Germany.

# GERMANY AND THE ROER RIVER
## (November 9-December 16, 1944)

After the Holland campaign, the division as an entity remained in rest during the remainder of November — the first relief from combat since August 14. The Division Artillery moved up to support offensive operations of the units in the XIII Corps zone. Other units, too, fought with neighboring divisions. The 40th Tank Battalion worked with the 84th Infantry Division and on November 29 captured Lindern, Germany, and repulsed several German counterattacks before the arrival of the supporting infantry. On December 1, elements of the 17th Tank Battalion moved in with troops of the 102nd Infantry Division to take Linnich, Germany, located on the banks of the now famous Roer River.

The entire division moved into Germany, and there followed a period of intensive planning in preparation for participation in the Ninth US Army's drive into the Rhineland, over the Roer River and deeper into the heart of the Reich. It was during this period that the maintenance crews of the 129th Ordnance Battalion were able, for the first time since the beginning of the campaign, to spend much-needed time in making necessary repairs to combat vehicles of the division — to make every vehicle of the command ready for the next mission. All this while, the troops of the division were experiencing conditions inside the enemy's homeland — a battered generality, a subdued and curiously dangerous-looking civil population, and eternal mud. It was while the division was thusly making itself ready for offensive action that it got alert orders — orders to move quickly and without warning of what was to follow to the general area of Vielsalm-St. Vith, Belgium, far to the south.

General Hasbrouck was at his headquarters at Castle Rimburg, just inside the German border near battered Ubach, when he got the movement orders late on Saturday afternoon, December 16.

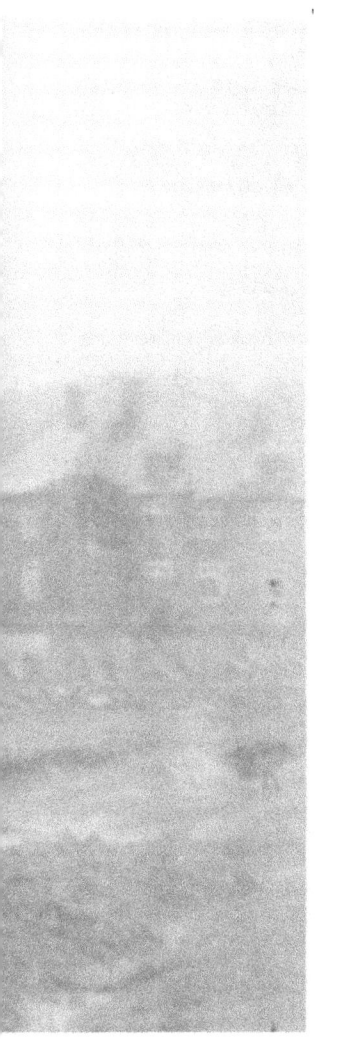

2nd Platoon, Co. B, 48th AIB standing in part of German Siegfried Line.

German Tiger Tank knocked out by the "Lucky Seventh."

Surveying one of our tanks after hitting a mine inside German border.

Before crossing the Roer River in Germany: Lt. Baker, Mau. Stump and Capt. Sveltz.

# THE TEAM

To military strategists an armored division represents the epitome of modern, complex fighting forces. But actually, the patch you'll soon be wearing on your shoulder tells the story. —

— **Blue of Infantry, the Queen of Battle.**

— **Yellow of Cavalry and its tanks, our Sunday punch.**

— **Red of Artillery with its cannon, the bigboys of the battlefield.**

— **All welded into the Lightning that has struck hard, fast, relentlessly against the forces of our enemy.**

That's the team that makes up the 7th Armored Division, together with the highly-specialized and important mechanized reconnaissance, engineer, signal, medical, ordnance and military police units. That's the team that brought war to the soil of Germany for the first time in over a hundred years and the team that will be in on the final push to victory.

At the command of General Hasbrouck and the members of his staff are over ten thousand men. For tactical purposes, the troops are grouped into three Combat Commands. Each one — Combat Command « A », Combat Command « B » and Combat Command « R » — can, if the need arises, fight alone and give a good account of itself. Generally, each has one battalion of armored infantry, one battalion of tanks, and an armored artillery battalion attached to it, together with various smaller detachments.

The « smaller detachments » are drawn from specialized units...

The mechanized cavalry reconnaissance squadron roams ahead and to the flanks of our columns, charged with the dangerous job of scouting for the enemy. Its men fight alongside our tanks and infantry.

The armored engineer battalion builds the bridges, maintains the roads, lays the mines, clears the minefields, and when all that's done, fights up on line with the infantry.

Communications, vital to high-speed operations, are maintained by the signal company

To the medical personnel is entrusted the task of caring for our wounded. From the aid man who races across the battlefield armed only with a medical kit, to the ambulance driver, litter bearer, surgeon — they're all devoted to one ideal, the saving of life.

Maintenance of an armored division that moves and fights on tracks and wheels is the mission of the ordnance battalion.

To help counter the Tiger and Panther Tanks of the enemy, a tank destroyer battalion is attached to the Division.

The military police control the traffic of our forces and take charge of the prisoners of war.

To discourage what's left of the Luftwaffe, an anti-aircraft battalion rolls along with the tanks, halftracks, self-propelled guns and trucks.

And to the trucking companies is assigned the important task of getting men and materiel to the front.

All fighting together to one end — the crushing defeat of the enemy's military forces.

Excerpts from the Orientation Booklet given to all

Almost new "royal King Tiger Tank" captured near Gersonweiler, Germany just prior to moving south into the Battle of the Bulge.

## THOSE TALL STORIES

Ever since the first fish was caught in American waters, our rod-and-reel sportsmen have been famous for the tall stories of « the one that got away ». As the fishermen sat around their evening campfire, the trout they didn't get was always far larger than the one sizzling in the pan.

Well, we're still the same Americans, although the campfires are thousands of miles from home and the game is Tiger Tanks instead of King Salmon. We still like to « embellish the yarn. »

And so, in your Government-sponsored tour of reinforcement depots, you've probably heard blood-curdling tales of front line life from GI's returning to their outfits. A guy with the Purple Heart on his shirt—badge of high courage and sacrifice, don't ever doubt that—has gathered a few new men together and proceeded to « embellish the yarn ». The hazards and hardships of combat are blown up until they'd make even an ETO veteran shake in his combat boots. According to that GI the Jerry tanks are as big as the side of a barn, he's never fought off anything less than a battalion ; every Heinie comes equipped with at least two machine guns. It makes a good story, but that's all it is—a good, tall story.

**So take it for what it's worth. Just file it away in your store of welltold fables, and, above all, don't let it scare you. There's only one person qualified to decide for you just how rough it is up front — and that's you, yourself. Until you get up there and find out for yourself, don't accept any secondhand information.**

You will come to know fear after you go into combat, but fear is a natural reaction. It happens to everyone. It stimulates physical reactions—the heart beats faster, breathing is more rapid; adrenalin flows from a gland inside of you, sugar is released from the liver and made available to the muscles for extra energy ; all parts of the body that are needed for a fight are literally put on a « war-footing » and made ready for instant, violent action.

Combat isn't easy, but don't forget there are over a million of your buddies up there fighting with you. There are a lot of things you'll have to learn and some you'll have to unlearn. But the oldtimers in your outfit will help you through the baptism. After that, its' up to you.

Siegfried Line

« And then there was the time when... »

"Replacements" joining the Seventh Armored Division in Combat

This is the last photograph Signal Corps Combat Photographer Cpl. Hugh F. McHugh (inset) ever made. He was killed by a sniper's bullet shortly after this picture was taken while accompanying Co. A, 23rd AIB, in the vicinity of Wallerode, Belgium, in the attack to recapture St. Vith. (Signal Corps Photo)

View of church in St. Vith, Belgium after the "Lucky Seventh" had recaptured the town, January 1945. (Signal Corps Photo).

# THE ARDENNES
(December 17, 1944-January 29, 1945)

### The Defense of St. Vith

The epic stand of the Seventh Armored Division at St. Vith, Belgium, in the face of Field Marshal Von Rundstedt's now famous "winter offensive" is well documented by military scholars and historians. General Hasbruck's detailed account of the action appears in Volume I of the Seventh Armored Division History.

Following is an Associated Press article of December 30, 1944, by Kenneth L. Dixon, which succinctly portrays the gravity of the situation and captures the fighting spirit of the division.

On the Belgian Front, December 30 (AP). They're all singing praise today for the soldiers of the Seventh Armored Division — those often orphaned waifs of the western front who have been bounced from army to army and had their noses bloodied at almost every turn.

For it was the scrapping Seventh, slung swiftly into the breach when Field Marshal Von Rundstedt's spearhead was stabbing deeply into Belgium's side ten days ago, which put the brakes on the Panzer plunge and finally split the German penetration, forcing the enemy to fight a two-way battle.

More than that the boys sat grimly there alone in the St. Vith sector taking a terrific mauling from half a dozen German divisions — denying them the use of that vital road junction, keeping them partly cut off from supplies and never letting them relax a moment to fight elsewhere.

Often their own supplies were cut off. Sometimes they were sliced into separate segments by attacking armor. But they ploughed through the enemy lines to reach supply dumps or traveled backroads at night. And when individual units were isolated, they formed deadly bands and wrought havoc among German forces until able to rejoin the main body.

### Fought Under Four Armies

Now commanded by Maj. Gen. Robert W. Hasbrouck, Kingston, N.Y., and boasting as its most famous guy, young Lt. Will Rogers, Jr., who is a popular platoon leader, the Seventh has fought under four armies, British and American, during its four months in combat.

It fought through Chateau Thierry and the Argonne Forest, encircled Reims and captured Verdun.

Somehow the Seventh always got hurt, the last big wound was late October when it was forced to hold a thin 25-mile line in the Weert sector of Holland, and had to face the brunt of an overpowering German attack which pounded it plenty.

On Sunday, 17 December, it was ordered to come quickly. Swiftly it split into two combat teams — one headed by Brig. Gen. Bruce C. Clark, and the other by Col. Dwight A. Rosenbaum. Clark's crew struck into St. Vith; Rosenbaum's covered the rear and north flank — both of which promptly became fronts.

Officially the Seventh was ordered to hold St. Vith sector for two days. It held five, despite all six surrounding Nazi divisions could do.

### A Most Savage Force

Although officially they scrapped almost alone without outside help, the Seventh's troops actually accumulated one of the most savage little armies ever seen on an allied front, straggling survivors of two semi-slaughtered units who had fought viciously back to the sector.

They formed a semi-circled front, fanning eastward around St. Vith, which formed the hub of a road network. Slowly the Germans' power crushed all around the Seventh — even back where the division's supply center was set up. The Germans came by the thousands. Col. Andrew J. Adams was in charge of supply trains — long lines of trucks carrying food and ammunition. He was assisted by Lt. Col. Austin A. Miller, as Quartermaster. Everybody turned in and manned a defense system. Finally after the fifth day the Seventh was relieved and ordered into a rest period.

The defense of St. Vith is presented from yet another perspective in the following story. This account was written by the DIVARTY S-3, Major Joseph Safer, as seen from his vantage point in the DIVARTY Fire Direction Center.

## THE BATTLE OF THE BULGE AS SEEN BY THE SEVENTH ARMORED DIVISION ARTILLERY OPERATIONS OFFICER (DIVARY S-3)
### By Joseph Safer

The time: December, 1944. The place: The Ardennes, Belgium. The story... The story concerns the 11,976 men of the 7th Armored Division, the attached elements, and of those American troops who chose to stay and fight it out where other Americans at the same time and place were shamefully abandoning their arms and taking off in a wild, panicky flight to the rear.

We — you and I — are out for what to us is a peaceful Sunday afternoon ride, miles behind the front lines. You are relaxing for the first time in weeks as your half-track moves near the front of Headquarters Battery, 7th Armored Division Artillery, following other vehicles on a well marked route to an assembly area in the rear.

The column stops — moves forward a hundred yards — stops. The executive goes forward to find out what is causing the delay. You notice for the first time noises in the distance: "BRRRRRRRP. BOOOOOM!"

To Major Berardi, the Division Artillery surgeon: "Say, Doc, what's going on? That sounds like German burp guns."

"Sound must be carrying a long way today — there aren't any Germans within a dozen miles of here."

"This column's been halted long enough. I'm going up ahead to find out what the story is."

As you move forward, you hear again the German burp guns, intermingled with a little of what might be artillery or tank gun fire, muffled by distance. It is true that the previous night's message from Corps had warned of enemy paratroopers heading for the area south of Aachen. We're south of Aachen now. You don't suppose...

About this time you find yourself in MALMEDY. You didn't get very far up ahead, any farther than MALMEDY, which was only a mile or two down the road. It was the first town of any size that you had seen since just after lunch. The country had become steadily wilder, more desolate, and colder since you had left EUPEN. Patches of snow had begun to appear, and tightly laced forests of fir trees had closed in upon the road as you rolled along; and now you are in MALMEDY's normally peaceful town square. A large green lawn surrounds a bandshell; large trees provide overhead cover to the square; and the tightly packed houses of the town are close to the street which encloses the square. You see the native population scurrying around, looking excited in a shocked, yet desperate sort of manner, and you are caught momentarily by surprise because you have no idea what has gotten into them.

Stopping a soldier, you find:

"Sir, the Germans have cut the road about three or four miles south of town. They have tanks... the largest thing we have is a bazooka... only a few engineers at a road block up ahead are between them and us... is there anything behind that can help?"

A pause to look around the square. Large, OD colored, 2½-ton trucks are jammed up almost bumper to bumper in the narrow streets ahead of your column, and some are trying to turn around by backing and filling — succeeding only in worsening the traffic jam. A truckload of trousered nurses passes by, coming from the direction in which you are heading, and moving at a high rate of speed through the square.

At this moment, you meet Major Scott, the Division Artillery Executive, standing in the square observing what is going on. Lt. Col. J.G. Dubuisson of the 434th Armored FA Battalion joins you shortly. Scott tells what he has found out about the situation. He verifies the engineer's report that the road up ahead is cut, and states that Lt. Col. Norman Hart's 440th FA Battalion has turned off the main road at this point and is taking a detour to reach the west column. Later reports indicated that the German Armor had followed the 440th part of the way on their detour, almost to STAVELOT, by not more than thirty minutes.

At this point, let's review the situation. Elements of the 7th Armored had been in position in the line north and east of GEILENKIRCHEN, GERMANY. We had been engaged for weeks in short bitter struggles, wresting tenaciously held ground from the Germans. Plans were being made for a quiet Christmas, although we were preparing for a large scale attack to be made at any moment — as part of XIII CORPS. On the 16th, we had received alerts to watch out for unusual German air activity, and had later received vague warnings of German paratroopers being dropped south of AACHEN. Sudden orders had sent the Division on an administrative march to an assembly area in the vicinity of ST. VITH. No combat was expected and, therefore, the various combatant units of the division were fitted into the two columns according to expediency, and not according to combat organization.

Now, back to MALMEDY, where we are holding a hurried conference. Should we follow the 440th, go into position to support the road blocks, or should we try to reach the division by a third route? The route taken by the 440th is decided upon as being unnecessarily dangerous, and all but impassable due to the traffic jammed up in the road ahead. Colonel Dubuisson is at first in favor of supporting the engineers, but after a little discussion, all agree that the mission of the artillery is the support of our own division and plans are made to retrace our route, detouring over back country roads to join the west column.

Radio silence is broken, as Major Scott advises Colonel Martin, the Division Artillery Commander, of the situation. A few minutes later, the radio operator gives Major Scott the answer: "Send in clear. Retrace route, join west column. Open command net."

You and I and Scott study our maps and pick out a possible route by which we could join the west column of our division. We go ahead in a peep (1¼-ton truck), followed by capable Lieutenant Zeilor, our Assistant Communications Officer. At the point where we are to begin our detour, we split our column, instructing the officer in charge of the unit just north of the road junction to remain in place until the last vehicle of the last serial has cleared the road junction.

At this point, we try — without success — to catch the eye of our Anti-Tank Officer, Major Weber, as he practically flies by in his peep, doesn't see us, and goes on in the direction of MALMEDY. Two days pass before we see him again, by which time we have given up for his safety — but he finally shows up with a tale of having been cut off front and rear, and of losing a ¼-ton trailer load of miscellaneous items in the excitement.

Our new route takes us along narrow roads, blacked out — for it is now dark, and much colder. The only illumination is from the weird looking

Three "Lucky Seventh" soldiers comfort an old Belgium woman who was found in the basement of a shattered building in Manhay, Belgium, December 1945. (Signal Corps Photo)

Captain Marvin Utter, Chaplain, 48th AIB assists medics in giving first aid to a wounded infantryman near St. Vith, Belgium. (Signal Corps Photo)

exhaust flames marking the path of the numerous buzz-bombs fluttering overhead continually. Now and then we find the roads blocked by large cargo trucks — and we quickly locate the Commanding Officers and order them to get the road cleared NOW. One turn is so sharp, so dark, and so dangerous that we stop to warn the Executive. It is fortunate that we do stop, for the lead driver does not see the turn and almost leads the column over the embankment. We are lucky that the combination of bad roads, sharp turns, and the black night does not cause any more trouble than it does — but as far as I know, only one major vehicle was lost that night. This was an M-7 self-propelled 105 howitzer of C Battery of the 489th, which had to be destroyed after it turned over on a bridge that later was blown in the face of the advancing Germans.

As if we were planning it that way and were right on schedule, we eventually reached the west route, tying on to the tail end of the west column. Now we think our troubles are over. We are on a road that is bounded on the left by a muddy ditch, paralleled by a high, almost vertical wooded ridge, and on the right by an equally steep and abrupt drop into a damp void, which must be a river some 40 to 50 feet below us. At this point, the stars hide from us, and it begins to rain in a slow, uncomfortable drizzle. We decide to push on and get to the head of the column.

Miles and miles of splashing, skidding, and squeezing bring us to the square of another little town. Vehicles of all descriptions loom up in the black mist, as we wind among the dark narrow canyons bounded by old stone buildings. This is VIELSALM.

You accidentally spot your S-2, who tells us that the Colonel is worried about our artillery's nonappearance in VIELSALM. He also tells us what little he knows of the situation, while he is guiding us to Division Headquarters. There we find Colonel

The ruins of St. Vith, Belgium, after Allied and Nazi bombardment of the town. (Signal Corps Photo)

Martin, who immediately asks where the artillery is.

You tell him the story in a few words. Nearby, in the same room, is the Division Commander, General Hasbrouck. He is studying the maps, and now and then asks a few questions. He is in this even deeper than we are, for the entire load of responsibility is on his shoulders.

Although the head of the west column has reached this town of VIELSALM, it has had difficulty going further because the roads leading forward are practically blocked by routed American troops. Our reconnaissance parties had gone forward and selected positions — but it is impossible to get up to them. I believe that the original idea was for us to get enough forward to support and relieve elements of the 106th Division which were surrounded and cut off. The congested condition of the road will cause our artillery to go into position quite a bit behind the areas originally selected.

You are taken down a pair of wet and muddy ruts two small two story buildings that suddenly loom up in the darkness. We are about a mile northeast of VIELSALM, at VILLE DU BOIS. Our command post is in the larger of the two houses, and some of the advance personnel (our billeting party) are lying around relaxing as much as they can. The fire feels good, but it is not long before we slide back into our uncomfortable bucket seats and leave to rejoin the column.

The trip back is quite wet and miserable. We slide into the ditch once or twice and proceed so slowly that we are able to catch low voiced bits of conversation as we pass the stalled vehicles. We finally pull up opposite our halftrack, dismount and locate the Executive. Another explanation of the situation, and then back to the halftrack to salvage a little sleep. It is then about 0200 on the morning of the 18th, and it seems as though we are barely sitting down before we are moving again.

Some time within the next few hours, we manage to get to VILLE DU BOIS, with our Headquarters Battery closing at 0530. It isn't long before the artillery battalions come roaring down the road, brightening up the situation with their presence. Even as these battalions are going into position just east of VILLE DU BOIS, retreating personnel and heavy equipment are pouring back in disorder on the main road, cutting the battalion areas. The narrow ribbon of road is completely covered by retreating vehicles and personnel. Materiel of all types is being abandoned — even the guns of an 8 howitzer battalion are left, complete with ammunition and in good condition, in the rapidly diminishing friendly area. One 8" howitzer has gone off the road between VIELSALM and VILLE DU BOIS. You stop, temporarily, the salvage attempts of the guns section in order to let the 434th go by.

At 0900 the 434th completes the final phase of its march, and occupies its firing positions. The battalion immediately begins firing on targets of opportunity and enemy installations. Lieutenant Klein is dispatched to the 17th Tank Battalion as forward observer, and the Battery Reconnaissance Officers are dispatched to elements of the 14th Cavalry Group and the 23rd Armored Infantry, who have established a defensive line in the vicinity of PETIT THEIR. Lieutenant Davis is sent out to establish contact with CCB, via a southern route at ST. VITH.

Close on the heels of the 434th, the 489th reaches VIELSALM about 0900, and moves into position as quickly as it can force itself against the flood of troops pouring back in the mad race to the rear. Observers are sent to CCA. After occupying position, fire is placed on observed targets only for the remainder of the day.

We later find out that the 440th had arrived in VIELSALM at approximately 0200 the 18th, going into position immediately prepared to repel any attack, and are now supporting CCR. They also fired only on targets of opportunity called for by their forward observers.

All during the morning, troops from other units (non divisional) continue to pass us going to the rear. Many hours are spent waking up weary drivers who have stopped in the middle of the road and have gone to sleep despite their headlong retreat.

Our efforts pay off, for finally the retreating columns thin out in the early afternoon, and we are left alone to ourselves, a semi-hostile population, and the enemy.

We later find out what had happened to the rest of the division up to this point. General Clark had gone ahead of the CCB column, reaching Headquarters, VIII Corps at BASTOGNE, at 0400. Finding out what little was known of the situation then existing, he set out for ST. VITH, arriving at 1030 — reporting to Commanding General of the 106th Division. There he was requested to launch an attack east from ST. VITH to take and hold SCHONBERG, so as to provide an escape corridor for the elements of the 106th Division that were then cut off from friendly troops. The attack by CCB was prevented by the American troops that were blocking the roads by their withdrawal — so that CCB could not reach the Line of Departure before dark. Even then, enemy patrols contacted CCB, and enemy tanks could be heard moving east of ST. VITH.

CCB then consisted of the 23rd and 38th Armored Infantry Battalions, the 31st Tank Battalion, B Company of the 33rd Engineers, the 87th Cavalry Reconnaissance Squadron (minus one troop), A Company of the 814th Tank Destroyer Battalion, and one platoon of the Reconnaissance Company of the 814th.

This force had been somewhat scattered by the night march over bad roads and there were a number of stragglers who continued to come in all night Sunday. The majority of the force was engaged Sunday afternoon.

The 275th Armored Field Artillery Battalion, commanded by Lieutenant Colonel Clay, was at OBER EMMELS firing on anything they could find — and they were finding plenty. The 275th was one of the few units that had been in the area since the beginning of the German attack and had chosen to fight instead of run away. They had already had some narrow escapes. At one time, German infantry attacking within 200 yards of the gun positions had been repelled by the fire of the 50 caliber machine guns mounted on the M7s (self-propelled 105-mm howitzers). As CCB came up into the attack, the forward observers contacted the front line units of CCB and immediately began giving them excellent artillery support.

CCA, coming along behind CCB, was sent to the vicinity of POTEAU to protect the north, or left flank. CCA had the 40th Tank Battalion, the 48th Armored Infantry Battalion, A Company, 33rd Engineers, and D Troop, 87th Cavalry Reconnaissance Squadron.

CCR, which had taken the same route as the Artillery originally was ordered to take, and had proceeded ahead of the Artillery Column, went directly to RECHT, through MALMEDY, evidently just clearing the point where the German column a few minutes later cut off the Artillery. CCR had the 17th Tank Battalion, C Company of the 38th Armored Infantry Battalion, C Company of the 38th Armored Infantry Battalion, C Company of the 33rd Engineers, and B Company of the 814th. Arriving in RECHT about 1300, CCR set up their CP and sent a peep driver out after Colonel Ryan, who was due in. The peep driver returned at 1530 reporting that he couldn't get through because of the presence of the enemy. CCR alerted their troops, established road blocks and posted guards.

About 1630, one of the guards stopped a soldier who turned out to be the driver for Colonel Mathews, our Chief of Staff. The driver told how he and the Colonel had run into an enemy column — with both diving out of their peep — the Colonel going one way, while the driver fell into a ditch by the side of the road. Approximately 75 enemy vehicles passed his position, he reported, including about 30 tanks. He then traveled on foot until stopped by CCR guards. It later developed that Colonel Mathews was killed about this time while firing at German infantry with a carbine.

The fighting Sunday and Monday was furious. The enemy had a large amount of armor and artillery along with large concentrations of troops. The enemy counterattacks were almost continuous. As a rule, tanks, and infantry in armored carriers or on foot, would attack, supported by artillery, anti-tank guns, mortars, nebelwerfers, self-propelled guns — everything the Krauts had. From various reports taken from prisoners, it was estimated that the enemy could muster more than 83,000 troops against us at this time.

And so, we come to the immediate situation on Monday, the 18th of December. At ST. VITH, CCB of the 9th Armored Division, the one remaining regimental Combat Team of the 106th Infantry Division (the 424th Combat Team), and 112th Regimental Combat Team of the 28th Infantry Division, are in position in a general quarter circle starting 2000 yards south of ST. VITH. Each of these three teams had been cut off from their parent units when the front folded and are putting up their best possible effort to stop the advancing Germans. In this general area are five artillery battalions not including our organic three. There are the 16th Armored Field Artillery Battalion of the 9th Armored, the 591st FA Battalion of the 106th Infantry Division, the 275th Armored FA Battalion which was attached previously to the 106th, and the 229th FA Battalion of the 28th Infantry Division. All of the above are 105-mm howitzers, and except for the armored battalions, truckdrawn. In addition, the 965th FA Battalion (155-mm howitzer) (minus one Battery until 22 December) is literally picked off the road and pressed into use. All of the above, except the 16th FA, are placed under control of the 7th Armored Division Artillery. The depleted state of their trains make it necessary for us to supply them at least partially — particularly with ammunition.

The next few days are repetitious of the first ones, but the action is developing into an even harder and

German tank still stands in Grandmenil, Belgium. Photo taken in 1983.

47

more bitter struggle. It is immediately evident that this general area and in particular, the towns of POTEAU and RECHT are of paramount importance to the success of the breakthrough. Through these towns and through the town of ST. VITH run the only two major roads in this sector. Failure on the part of the Germans to control these roads would necessitate long detours on the part of combat units and especially the supply vehicles. This makes for the double disadvantage to the Germans of additional time and especially additional gasoline.* In addition, these roads lead to the main objectives of the!German breakthrough, and are on the main route to LIEGE. ST. VITH is also the hub of a rail network and the only rail center between the Rhine and Ardennes capable of serving as a rail depot to support the entire counter-attack. From the German point of view, they must control this area or have their entire operations seriously threatened.

We are already out of touch with ARMY, and for a short while, are in touch with only Corps. Extra artillery is promised us by Corps, but it never comes. You think of what Corps Artillery Liaison Officer — his two short, nervous visits to us, and his rapid departures from our CP on most urgent business to the rear. After his second departure, we never see him again, nor do we hear from Corps anymore.

Tuesday, the 19th of December, is again cloudy and rainy, with poor visibility. The 434th is attached to CCB together with the 275th and 965th (Minus 1 Battery), which are formed into a group under the control of the 434th. The 440th is placed in direct support of CCR and the 489th is in direct support of CCA. In order to achieve maximum support, the 434th is moved to the vicinity of CROMBACH and the 275th to HINDERHAUSEN.

Tuesday morning is relatively quiet, consisting mostly of patrol skirmishes and occasional enemy artillery. Most of our vehicles that had been missing on the march begin to show up. By early afternoon, activity has increased, with the enemy starting to counterattack again — especially on the CCA area, where CCA is massed to meet a determined effort at a breakthrough into VIELSALM near POTEAU. T.F. Albright is organized in the vicinity of PETIT THIER — being made of combat engineers, tank destroyers, remnants of an AA Battery, and what other miscellaneous troops that can be found. This task force is typical of our defenses — which have taken advantage of anything and everything available.

One typical incident is that of the ten engineers holding TROIS PONTS. Reports tell of their blowing the bridge northeast of town and being ready to blow the rest. These ten engineers established a road block on the TROIS PONTS-STAVELOT road to the east of the bridge they have blown. At this roadblock, the reports say, these engineers held off seventeen German tanks and an unknown number of German infantry, until relieved. Such acts as this were typical results of the determination of those Americans fighting the enemy.

Although our artillery fires a lot on this day, most of it is on targets of opportunity, including infantry and tanks, and on enemy counterattacks, which are constantly increasing in strength — especially in the ST. VITH area. There is still no registration — a cotton wool fog shrouding the country and limiting visibility. It is apparent that the supply situation is reaching a critical stage at this period, with all elements in dire need of ammunition and gasoline. In the smaller units, information on the big picture and on adjoining units is nil, with only an occasional unsubstantiated report filtering through the cauldron of rumors. Word is received that an enemy roadblock has been established at SAMREE, with

*The Germans almost captured a huge gasoline dump near STAVELOT, but apparently didn't realize the prize that they almost had in their grasp.

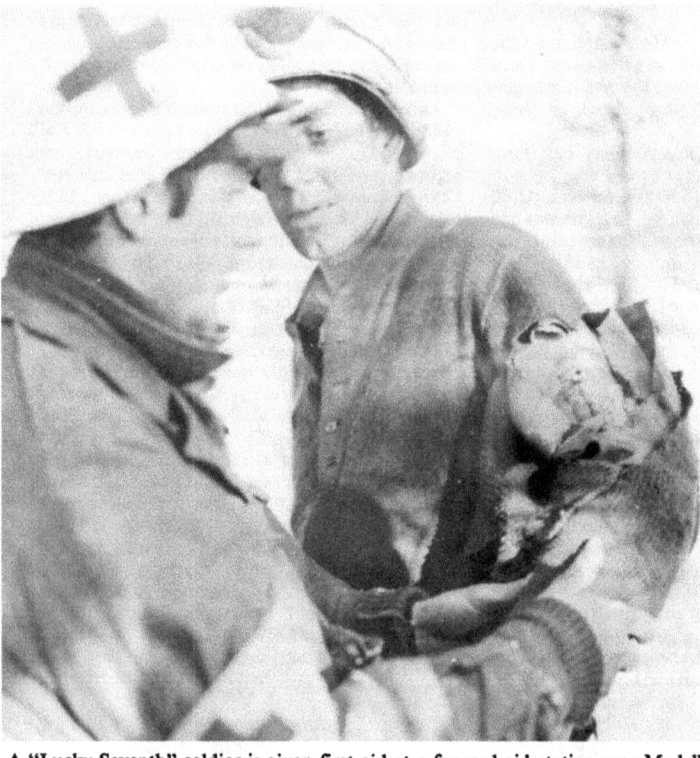

A "Lucky Seventh" soldier is given first aid at a forward aid station near Medell, Belgium (Signal Corps Photo)

Blasted vehicles in the shattered town of Manhay, Belgium, scene of bitter fighting after St. Vith fell, December 1944. (Signal Corps Photo)

Manhay, Belgium, January 1945.

This American M-8 reconnaissance car had been captured by the Germans in their break-through near St. Vith, Belgium, and used by them until it was knocked out by our artillery. (Signal Corps Photo)

The debris of what was St. Vith, Belgium, when the "Lucky Seventh" recaptured the town. (Signal Corps Photo)

Knocked out German Mark V tank.

the result that trains are cut off.

Wednesday is again cloudy with very poor visibility. By this time, the enemy has evidently decided the force in front of them is of major importance and must be destroyed at all costs. Twenty-one counterattacks are launched against us from the north, east, and south. Tanks are coming in on us from every direction. Infantry, mounted and dismounted, press in on us. Enemy artillery activity has increased to a point where it now is used quite liberally.

A glance at the situation map, now more complete, shows a red tide gradually encircling the blue bulge. In face of all this, our troops are still holding their ground and inflicting very heavy damage on enemy material and personnel. Reports of knocked out enemy tanks and infantry caught in assembly areas are coming in constantly. Many vehicles are burning and as fast as the Germans come in, our artillery and our troops in defensive positions, giving no quarter, are fighting the enemy so fiercely that they are forced to fall back without their penetration.

News comes that an enemy armored column is approaching us from the south. TF Jones, commanded by Lt. Col. Jones of the 814th TD Battalion, is formed at 0900, and at 1200 moves south through VIELSALM and SALMCHATEAU, to positions at GOUVY and CHERAM. They have occupied these towns, establishing road blocks and repulsing enemy infantry trying to infiltrate their positions. The firing batteries of the 440th, which are now supporting TF Jones, go into position near BOUVIGNY.

In general, on Wednesday, CCA is continuing the defense of POTEAU and vicinity, controlling the crossroad by fire only. CCB continues to defend their positions, repulsing four counterattacks from the vicinity of CHER EMMELS and NEDER EMMELS. The 17th Tank Battalion is withdrawn to RODT early in the morning and is sent to TF Jones minus one company of medium tanks, later in the day. D Troop of the 87th, which was sent to protect our Division trains, has made contact with and intercepted an enemy column moving on our installations at SAMREE from the east. While D Troop is engaged with the enemy column, Division trains are maintaining their road blocks and security patrols and are engaging the enemy west of SAMREE.

Supplies of all kinds are becoming shorter, and all units are now ordered to be prepared to operate for three days without resupply. Word is received that there is an abandoned Class 1 dump at GOUVY, and units restock themselves with food and large supplies of cigarettes. Ammunition especially is becoming tight, and all battalions are trying to cut down on ammunition expenditures. The situation is still so fluid that the FA Battalions are organized for position defense, prepared to fight and fully expecting to meet enemy patrols operating within our positions.

The odd units, scrambled from the remains of other divisions, that are still operating in our area, are placed under the control and command of the 7th Armored Division at 1030 on order of FIRST ARMY. All this time, the bad weather has prevented our planes from joining us. Although we get an occasional stretch of clear sky, when we could use our observation planes with excellent effect, the general overall weather picture still prevents them from coming.

Thursday, the 21st, is again cold and overcast with very poor visibility. The enemy is fairly quiet before dawn, there being recorded only movements behind the lines, patrolling, infiltration, and small arms fire. Pressure is resumed during the morning and aggressively maintained the rest of the day. Numerous attacks are launched from every section of the front. Most of these attacks are repulsed at considerable loss to the enemy, and at no loss of ground for us. However, the enemy flood is rising dangerously close to the top of our "dike" at ST. VITH — coming from due east and from the south.

All during the day, reports indicate that the enemy is gathering his forces for an assault against CCB positions, and attack after attack is turned by the massed artillery fires of the 434th's Group. At 2100, the Germans attack in strength against CCB, and the 489th switches to their support to help repulse the effort. At 2200, Lieutenant Morse of the 434th returns to the battalion on foot after having been forced from his OP by enemy action, first having destroyed his radio with his pistol. At midnight, Lt Col Dubuisson of the 434th calls a meeting of his staff and battery commanders, and informs them that the situation is critical, and that due to the vigor of the enemy's attacks on ST. VITH, the only alternative left is to prepare for a retrograde movement. Positions will be in the vicinity of COMMANSTER, and the attached 965th and 275th FA Battalion will displace to firing positions in the vicinity of the 434th in that order.

On the CCA sector, POTEAU, lost temporarily during the night, is retaken — or at least encircled. Enemy artillery still makes it unfeasible to go into town. In the area defended by TF Jones, road blocks stop an enemy column early on the morning of the 21st. Lieutenant Collins, forward observer from the 440th, immediately smothers it with fire, destroying a large number of enemy vehicles and personnel. The enemy counterattacks here in five places, and the left flank of TF Jones is forced to withdraw to better positions. Service elements are attacked near SAMREE by enemy paratroopers and forced to displace. Concentrations of German infantry are noted at numerous points behind our lines. Enemy paratroops and patrols have been ambushing single vehicles, especially on the main roads in the area to the east, on our side of the front line. One officer has been captured by a strong enemy patrol operating in our supposedly friendly territory, losing to them the new Division Field Order giving our latest plans of defense, almost before the ink on the order is dry.

In general, enemy armor is very aggressive. Tanks are involved in every action in direct proportion to the intensity of the attack, and generally number from three to ten. Much movement of them is noted behind their lines — generally to the east. The artillery is even heavier than on the 20th.

Heavy concentrations are received by us on the east front with a good amount of harassing from everywhere. Much direct fire of high velocity weapons is encountered and some counterbattery fire is received. The enemy infantry is also especially active, being used recklessly and always in strength. Long columns of enemy armor are under constant surveillance. At one time, there is a report of 10 tanks massing at NEDER EMMELS. There is no doubt that the enemy is present in great strength.

Pressing on three sides of us we now have the II SS Panzer Corps (9th SS PZ Division, and 2d SS PZ Division) assisted by the LXVI Corps (18th and 62d Volks Grenadier Divisions, and the Gross Deutchland Brigade) plus elements of the LVIII Panzer Corps, plus an estimated 20,000 service troops. Altogether, our intelligence estimate approximately 87,000 Germans are operating directly against us.

The 22nd of December is again cold with snow and extremely poor visibility. The ammunition situation is critical. We are at one time down to less than 20 rounds per gun, which is liable to be expended at any time. All ammunition trucks have been sent back for ammunition, but because of the very difficult route — that for all we know the enemy has cut — we are doubtful whether they have been able to get through.

About this time, the incident of the propaganda shell occurred. Enemy infantry was attacking. Our situation was desperate, with the 434th's forward observer frantically calling for fire. A few moments of delay — and then the welcome sound of our shells whispering overhead. To the amazement of all, especially the Germans, the shells did not burst like HE, but instead, erupted a shower of propaganda leaflets. The leaflets, in German, advised the Germans to surrender, as they were hopelessly "surrounded."*

A force of 300 paratroopers with mines, panzerfausts, flame throwers, etc., is reported to have dropped somewhere between VILLE DU BOIS and ST. VITH. Enemy artillery is coming in in ever increasing quantities. Enemy infantry and tanks are assembling in all key points and columns of tanks and armored vehicles are trying to break through our defensive strong points to the north, east, and south. Our elements send in continuous requests for fire.

At 0100, the 434th is instructed to send a guide to the 440th, for four trucks of ammunition, of which the 440th has relative surplus, while the 434th is almost depleted. Around daylight, the 434th begins a displacement to previously reconnoitered firing positions, and the start of the withdrawal of armored elements of CCB is begun. The CO, CCB had instructed that the armor of CCB fall back to a line HINDERHAUSEN-CROMBACH, while a small task force of tank destroyers and dismounted troops deploy south of the railroad vicinity of CROMBACH. The remaining elements of CCB are

*Major Oscar C. Tonetti, S-3 of the 434th, stated at the time he had practically no ammunition left, and that the propaganda shell was all that was available at the moment.

Two "Lucky Seventh" GIs passed a wrecked German ambulance in St. Vith, Belgium January 1945. (Signal Corps Photo)

to withdraw through this line and assemble in the vicinity of BRAUNLAUF.

The 434th closes into firing positions in the vicinity of COMMANSTER, at 1300, and with the closing of the battalion, the ammunition trains begin arriving with 5000 rounds of sorely needed ammunition and the shortage is relieved. The battalion commander then instructs Lieutenant Shively to observe for tank destroyers and dismounted elements then south of the railroad at NEUNDORF. Lieutenant Foss is dispatched to the 17th Tank Battalion as observer.

Displacement of the 275th and 965th FA Battalions to the vicinity of VIELSALM is begun in the early afternoon. Later in the day, orders are received for an impending march order which will place the 434th in firing positions west of the SALM RIVER, presently defended by the 82d Airborne Division. The 434th is to cover the withdrawal of elements of the 7th Armored Division, and is to reinforce the fires of the 440th FA Battalion (which has withdrawn to positions at SALMCHATEAU), who are in direct support of TF Jones at BOVIGNY. During the day's action, Lieutenant Shively is killed by enemy action.

The 489th is placing down heavy fires throughout the night of the 21st-22nd. CCA has a number of fires on call, and all concentrations are observed by the forward observers. CCA moves their headquarters to PETIT THEIR. At 1800, orders are received by the 489th from Division Artillery for a withdrawal to the rear along the road VIELSALM-GARONE-ODRIMONT. The time for the withdrawal is to be late the 23rd.

At 2400, the 434th has given march order for all elements east of the SALM RIVER. The mission of the 434th is to cover the rear guard of CCB composed of elements of the 87th Reconnaissance Battalion and the 31st Tank Battalion. Battery B is to remain in firing position until relieved by the covering force. The alternate plan in event that positions at SALMCHATEAU are untenable provides for occupation of positions in the vicinity of LA CHAPELLE.

During the day, the Germans have been pouring into ST. VITH, which we have been forced to evacuate. Enemy attacks are being pushed in strength from so many different directions that it is becoming nearly impossible to deal effectively with all of them. The accurate fire our forces is delivering is slowing up the Germans, but today is not stopping them entirely. Infantry, tanks, vehicles of all kinds are being knocked out. Of course, we are losing vehicles, especially, and some personnel in this exchange of fire — but we are exacting a terrific toll on the German forces. However, Jerry is continuing to push on in such numbers and at so many places that it is becoming evident that they will soon be able to overrun us by sheer weight of numbers. Nevertheless, our troops tenaciously are defending every square inch of ground and regardless of the number of the enemy or the frequency of his attacks, are refusing to give any quarter at all.

That our defenders have been in a hard fight is easily verified by the number of knocked out German vehicles (later estimated at 133 enemy tanks destroyed and 30 damaged) and by the number of their personnel that have become casualties. There is no certain way of knowing the exact toll that our division has exacted, but from every source it is acknowledged to have been very heavy.

Four of our liaison planes join us for the first time in the late afternoon of the 22d. They have been sorely missed in the few spells of clear weather that we have had since we had occupied position in the area, but from the 23rd and on, they are of immense value.

At 0015 the 23rd of December, the withdrawal instructions are issued. Previously the first units to withdraw had been notified and are making necessary preparations. In general, the 7th Armored Division and attached units are to withdraw west of the SALM RIVER to an assembly area in the general vicinity north of LIERNOUX. The attached units of the 9th Armored Division, 106th Infantry Division, 28th Infantry Division, and the 14th Cavalry Group generally are to pull out first, followed by our CCB which has a covering force out to protect the withdrawing units. As CCB clears through the center, CCA is pulled down from the north flank and folded into the withdrawal immediately behind CCB, leaving a covering force of CCA until their units have successfully withdrawn. As CCA withdraws, CCR from the north is to fall back relieving CCA's covering force and providing one of their own until all units are across the river. Therefore, in effect the withdrawing force is drawn from the center leaving no unexposed flank, each flank folding back in turn to the center and pulling on through until eventually the flanks form the center. This in itself requires superb coordination on the part of all units. Covering the south flank in this operation is TF Jones which in turn is to fold back on the withdrawing forces of CCR and furnish the rear guard in the withdrawal. It is necessary, therefore, for the artillery battalions to be among the last of the units withdrawn, and even when they are to withdraw, other artillery units in position must take over support missions until the withdrawal has been successfully completed.

Before the withdrawal of CCB, the 965th is withdrawn to the west side of the river late the 22d of December. On the 23rd, the 965th has gone into position in the vicinity of CHEVRON where they are supporting the balance of the withdrawal. The 275th has moved back before CCB, going into position just west of the river opposite VIELSALM, and later, as the withdrawal is successfully nearing completion, withdrawing to the general area of AMCOMENT. The 434th FA Battalion, accompanying CCB in their withdrawal, has displaced at 0935 from positions in the vicinity of COMMANSTER as the enemy closed in. Battery A's command half-track has fallen out as a road failure, and, after all essential equipment had been evacuated, has been destroyed to prevent falling into the hands of the enemy. The march is well disciplined and made without confusion — a tribute to the leadership provided by CCB. At 1200 the battalion closes into positions at HIERLOT due to the fact that the positions selected at SALMCHATEAU are under fire. However, at 1530 the battalion displaces to more suitable positions in the vicinity of LA CHAPELLE, due to the inadequacy of supply routes at HIERLOT. The complete march has been made over improved highways under excellent weather conditions.

At 0400, the security guards of the 440th report enemy paratroops landing near their positions. All men are alerted, but no paratroopers are seen. However, some parachutes are definitely seen on the ground. As the 7th Armored Division withdraws, the 440th is used as covering protection. By 1400, the 440th begins to withdraw to GORENNE. The firing batteries are sent ahead singly, as Jerry has the escape route zeroed in and is firing interdiction fire continuously. As C battery (the last to displace) pulls out, they encounter small arm fire from a clump of woods not fifty yards away. Mortar fire scored a direct hit on a C Battery M-7, destroying it and causing six casualties. Firing begins immediately after the 440th has gone into position at GORENNE, as Task Force Jones needs help desperately. Although Lieutenant Schwartz's transmitter is out, he manages to conduct fire by a series of taps and clicks for range and deflection changes. For four hours, the battalion fires almost continuously, and finally manages to extricate TF Jones almost intact. Lieutenant Schwartz has his tank (his third) disabled by enemy fire and burned. Luckily, none of his crew members are harmed.

At the time of the 440th's withdrawal, all but one bridge across the SALM RIVER has been destroyed — including the one the 440th is to use. It is while taking an alternate route, that the M-7 is destroyed by enemy fire.

The 489th is firing almost continuously, with the 275th reinforcing its fires. At 1000, Lieutenant Donald R. Bauer, one of the newly commissioned lieutenants, is killed by a direct fire tank hit on the house from which he is observing in POTEAU. An infiltration of unnecessary vehicles is started to the new position in the vicinity of ODRIMONT. At 1500, CCA starts its disengaging movement and tanks and armored vehicles start pouring through the 489th's area. At last come the 489th's turn, and their M-7s and lesser vehicles pull out of the fields and orchards and cross the bridge between PETIT THIER and VILLE DUBOIS, which the engineers are waiting to blow up. The whole movement is flawlessly executed and no equipment is lost in the process. At 1700 that evening, just as darkness is setting in and just as a three-quarter moon is starting to rise, the 489th reaches its destination at

ODRIMONT.

Headquarters and Headquarters Battery, Division Artillery, infiltrates to the assembly area during the day. The last to leave is the Fire Direction Center, which continued in operation at VILLE DU BOIS until 1600. Earlier in the day, our observation planes had reported enemy columns moving at high speed and with several hundred yards between vehicles. The FDC caused interdiction fire of one round of 155s every minute to be placed on the road, for 15 minutes. At the end of 15 minutes, the planes reported that the road was now nicely congested with German vehicles, at which time the closed up German column was worked over with artillery, with good effect. At the time that the FDC is withdrawing, the outpost to their immediate north has just been overpowered. At the time of their withdrawal, there is nothing on either flank but two good roads occupied or about to be occupied by the Germans. Most of the remaining personnel leave in one half-track, which contains — besides key fire direction center personnel, key communications and key motor personnel — the valuable radio sets which are used to tie in all units. This half-track conveniently chose to break down in VIELSALM, and it is not until the last elements of the division were pulling out that it began moving again. Even at that, we think we might have to abandon it, for it is barely able to move. One peep, pushing another disabled peep, gives a good comparison of how slowly we were able to move, for they fairly breeze past us. Had this vehicle with its radios been lost, not to mention the key personnel, we might have suffered a serious setback a little later (as I will presently bring out).

The 24th is again cold and clear with good visibility. At 0731, the 440th moves to LA FALIZE where they take the enemy under fire almost immediately, causing great damage and destruction, especially on enemy columns.

Early in the day, the 434th receives orders to dispatch one Forward Observer and one Reconnaissance Officer to TF Carlson at MANHAY. Lieutenant McLemore and Lieutenant Snyder are assigned the mission and set out from the battalion at 0800. Later in the day the battalion displaces from its position at LA CHAPELLE and closes into the new position at FAGNE at 2100, travelling thirteen miles blacked out over improved highways under excellent march conditions. The 434th is to reinforce the fires of the 489th, who are in direct support of CCA at MANHAY.

The 489th opens the day with its guns laid west and southwest in order to cover the withdrawal of CCA to MANHAY. Registration is completed, and some support is furnished to the 82d Airborne Division to our direct south. Here, German armored columns are steadily advancing despite heavy losses. What remains of the unfortunate covering force straggle through the positions all day.

By dark, all battalions are displacing or are under orders to displace to new positions which all were in the general vicinity of HARRE. Headquarters and Headquarters Battery of Division Artillery is displacing by infiltration to HARRE.

In our particular party are the S-3 half-track with its radios, the personnel of the S-3 section, and some LN O's with their vehicles and sections. Somewhere along the route, with the help of an MP who says that our other headquarters vehicles have gone down a road to our left, we turn off on the wrong road. We pass through a couple of tank assembly areas, and then for awhile, we see no one. Eventually, a Captain of Engineers stops and cautions us about driving off the center of the road, as the edges of the road are mined with "Daisy-Chains" of several AT mines wired together. At this point, we stop at the biggest house of a small group, and learn that we are at VAUX CHAVANNE. MANHAY is just a short distance to our left front, but we cannot see it from where we are.

We immediately turn and, careful to keep in the middle of the road, retrace our tracks and eventually arrive at our new CP in HARRE. On the way, we receive a radio message from the 489th, asking for permission to remain in their present positions at the request of Colonel Rosebaum of CCA. After contacting Colonel Martin, approval is given to remain in their positions. Later that night, about 2100, the 489th hears several loud explosions nearby, and find upon investigation that the 82d Airborne Division is withdrawing along the only route to the rear, with orders for their covering forces to clear by 0400 and then to blow up all bridges. Lt Col Milner of the 489th immediately asks CCA for permission to retire, and at 0100, receives word that it

British 30 Corps with German prisoners near Nieder-Emmels, Belgium, January 1945.

Badly damaged German Hetzer in Wallerode, Belgium, January 1945, in sector of attack at Co. A, 23 AIB.

The wreckage of three German tanks and a Volkswagon lies to the side in the Ardennes, December 1944.

is all right. At 0115, the 489th is on its way to the positions that had been previously selected for it.

While all this was going on, we are setting up our fire direction center in HARRE, but we are not really expecting any enemy action that night. Lieutenant Zeilor, our communications expert, dropped in by the CP and asked what I thought about extending wire communications that night. It is very cold, the night is black, the roads are slippery with ice, the men have been busy for days keeping up communications in the ST. VITH area, and are dead tired, and it is Christmas Eve. In spite of all the possible reasons for not laying wire, you tell Zeilor to get the wire in anyway — feeling like a heel when you tell him. However, a few hours later, we all are thankful that we decided to lay the wire.

Bill Zeilor had dropped in at the CP later in the evening to report that the wire was in. We are just ready to leave the CP and go to bed, and are waiting for the duty officer to show up. While we wait, we are opening Christmas packages which have just been received. We could hear the usual message traffic on the radio, when suddenly we hear: "If we could only get some artillery." That statement had come in as a result of a bit of cross-talk due to CCA's radio channel overlapping ours. We tune in to CCA's channel, and what we hear going on in the clear would convince anyone that some unknown, deadly scramble was going on in the dark. We call CCA, and tell them that we are Division Artillery, and will give them what they want if they will tell us where to put it. The only verification that we have is the recognition of your voice by Major Ford of CCA, and your recognition of his voice. Lt Col Rhea, commanding the infantry battalion in CCA, finally gets on the radio and says that all hell has broken loose and that he has been unable to get any artillery support. In the confusion and darkness, he has lost his map and cannot tell us where to place fire, although if we can mention a few names to him, he believes he can tell us. A few words later, we have agreed that he wants fire along the road from VAUX CHAVANNE to MANHAY, and in MANHAY itself. In a matter of minutes, we have divided up the sector among our battalions and have told them to fire when ready along their parts of the road. As a matter of interest, no one has had a chance to register in our new positions, and we are going solely on our survey and our metro message. The data must have been good, for we receive reports that our fire is extremely effective. After a few hours, Colonel Rhea calls us up to tell us that his observers are reestablished now, and that he can now get by without our help.

We later find out what had happened. A strong force of Germans was pushing into the MANHAY area. It actually was led by some captured American Sherman tanks, with some Tigers mixed up in the column. Some of the personnel of CCA had actually called out to the Tiger Tanks trying to engage the personnel in conversation, and had assumed that the engine noise was too great for the tank personnel to hear them. They had assumed that the Tigers were captured tanks manned by American personnel, whereas actually there were Germans inside, manning the tanks. Other personnel of CCA told of hearing backfires behind them in their column. They also erroneously assumed that these noises were from cold tank engines, but they awoke to cold reality too late when an 88 exploded on the ground just behind their halftrack. The Germans were simply moving in the column, picking off vehicles one by one from the rear.

The 489th's and 434th's observers' tanks are knocked out almost immediately. The enemy is using both tanks and infantry in force. CCA is forced to withdraw about 2000 yards north of MANHAY in face of the German attack.

Later, CCB is ordered to assume control and to reorganize the defenses of the 7th Armored Division Sector. The forces of CCB are disposed for the defense with the 23rd and 38th Armored Infantry Battalions situated west of the WERBOMONT-MANHAY road, north of MANHAY, and elements of the 106th points, and artillery observers are sent with the troops manning the blocks.

The thundering roar of TOTs ushers in Christmas Day.

The early morning sees the fighting continuing hot and heavy, with our artillery constantly working over the area to the detriment of the enemy. By daylight, the German attack has been stopped, and later in the day our forces counterattack and regain about 1000 yards of ground.

At 1900, the enemy counterattacks and massed defensive fires by the artillery repulse the enemy.

Our liaison aircraft again demonstrate their worth. Numerous German vehicles are observed turning off the main road at a certain point, and pausing — evidently to check their maps — before continuing into the woods just south of MANHAY. One battery of the 275th is registered upon this point, later being credited with knocking out several German vehicles which had, as usual, stopped to check their maps. A long stretch of road is broken down into individual battery concentrations, but is covered by all of the Division's Artillery. This interdiction fire, a TOT, is called for by our liaison planes when the road is jammed, costing the Germans numerous vehicles, with the airplanes reporting as many as twelve vehicles knocked out at one time by one TOT. This particular TOT is known by the code name of George. The woods south of MANHAY are raked with TOTs, especially along the numerous roads and trails — and the varied colored flares that the Germans frantically send up after these concentrations are heartening to us and show evidence of the effect of our fires. A call for Hitler, Himmler, Goering (or others), is a signal for our massed fires to come crashing down simultaneously on a specific area. Up to 18,000 pounds, or more, of High Explosive shell would land within a few seconds of each other, as quickly as "3 rounds" could be loaded and fired.

The 26th of December is again cold and clear with good visibility. There is considerable movement in and around MANHAY, VAUX CHAVANNE, and GRAND-MENIL. Our Artillery places TOT after TOT on these points, enemy columns, infantry assembling, enemy tank assembly areas, and on all enemy movements. The enemy is building up his strength in preparation for an attack, but is dispersed at each instance by our artillery fire. Numerous vehicles are knocked out and large numbers of the enemy are killed. Burning vehicles are spotted over the entire area. German prisoners brought in declare that our artillery fire is more intense and more demoralizing than any other military fire that they had ever encountered — including that on the Russian Front.

Warning messages are received from higher headquarters, alerting everyone to be suspicious of

Troops of the 509th Parachute Infantry Bn. supported by an M5A1 light tank of the "Lucky Seventh," push against German positions beyond St. Vith, Belgium, January 1945.

Knocked-out German Mark IV tanks.

Didenberg, Belgium, in July 1981.

all vehicles, due to the infiltration of the enemy into our lines. As a result, guards are instructed to halt all vehicles and ascertain the identity of the occupants. Dog tags and identity cards have to be inspected — possession of U.S. vehicles, or uniforms, or insignia of rank is not enough to identify the occupants as being friendly.

Among the troops opposing us in this sector are the 2d SS Panzer Division, the 11th Panzer Division, and the Gross Deutschland Brigade. These are Hitler's best. They try numerous counterattacks, but each time the attacks are broken up by our massed fires almost before they start. At one time, two of our liaison planes report a German attack starting up — just as we launched one of our TOTs. Almost immediately they report the results of our fires — the enemy machine guns knocked out and the infantry dispersed. In this typical example, the attack was broken up before it really began.

We receive reports of one of CCA's officers who had been held captive in MANHAY. He had been held in a cellar, and had had a good chance to observe the Germans with him. At first, it seemed that every time they started to leave the cellar, a TOT would come down on MANHAY, with the result that they would come tumbling down the stairs in terror. After a little while, they were literally shivering from the heavy shocks, and were huddling pathetically in the cellar. It was immediately after one of our TOTs that this officer made good his escape.

During this time, our artillery now consists of six battalions of 105s — our own organic three, plus the 275th, the 591st, and the 229th. In addition, Corps — the XVIIIth AIRBORNE CORPS — has given us the use of the 965th (155-mm Howitzer) on reinforcing missions. A scrappy 75-mm pack howitzer battalion of the 82d Airborne Division, whom we knew only by their code name of CIRCLE, also is firing with us, having given us their fire support in return for our laying a wire to them.

On the 26th, word is received of a plan to seize MANHAY with the 517th Paratroop Infantry, a separate regiment, during the night. The 489th is to fire in direct support of this effort. In the early morning hours, after an extremely heavy artillery preparation, the coordinated attack sweeps down from the high ground north of the town and seizes the objective in twenty-seven minutes.

The 27th brings some more German counterattacks, but they never stand a chance in the face of our artillery fire. By the 28th, the Germans no longer feel free to move about in daytime, and we enter into a period of comparative quiet. Orders to relieve the division are received, as the defensive phase is now over and fresher divisions are preparing to launch a general counterattack. Division artillery remains in position in general support of the 75th Infantry Division, who have taken over our sector. On the 31st, the sector is very quiet. At midnight, as the old year passes into the new, a special TOT is fired with CORPS, as the artillery's own way of sending New Year's greetings to Jerry.

And so, our story comes to a close. The 7th Armored had met the best that the enemy had, had stopped cold overwhelming numbers of the enemy — even in the face of a most severe ammunition shortage — for five long, decisive days, and had again met the enemy and stopped his best troops in their last frantic attempt to get going on the main road to LIEGE.

Bradley, Montgomery, and Eisenhower sent congratulatory messages to the division for its magnificent stand. Elements of the division were given a Presidential Citation. For one small group of men, thrown into the breach without prior warning, had made possible the rallying of American-British strength and had been the margin between victory and defeat in ARDENNES.

Cook and kitchen truck, getting ready to serve "chow" in the snow.

German prisoners carry one of their wounded in blanket sling after their capture by the 23rd AIB near Wallerode, Belgium, January 1945. (Signal Corps Photo)

Moving into Didenberg, Belgium, January 1945.

# THE RECAPTURE OF ST. VITH

On January 23, 1945, one month to the day after a division of weary warriors had been ordered to withdraw from St. Vith, the Seventh Armored fought its way back into the now bomb-wrecked village.

The Seventh's return to St. Vith climaxed a four-day drive from the north during which heavy opposition was beat down in the bitterest kind of weather. Snow was everywhere, having drifted in some places to a depth of six feet. Through it, and through the positions of a determined enemy, the men and tanks of the Seventh Armored pushed to St. Vith.

The Seventh's capture of St. Vith marked the virtual demise of Von Rundstedt's winter offensive. The enemy forces had been battered back for 50 of the 55 miles that they had gained, and their losses of men and material had been high. The fields over which the soldiers of the division fought bore mute testimony to the German losses. Vehicles and equipment of all descriptions that had been knocked out one month earlier strewed the ground, only to be added to by the new toll exacted by the weapons of the Seventh in the recapture of the scene of its gallant, historic December stand.

When the division had finished its job in the St. Vith area, it was pulled out of action and assembled in the Eupen, Belgium, area, where the men of the command were given the opportunity of resting and getting equipment back into combat shape.

While much has been written on the defense of St. Vith, very little has been documented on the recapture of this vital road junction. The following narrative prepared by the Research and Evaluation Division, The Armor School, Fort Knox, Kentucky, tells the story of the Seventh Armored Division's heroic fight to retake St. Vith one month after its loss.

Road in 17th Tank Bn. sector near St. Vith, Belgium December 1944.

L-4B Cub nosed over on landing at Haar, Belgium, December 1944. No injuries.

This printing is not clear but the sign over the road states "You are entering St. Vith through the courtesy of the 7th Armored Division." January 1945.

Staff Sgt. Samanie and Tech/5 Orvin look over L-4 Cub after engine failure on take-off at Robertsville, Belgium December 1944.

Troops of 23rd AIB take cover behind a tank as they capture the town of Hunnange, Belgium on the road to St. Vith, January 1945. (Signal Corps Photo)

Retrograde movement from St. Vith, Belgium, December 1944 (Signal Corps Photo)

# THE RETURN TO ST. VITH*

Among the famous historical examples of indomitable courage and outstanding leadership during the recent war, the back-to-back stand of the 7th Armored Division at St. Vith, Belgium, during the period 17 December to 23 December 1944, has a place high in the annals of military historians.

St. Vith, Belgium — focal point of the bitter fighting found in the swirling snows of the "'Belgian Bulge" — will long be remembered as one of the key points whose staunch defense by the 7th Armored Division broke the prongs of the mechanized might of Von Rundstedt's abortive blitz.

After a gallant stand of six days, the 7th Armored Division on orders relinquished its hard-won ground and again drove into the German line in the vicinity of Manhay, Belgium, and whittled at the German Army until relieved on 30 December 1944. Particularly notable is the fact that at this time, the gallant 7th Armored was fighting with understrength units, for only 70 percent of the combat personnel was effective and medium armor was 56 percent below normal.

Von Rundstedt's lightning armored columns were blunted and disorganized as they probed at the 7th Armord's defense, and the methodical German planners found themselves thrown six days behind schedule because of the 7th's stonewall ring of fighting personnel around St. Vith.

Not content to rest on its laurels, the 7th Armored Division began the task of "seek and destroy" as it eliminated pockets of resistance and feeble attempts of the enemy to regain the remnants of their lost mission.

When the 7th Armored Division was withdrawn from the line at the end of January, it had forced the enemy back to within seven kilometers of the German border.

Although St. Vith received far less publicity than Bastogne, it was the opinion of many of the German field Marshals, including Hitler himself, that St. Vith was far more important strategically than Bastogne. The most important fact to consider is that Bastogne could be by passed and St. Vith could not. Not only to the German

S/Sgt Adan Calinka, Pvt. Eorley Thompson and Pvt. Gordon Harris guard German prisoners just brought into St. Vith, Belgium, January 1945.

High Command was this a paramount issue, but to the Allied Supreme Command as well, for the same reasons that the German Ardennes offensive begged down when denied this road and rail center, any large Allied counteroffensive to drive the enemy from Belgian soil would beg down unless St. Vith were in friendly hands. The German mission was to deny the Allied Forces the use of the road net, and to "defend to the last round" this all-important town.

Primarily the enemy employed delaying actions and small determined pockets of resistance to hold off the advance of the 7th Armored Division. The units so engaged were to fall back on St. Vith and hold at all costs. Consequently, when Combat Command B attacked and took St. Vith it encountered well-organized resistance. It had advanced into the area of prearranged artillery, Nebelwerfer, and automatic weapons fire. The enemy had taken about two weeks to organize the defense of St. Vith with all the cunning and sound military knowledge available in well-trained Prussian minds.

In addition to the strong enemy resistance encountered, the 7th Armored Division faced the added hardships of a bleak, biting winter. The entire operation was impeded by drifts of snow from two to three feet deep. Men shivered in foxholes as the temperature dropped to the zero mark, and yet kept their faces and weapons toward the attacks of the German forces.

## RECUPERATION AND PREPARATION

January 1945 found the 7th Armored Division as XVIII Airborne Corps reserve in the vicinity of Aywaille, Belgium, preparing for the coming counteroffensive.

Replacements in men and material were absorbed by the division at this time, and an intensive training program with emphasis on maintenance and firing was begun. The extreme cold, lack of suitable billets, and icy and hazardous operating conditions caused the division many hardships.

However, preparations and training for the offensive to clear the last of the enemy from Belgium soil rapidly transformed a weary, battle-scarred division into a well-trained and hard-fighting team.

Ingenuity was necessary in the cold weather operations, and two officers in the division devised a very feasible makeshift for "grousers" to enable track-laying vehicles to operate satisfactorily over the ice-covered roads and countryside. Extensive reconnaissance and analysis of the terrain were made to determine the most effective manner of operation. The poor road net, heavily wooded areas, and rugged terrain dictated the employment of small infantry-tank-engineer teams. Where mass employment of tanks would be impossible, these small teams could operate over roads or trails and gain the rear of the enemy forces to make surprise seizures of important road centers or defiles.

Organizing small task forces and conducting training problems to study the proper uses of these units, the combat commands of the division prepared themselves for the coming counteroffensive during the first half of January. A US First Army camouflage team visited the division during this time and assisted in the solving of winter camouflage problems. Each line infantryman and all key personnel of tank battalions, artillery battalions, the engineer battalion, and the cavalry reconnaissance squadron were equipped with white outer garments to blend with the snow. The tanks of the 7th Armored were the first in the US First Army to be painted white.

On 19 January 1945 the 7th Armored Division had completed all preparations for its attack. The division was poised and ready for the assault.

## THE RETURN TO ST. VITH

Task forces were organized and the division awaited Corps order for the attack. Combat Command A and Combat Command B were organized as follows for the coming operation:

### COMBAT COMMAND A

#### TASK FORCE W (WEMPLE)

17th Tank Battalion (— Companies B and C; 1st Platoon, Company D)
Company B, 23d Armored Infantry Battalion
2d Platoon, Company B, 33d Armored Engineer Battalion
2d Platoon, Company A, 814th Tank Destroyer Battalion

#### TASK FORCE R (RHEA)

23d Armored Infantry Battalion
Company C, and 1st Platoon, Company D, 17th Tank Battalion
1st Platoon, Company B, 33d Armored Engineer Battalion
1st Platoon, Company A, 814th Tank Destroyer Battalion

#### TASK FORCE S (SEITZ)

2d Battalion, 517th Parachute Infantry Regiment
Company B, 17th Tank Battalion
3d Platoon, Company B, 33d Armored Engineer Battalion
3d Platoon, Company A, 814th Tank Destroyer Battalion

### COMBAT COMMAND B

#### TASK FORCE A (CHAPPUIS)

48th Armored Infantry Battalion (— Companies B and C)
Companies A and D, 31st Tank Battalion
1st Platoon, Company A, 33d Armored Engineer Battalion
1st Platoon, Company C, 814th Tank Destroyer Battalion

#### TASK FORCE B (THOMASIK)

509th Parachute Infantry Battalion (— Company C)
Company B, 31st Tank Battalion
Company B, 48th Armored Infantry Battalion
3d Platoon, Company A, 33d Armored Engineer Battalion

#### TASK FORCE C (ERLENBUSCH)

31st Tank Battalion (— Companies A, B, and D)
Company C, 48th Armored Infantry Battalion
Company C, 509th Parachute Infantry Battalion
2d Platoon, Company A, 33d Armored Engineer Battalion

The division command post moved to Waimes on 19 January, and Combat Command A and Combat Command B moved into final attack positions in the vicinity of Waimes during the night of 19-20 January.

The general plan of attack was to have Combat Command A on the left and Combat Command B on the right. The division objective at this time was to occupy a frontage of about 10,000 meters extending from the high ground north of St. Vith, and thence to the north and east to the town of Ambleve.

20 January 1945

On the morning of 20 January at 0730 the 7th Armored Division began its coordinated attack through the sector held by the 1st and 30th Infantry Divisions. The weather had not moderated, being very cold with snow flurries and visibility ranging from fair to poor. Icy conditions and

Tank crew gas-up their tank in deep snow near Weims, Belgium, January 1945. (Signal Corps Photo)

Men of "Lucky Seventh" look at a dead horse and cart it was pulling in Hunnange, Belgium, January 1945. (Signal Corps Photo)

near zero temperatures made movement of tracked vehicles extremely difficult.

Task Force Wemple jumped off at 200730 January for Diedenberg; meeting only light enemy resistance, it occupied Diedenberg by 1030. Task Force Rhea succeeded in securing the high ground southeast of Diedenberg by 1530, although it met heavy resistance from strong points established in houses located in its zone of action. During the remainder of the day Combat Command A consolidated its positions and made preparations for the attack on Auf der Hart Woods.

Combat Command B was to attack Born with two task forces: Task Force A (Chappuis) astride the road from the west and Task Force C (Erlenbusch) from the northwest. However, because of last-minute changes the attack was postponed; Task Force B (Themesik) patrols encountered difficulty in returning from enemy reconnaissance, and the 120th Infantry Regiment, through which Combat Command B was to pass, had changed its plans just prior to the scheduled attack. At 1130 the attack was launched through the 120th Infantry Regiment. Task Force B approached Born without serious difficulty, but Task Force C encountered mines and terrain impassable for armor. At 1630 the assault was launched on Born by Task Force B and the infantry of Task Force C. Both forces encountered heavy small-arms fire from the enemy and by 1800 the attack had bogged down.

Brigadier General Bruce C. Clarke, commanding Combat Command B, directed the task forces to reorganize and be prepared to continue the attack on order that night. From 2300 to 2345 an intense artillery preparation was laid on the town, utilizing 13 battalions of division and corps artillery. The attack was again launched, this time encountering severe enemy resistance which included tanks, self-propelled guns, and infantry. Both task forces succeeded in reaching the outskirts of Born at 210132 January. The remainder of the night was spent consolidating the hard-earned positions. During this day's operation the task forces captured 115 prisoners who were components of the 18th Volks Grenadier and 3d Parachute Divisions.

21 January 1945

Combat Command A's Task Force B crossed its line of departure at 210400 January toward their objective, the Auf der Hart Woods. Only light opposition was met, and by 0900 it was on its objective. At 0800 Task Force Wemple and Task Force Rhea moved forward from their positions to tie in with Task Force Seitz, and the Auf der Hart Woods were occupied 211400 January. In clearing the objective Task Force Seitz met moderate enemy resistance, consisting of small-arms, mortar, and artillery fire. Five members of an enemy patrol were captured, and the identity of the enemy force was learned for the first time. The enemy soldiers were from units of the 12th SS Panzer Division, I SS Panzer Corps, who a month before were racing across the Ardennes toward the Meuse River.

Combat Command B was meeting considerable resistance in trying to enter Born. After consolidating positions during the early morning hours, Company A, 48th Armored Infantry Battalion, was given the mission of clearing that part of Born east of the railroad which ran from north to south, and Task Force C was ordered to clear the area northwest of the railroad. At 210545 January the attack began as scheduled. No sooner had the attack developed than it was quite evident that the enemy had brought up considerable reinforcements during the night. Later, from prisoner of war sources, it was learned that one full battalion of infantry had been moved into Born under cover of darkness. Artillery, Nebelwerfer, and mortar fire was far more intense than during the previous day. Evidently the Germans were determined that Born should be held at all costs. In anticipation of fierce resistance by the enemy, at 0830 the 38th Armored Infantry Battalion was attached to Combat Command B and moved to an assembly area within quick striking distance of Born. Stubborn last-ditch resistance by the enemy held up operations east of the railroad. Fighting was intense, and every house was a fortress in itself where hand-to-hand fighting developed. Born was a much different type of town from those heretofore fought through by the 7th Armored Division. Born consists of houses surrounded by gardens and yards, very much like an American town. This meant that the assault troops had to cross open ground in

Manhay, Belgium, January 1945.

Troops of the "Lucky Seventh" look over an undamaged German tank, captured on the road to St. Vith, Belgium, January 1945. (Signal Corps Photo)

Engineers working at Grandmenil, Belgium, January 1945.

advancing from house to house. There Germans chose to organize each house as a strong point and defend it from the cellars. It was virtually impossible to assault these positions in the usual manner. To clear out the resistance, a tank destroyer was placed in a commanding location on a hill just outside of Born. One delayed-action round was fired into each house at the cellar and ground floor line. Mopping up behind this fire came foot troops to clean out any overlooked pocket of resistance. Clearing of the northwest section of Born proceeded with somewhat less resistance and by 0945, Task Force C was given the mission of continuing forward and clearing the east section of Born. The balance of this day's fighting, however, was bloody; and Company A, 38th Armored Infantry Battalion, was called in to assist Task Force C at 1700 to clear Born of all organized enemy resistance. Testifying to the severity of the day's fighting, one company of the attacking forces lost 80 men. Combat Command B immediately organized defensive positions in preparation for any enemy counterattacks.

The 7th Armored Division knocked out seven tanks and several self-propelled guns during this operation and damaged several other armored vehicles by artillery fire. Only 78 German soldiers were captured as a result of the close-quarter action. At 212325 January the 508th Regimental Combat Team* relieved Combat Command A and assumed defense of the Diedenberg-Eibertingen area.

## 22 January 1945

The Reserve Command, which up to this time had been in division reserve, moved into the area Monteneau, Deidenberg, Eibertingen, and assumed defensive positions. The 508th Parachute Infantry Regiment was attached to the Reserve Command.

Combat Command A and Combat Command B were ordered to secure Hunningen and the high ground to the east and west of the town.

The order for the attack was for Combat Command A to attack from the northeast and Combat Command B to attack from the north. Combat Command B was to organize Task Force Beatty**, which would wait for the arrival of troops of Combat Command A (Task Force Seitz and Task Force Wemple), before attacking. Combat Command A moved out from the high ground east of Born at 1000 and ran into small-arms, antitank, and artillery fire, which held it up so that it was not until 1700 that both task forces were ready to jump off toward Hunningen. In the meantime, Task Force Beatty, Combat Command B, was ordered by the division commander to jump off at 1430 without further waiting for Task Force Seitz and Task Force Wemple of Combat Command A. Speed in the advance was the order of the day, and enemy resistance was either quickly overrun or by-passed. The daring aggressiveness of the attackers did much to disorganize the defense of the enemy, and by 1730 Task Forces Beatty, Seitz, and Wemple were on their objective. By 1900 all enemy resistance was completely crushed, and the town was organized for defense.

*Composed of:
  508th Parachute Infantry Regiment
  319th Field Artillery Glider Battalion
  Company D, 307th Engineer Battalion
  Company B, 80th Antiaircraft Artillery Battalion
**Composed of:
  Company C, 31st Tank Battalion
  Company B, 48th Armored Infantry Battalion
  1st Platoon, Company A, 33d Armored Engineer Battalion
  1st Platoon, Company C, 814th Tank Destroyer Battalion

Additional enemy units identified on 22 January 1945 were: 18th Volks Grenadier Division, 246th Volks Grenadier Division, 3d Parachute Division, and 25th SS Panzer Grenadier Regiment.

So rapid was the advance that seven 88-mm antitank guns were overrun. The fleeing enemy had left these guns in their original emplacements, with an ample supply of ammunition at the gun site. No attempt had been made by the enemy to destroy these pieces and deny them to the American forces.

## 23 January 1945

The long-awaited chance of the 7th Armored Division to retake St. Vith came on 23 January. Just one month previously, 23 December 1944, Combat Command B, commanded by Brigadier General Bruce C. Clarke, bearing the brunt of the defense of St. Vith, had been ordered to withdraw west of the Salm River with the balance of the 7th Armored Division and the other defending elements of this important road and rail center.

The original plan called for Combat A to retake St. Vith, but a last-minute change in plans gave Combat Command B the honor. Combat Command B was organized into three task forces for the mission:

### TASK FORCE CHAPPUIS

48th Armored Infantry Battalion (Company B)
Companies A and B, 31st Tank Battalion

### TASK FORCE BEATTY

Company B, 48th Armored Infantry Battalion
Company C, 31st Tank Battalion
1st Platoon, Company C, 814th Tank Destroyer Battalion
1st Platoon, Company A, 33d Armored Engineer Battalion

### TASK FORCE RHEA

23d Armored Infantry Battalion (Company B)
Company C, 17th Tank Battalion
1st Platoon, Company D, 17th Tank Battalion
1st Platoon, Company B, 33d Armored Engineer Battalion
1st Platoon, Company A, 814th Tank Destroyer Battalion

The attack on St. Vith called for a full-scale attack by Combat Command B. Task Force Chappuis was to attack parallel and west of the Hunningen-St. Vith road; Task Force Beatty was to attack astride this highway; and Task Force Rhea was to attack due south of the Kinnelberg woods. The plan was to completely envelop St. Vith without exposing attacking troops to the suspected enemy concentrations east and southeast of the town.

The attack moved forward at 1415 preceded by a heavy artillery preparation. Just prior to and during the attack, the enemy resisted by the use of heavy artillery and Nebelwerfer fire. These enemy fires were ascertained to be coming from the vicinity of Wallerode, and an air strike was called for. The air force bombed and strafed likely-looking targets and targets of opportunity in this area, with excellent results. Small-arms and machine-gun fire were the main weapons used by the German defenders of St. Vith. Heavy to moderate resistance was met, but by 1745 all task forces had gained their objectives and were tied in.

Now that St. Vith had been recaptured by Combat Command B of the 7th Armored Division, the Germans were determined to retake it. From 2015 to 2250 the enemy launched three vicious counterattacks at the American troops. These attacks consisted of infantry supported by armor, artillery, and Nebelwerfers. The artillery fire was heavier than had been delivered before, since Combat Command B's advances into St. Vith had carried it into range of the organized artillery defense plan of the enemy.

By 2400, 157 prisoners were taken; one tank and four assault guns were destroyed; and one assault gun was captured intact. This again reflected the shattering force of the 7th Armored against the enemy.

24 January 1945

Combat Command A, commanded by Colonel W.S. Triplet, Infantry, composed of Task Forces Seitz, Rhea, and Griffin with Task Force Wemple in reserve to support by direct fire, jumped off at 1000 to seize and defend Wallerode and the high ground north and northwest of the town. Small-arm, machine-gun, and artillery fire resisted the advance of the troops, but in spite of this and the heavy mortar and Nebelwerfer fire, all task forces secured their objectives before nightfall. The ground operation of the enemy in this attack on Wallerode and vicinity consisted mainly of well-dug-in infantry whose emplacements were connected by tunnels and studded with dugouts. The points of high ground were well defended by dug-in infantry, supported by mortars and machine guns. In addition, the houses along the routes of advance were organized by defense. However, the well-planned, well-coordinated, and brilliantly executed attack met with resounding success as had all others in this operation.

At 1000 on 24 January 1945, Combat Command B was given the mission of taking three objectives, namely: the high ground to the southwest, the ground to the south, and the high ground to the east of St. Vith, all of which were about 1500 meters from the town proper. Combat Command B, under Brigadier General Clarke, was organized as follows:

### TASK FORCE ERLENBUSCH

31st Tank Battalion (— Company A)
509th Parachute Infantry Battalion

### TASK FORCE CHAPPUIS

48th Armored Infantry Battalion
Company A, 31st Tank Battalion

### SUPPORTING TROOPS

Company C, 814th Tank Destroyer Battalion
(support 48th by fire) Company A, 33d Armored Infantry Battalion (general support) Company D, 87th Mechanized Reconnaissance Squadron

The high ground to the southwest (WALT) and south (NINA) was to be taken on the night of 24 January. The high ground to the east (CORKY) was to be taken on the morning of 25 January. WALT, NINA, and CORKY were the code names used

Artillerymen enjoy lull in the fighting in the Ardennes, December 1944.

Troops of 23rd AIB in Hunnange, Belgium, January 1945

Light tanks of CCA moving into Weims, Belgium, January 1945. (Signal Corps Photo)

Cpl. Orvin Traver, DIVARTY, uses M-4 tank with dozer blade to clear airstrip for our light planes, Robertsville, Belgium, December 1944.

for easy reference in this operation.

At 1630, Task Force Erlenbusch advanced toward the dual objectives of WALT and NINA, both being the high ground to the south. At 1910 Task Force Erlenbusch reported it had captured ALT. This mission was accomplished by Company C of the 509th Parachute Infantry Battalion because of the deep snow and rugged terrain which precluded the immediate use of armor. At 2015, NINA was taken by the remaining half of Task Force Erlenbusch, but the resistance was so great it was forced to withdraw shortly before dawn to the railroad tracks just south of St. Vith. The Reserve Command was called upon to furnish troops to fill the gap between NINA and WALT.

## 25 January 1945

At 250615 January 1945, Task Force Chappuis jumped off on its attack to CORKY. The southern half of CORKY was captured by 0900, but the northern sector offered such great resistance that the attack was halted short of its objective.

In the south Companies B and C of the 509th Parachute Infantry Battalion and Company C of the 87th Cavalry Reconnaissance Squadron had attacked NINA at 1530, and at 1635 had taken the high ground and were consolidating their positions.

## 26 January 1945

It was believed that Prumerberg and the surrounding ground was the key to the German defense of the area east of St. Vith. If this objective could be taken it was felt that strong organized resistance by the enemy would be reduced. At 260700 January, Task Force Chappuis committed its reserves and launched a final all-out assault on Prumerberg. The objective was taken at 0810, and by 1030 Task Force Chappuis had made contact and tied in with Combat Command A on the left.

It was expected at this time that elements of the United States Third Army would relieve the division. However, inasmuch as they had not arrived, Combat Command B was ordered to coordinate an attack of the 82d Airborne Division, which was to advance through Combat Command A and secure its right flank as it advanced through the heavy woods and incised terrain in the Bois de St. Vith. The objective of General Clarke's Command B was some 4600 meters east of St. Vith.

## 27 January 1945

Elements of Combat Command B jumped off at 1025 and immediately encountered heavy small-arms and artillery fire. The attack made slow progress in the thick woods that seemed to hide a determined enemy rifleman behind every tree, and soon the attacking troops had met with resistance far greater than their strength. General Clarke, the Combat Command B commander, notified division that reinforcements were sorely needed to continue the attack.

Additional troops were attached, and another full-scale attack was immediately launched. By 280355 January, the hard-fought-for objective was in American hands.

At this time the communications were extremely poor, and the disposition of friendly troops was very uncertain. When Company B of the 38th Armored Infantry Battalion moved out to cut the Prumerberg-Setz road, it was brought under devastating small-arms and automatic weapons fire. So fluid was the situation, in the waist-deep snow and trackless forests of Belgium, that the attacking forces actually believed at first that they were being brought under friendly fire. Investigation proved otherwise; and in conjunction with a platoon of medium tanks, an attack was launched on this enemy pocket. By 1800, despite heavy enemy artillery fire bursting in the treetops and raining death in every direction, the well dug-in Germans were eradicated.

Elements of the US Third Army relieved Combat Command B on 29 January 1945. When they took over the sector of the 509th Parachute Infantry Battalion, 26 battle-weary paratroopers moved to the rear from their foxholes. These 26 combat heroes were all that remained out of an original complement of 400.

During these last days of bitter winter fighting, in which Combat Command B was the only element of the 7th Armored Division in continuous attack, 60 prisoners of war were captured.

A great deal of small arms equipment was taken, but the Germans committed none of their armor or assault guns, and denied the American forces the opportunity of capturing them. At times the enemy armor would engage American armor in extremely long-range duels, where he believed his 88-mm rifle would give him a slight advantage, but at this he proved highly ineffective.

## ST. VITH — THE KEY TO VICTORY

It was only through brilliant generalship and the courage of the attacking troops that the enemy was defeated and driven from his established positions.

The dashing, sometimes highly unorthodox attacks of American armor, which almost invariably seemed to meet with uncanny success, were employed in the operations of the 7th Armored Division.

The division gained the initiative on 20 January 1945 and never relinquished it until relieved on 29 January 1945. Attacks were launched continuously and with such rapidity that the enemy was hard pressed at all times, day and night.

The entire campaign — *The Return to St. Vith* — was one of great pride and honor to the 7th Armored Division. To those who had shown the world that they had the indomitable courage to stand and fight and stand to fight again in death-laced battles to retake that town, St. Vith and its capture will remain a never-to-be-forgotten episode in the minds of the fighting men of the 7th Armored Division.

*This documentary narrative was prepared by the Research and Evaluation Division, The Armor School, Fort Knox, Kentucky, 25 June 1948.

Artillery Battery firing position during the defense of St. Vith, Belgium, December 1945.

First troops of the "Lucky Seventh" walk up the silent streets lined with wrecked buildings, testimony to the battle that raged for the town. January 1945.

St. Vith, Belgium, in rubbles after recapture by the "Lucky Seventh" January 1945.

Machine Gun Squad, 2nd Platoon, Co. C, 38th AIB, in Verviers, Belgium 1945

A tank of the "Lucky Seventh" guards a road in Born, Belgium, north of St. Vith, January 1945. (Signal Corps Photo)

Preparing to move out of a bivouac area for the "attack."

Neider-Emmels, Belgium taken by the "Lucky Seventh," January 17, 1945.

T/5 Kurfiss, DIVARTY with camouflaged aircraft workshop in the background, Haar, Belgium, December 1944.

T/3 Kerwin Samanie and T/Sgt Ken Danielson, (past President, 7th A.D. Assoc.) DIVARTY, plowing the airstrip at Robertsville, Belgium, December 1944.

The Ardennes Forest after the snow had melted and fallen from the trees.

Members of Troop D, 87th Recon, on the outskirts of St. Vith, Belgium.

"Horses," a common mode of transportation for the German Army.

Co. C, 48th AIB Command Post in St. Vith, Belgium.

Extract from Department of the Army General Order No. 43, Washington, D.C., 19 December 1950.

## 7th ARMORED DIVISION

CITED IN THE ORDER OF THE DAY of the Belgian Army, in Decree No. 7253, 13 July 1950, by Charles, Prince of Belgium, Regent of the Kingdom, with the following citation:

During the crucial period of the German offensive of the Ardennes, in 1944, the American 7th Armored Division, attacked by enemy forces estimated at eight divisions, among them 3 SS Panzer and 2 Panzer Divisions, held the important center of St. Vith, preventing any advance and any exploitation on this main line, thus dooming the German offensive to frustration and, by its sacrifice, permitting the launching of the Allied counteroffensive.

CITED IN THE ORDER OF THE DAY of the Belgian Army, in Decree No. 7253, 13 July 1950, by Charles, Prince of Belgium, Regent of the Kingdom, with the following citation:

Passing over to the attack on 20 January in the St. Vith sector where it had fought previously, the 7th Armored Division pushed the enemy out of the position that it had been organizing for two weeks and pushed it without respite seven kilometers beyond the Belgian frontier, inflicting heavy losses on this enemy. During these nine days it captured more than one thousand prisoners.

BELGIAN FOURRAGERE (1940), awarded by Decree No. 7253, 13 July 1950, by Charles, Prince of Belgium Regent of the Kingdom.

(What follows deals with the second CITATION. The first CITATION was covered on pages 91 to and including 105, "THE LUCKY SEVENTH.")

The frozen body of an American Soldier still lies across this tank of Company A/17th Tank Battalion, Seventh Armored Division, southeast of Born, Belgium — 22 January 1945. (US Army Signal Corps Photo)

# 7th Armored Takes St. Vith

## Tanks, Joes Win Vital Road Hub

By Russell Jones
Stars and Stripes Staff Writer

WITH FIRST ARMY, Jan. 23—St. Vith, the Germans' last stronghold of any consequence on the First Army's sector of what once was a «bulge», was recaptured today by the Seventh Armd. Div.

Tanks and armored infantry drove 1,000 yards into the key road hub early in the afternoon. After a house-to-house battle which lasted three hours and 45 minutes, the forces under Brig. Gen. Bruce C. Clark, of Syracuse, N.Y., had cleared it of the enemy.

Meanwhile the 75th Div. took Braunelauf and Maldange and was fighting tonight in Aldringen, three and one-half miles southwest of St. Vith. The 30th Inf. Div. moved 2,000 yards to points southwest of St. Vith.

### Planes Blast Vehicles

Ninth TAC flew 466 sorties today against an estimated 2,500 enemy vehicles, after having a record day yesterday along the road north of Prum to Bonn. It claimed 652 motor transport vehicles destroyed, 749 damaged; 26 armored vehicles destroyed, 19 damaged; 80 railroad cars destroyed, 178 damaged; three locomotives destroyed, one damaged; one fuel dump and one ammunition dump destroyed, railroad breaks in 14 spots, and destruction of six gunsites while three more were damaged.

Seventh Armd's attack started at 2 PM with simultaneous drives by task forces under Lt. Col. Richard Chappius, of Lafayette, La., coming down the Malmedy-St. Vith road, and under Lt. Col Marvin L. Rhey, of Chicago, coming from the patch of woods 1,500 yards straight north of St. Vith.

The task forces, made up of tanks and armored infantry backed by parachutists commanded by Lt. Col. Richard T. Seitz of Leavenworth, Kan., pushed into the outskirts of the town in the face of small arms fire from Germans dug-in on the eastern edge and with artillery fire hitting them from the vicinity of Wallerode, 4,000 yards to the east.

### THIRD CLEARS ITS SECTOR

PARIS, Jan. 23—Third Army forces, paced by the four-mile advance of the 17th Airborne Div., drove the enemy out of all Belgian territory today between Houffalize and the Luxembourg frontier.

American artillery joined fighter-bombers in blasting fleeing German convoys which choked the snow-packed roads toward Germany. The remaining salient in Luxembourg was tottering under Third Army blows north of Diekirch.

In the graveyard of the Ardennes was buried the striking force of three powerful German armies and the hopes of the German High Command of a stalemate in the West.

While the German withdrawal was even and methodical, the fact that armor and transport were being rushed out in daylight was evidence that mounting Allied pressure had made the German position west of the Siegfried Line critical.

In Holland, attacking British troops extended their right flank toward Heinsburg, an important road center, and captured Valdenrath, Laffeld and Obspringen as well as a string of four villages lying between these towns.

In Alsace, powerful French forces continued their attack along the Mulhouse-Thann road.

## In Again

## Last Out, First In —7th at St. Vith

By a Staff Correspondent

ST. VITH, Jan. 23—The Seventh Armd. Inf. was back in town tonight, one month to the day from the night they evacuated after holding five days—three days longer than they had been ordered to—and knocking the German break-through so far off schedule that other First Army units were able to get farther west where they stopped the threat.

The last Seventh Armd. outfit to pull out of St. Vith that cold night of Dec. 23 was an armored infantry battalion under Lt. Col. Richard D. Chappius, of Lafayette, La. Today Chappius commanded the task force which spearheaded the attack on the town.

### Bitter Fight Going and Coming

The Germans were swarming over the Seventh's positions when they evacuated St. Vith and Chappius had to fight hard to get out. Today, although the Germans are retreating, they had to fight to get back in. The armored infantry led the attack, jumping off from Hunningen, 1,000 yards up the Malmedy-St. Vith road.

When they moved off the road into the fields, some of the men seemed to disappear into shadows which left tracks as they struggled over the snow. They were the men with the new snow suits. Others were yellow blotches in the white glare because their suits were stained with many wettings of snow melted in the dim heat of foxholes.

The infantry moved slowly, ducking briefly during the intermittent screaming of the Nebelwerfers—six-barreled mortars—hitting the road junction behind them, the road in front of them, and sometimes hitting them. They were armored infantry but right then they were like any other infantry—plodding toward the enemy with only their weapons to protect them.

### Supported by Tanks, Paratroopers

Behind the infantry were the tanks and parachutists under Lt. Col. Richard J. Seitz, of Leavenworth, Kan.

The infantry and the tanks and the parachutists moved against the town, dipping out of sight in the hollows of the rough ground, coming up on the hills, going through the woods and finally disappearing for good into the houses on the edge of St. Vith. And while they moved, the constant roar of artillery and mortars was punctuated by small arms fire, the rapid staccato of German guns breaking through the heavier rattle of the Americans'.

The Seventh's armored infantry was in St. Vith again.

---

### "HALT — GIVE THE PASSWORD!"

The Ardennes Offensive, better known as the "Battle of the Bulge", not only made military history but will forever remain in the memories of all those who participated. For one reason or another the events of that period stand alone without parallel in humor, tragedy and pathos.

Those who were engaged in the supply network strained to maintain inventories of the essential needs of the division and were, in most cases, continually on the run seeking and then delivering material.

In all small task during regular battle assignments the fluidity of the situation in the Ardennes compounded everyones' risks and particularly jeopardized the movement of those whose duties required daily traveling through areas believed to be infiltrated by enemy paratroops disguised as Americans.

The Supply Sergeant of the 147th Armored Signal Company, on a supply run with his Wisconsin-born driver, experienced some exciting moments when routinely stopped at road blocks by guards on the alert for English speaking Germans in American uniforms. Sometimes, being on the road for several days, and therefore not knowing the current password, questions starting with individual names for identification were the beginning of an interrogation. Imagine the reaction to "Edelmann" and "Hochstein!" Usually this brought out the Sergeant of the Guard and the Officer of the Day — but quickly — as the nervous road guard demanded exiting from the vehicle, hands on head.

The presentation of I.D. cards and the correct answers to several questions would eventually overcome the apprehensions of the challengers but the most convincing rebuttal to a challenge was, "If we were Germans masquerading as Americans, do you think we would use our real names?"

Blue-eyed and blond, Harry "Bud" Edelmann and Oscar H. Hochstein, both of German ancestry, during desert maneuvers in California.

DIVARTY Air Section at Lammersdorf, Germany, just across the Seigfried Line. Standing L to R: Lt. Sumter, Capt. Alton, Lt. Crockett, T/Sgt. Danielson, T/3 Samanie, T/5 Traver. Front row L to R: Maj. Neal, C.O. Cpl. Blackburn and T/5 Traver. January 1945.

Troops of 23rd AIB in Hunnange, Belgium, as they continue the attack to St. Vith. January 1945.

T/Sgt Ken Danielson and Cpl. Orvin Traver, DIVARTY Air Section, and Belgian couple they were billeted with in Haar, Belgium, December 1944.

Typical winter scene during the Battle of the Bulge.

Members of the DIVARTY Air Section in front of their "office/workshop" at Haar, Belgium, December 1944.

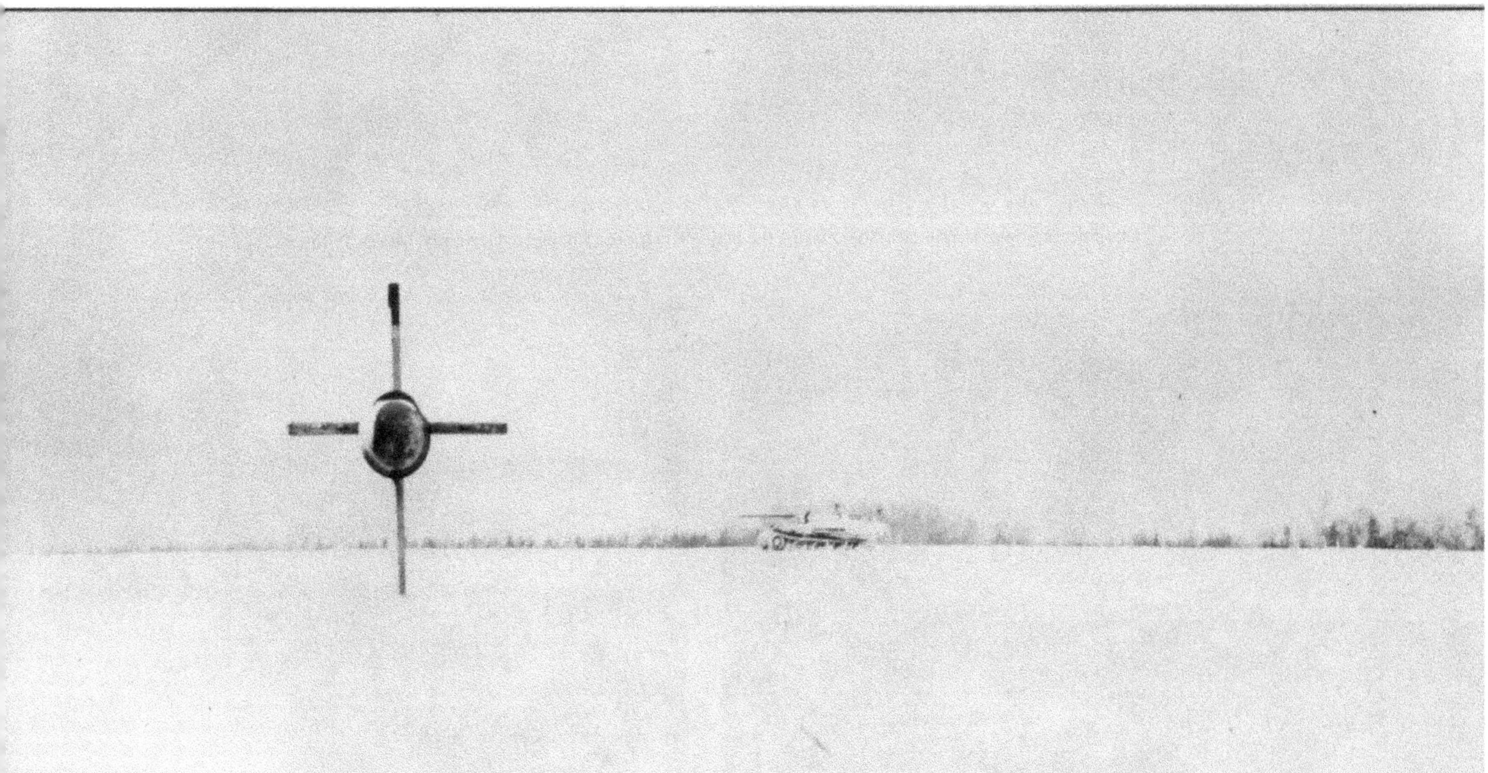

The snow covers this lone German grave near Recht, Belgium, on the road to St. Vith. A knocked-out German Mark V tank is in the background. January 1945. (Signal Corps Photo)

Engineers preparing pontoons for crossing the Rhine River near Remagen, Germany, March 1945.

Members of the 33 Armored Engineer Bn., with the aid of men of the 17th Tank Bn., work at a stone quarry near Schmidt, Germany to provide crushed stone for road repairs, February 1945.

33 Armored Engineers and 17th Tank Bn, crewmen working on roads in First Army area, February 1945.

# THE RHINE RIVER PLAIN
(March 5-April 4, 1945)

On March 5, the Seventh Armored moved up to aid in clearing the enemy from the territory west of the Rhine River. Collapse of general enemy resistance between the Roer and the Rhine left the Seventh without a seriously defended objective, however, and simplified the job to a major degree. The only fighting that was of any consequence entered into by troops of the division was in the area to the southwest of Bonn, where a stubborn pocket held out in an attempt to keep an escape avenue to the Rhine open. The pressure of the Seventh's troops forced a collapse of this resistance; the offensive power of the division could not be stemmed — the enemy it faced was destroyed.

While awaiting further assignment, the Division occupied the area around Bad Godesburg, a resort and health center on the west bank of the Rhine, establishing control over the population and combing the area occupied for enemy soldiers who had been unable to escape across the Rhine. Nearly a thousand prisoners were taken during this period — most of them having masqueraded in civilian clothes to escape their ultimate destiny. It was while the Seventh Armored was deployed along the west bank of the Rhine that the 203rd AAA Battalion was called on to augment the anti-aircraft defense of the famous Remagen Bridge. The 203rd, which had been attached to the Seventh in Normandy, had seen all of the hardships that the division had seen, and was to see all of those in the future, was, for all practical purposes, one of the division's own units. It added the weight of its weapons to the array that saved the Remagen Bridge from the constant, but vain, attempts of the Luftwaffe.

The Seventh Armored went back into action on March 26 — into the sort of action for which it was designed — and with a vengeance.

Launching out as the center spearhead of a coordinated attack along the entire First Army front, the Seventh broke out of the Remagen bridgehead and drove on unchecked for five eventful days — roared on until it was ordered to halt. During those five days it led the offensive, bore the brunt of the resistance that the enemy offered, changed directions three times and covered 148 miles of German countryside, leaving it littered with the remains of a once-proud enemy fighting machine.

The drive was not unopposed; it was simply an impossibility for the Germans to successfully cope with the speed and daring of the division's attack. There were stubborn defenses met at many points, and these defenses were completely crushed by the Seventh's driving power.

The climax to the drive from the Rhine came on the fifth day. The division bowled over all resistance to reach — and capture intact — the great Eder See Dam, 25 miles north of Kirchain.

This five-day dash represented the ultimate in an armored division's effectiveness. All points of resistance had been neutralized; the enemy's will to fight was broken, and his material power smashed. Thousands of prisoners were herded to the rear; other thousands surrendered to infantry divisions which followed up the Seventh as it tore through the enemy's ranks.

Hq. Battery, Seventh Armored Division Artillery, taken at Villip, Germany, March 18, 1945.

Pontoon Bridge across the Rhine River used by units of the "Lucky Seventh."

German civilians evacuating town of Bad Godesberg as "Lucky Seventh" provided artillery support.

Destroyed German tank.

General Hasbrouck visiting troops in the field.

The Remagen Bridge which collapsed after the 9th Armored Division crossed the Rhine River. "Lucky Seventh" provided artillery support.

Crossing the Rhine River.

Destroyed bridge over Rhine River.

Bridge constructed over the Roer River at the time of big March 1945 push to the Rhine River.

The M-7-105 Howitzer "C.O.D. Berlin" rounded out 3,100 miles. With the tank is the crew — "The Dirty Eight." Bottom row: L to R: Howard McFarland, Earl McMahon, Charles Baldga, Davis. Back row L to R: John Andrye, Levi Kresler, Louis Theobold, and Antony Villanova. All were members of C Battery, 434th Armored Field Artillery Bn.

View from the tower of the Remagen Bridge showing engineers constructing a pontoon bridge across the Rhine River.

German boat on the Rhine River.

General Hasbrouck meeting with staff officers and commanders during the Ruhr Pocket Campaign, April 12, 1945. Lt. (later Colonel) Bob Freeland, aide to General Hasbrouck, is on the extreme right. (Signal Corps Photo)

# OPERATIONS AGAINST THE RUHR POCKET
(April 5-April 17, 1945)

The pause of the division in the Eder See area was brief; the pocket around the Ruhr industrial area had been closed and orders came for the Seventh to aid in wiping out an estimated 100,000 Wehrmacht cornered there. CC A was the first element of the division to go into action against the pocket, under attachment to the Ninth Infantry Division.

On April 5, the Seventh went into action, attacking, from a southwesterly direction, the pocket it had helped to create. The enemy was fighting in a sector well adapted to the defense, and he was desperate in his defense of every point of terrain, watching keenly, and massing troops for a chance to break out. As was said at the time, the forces were fighting on a "one-tank front," battering slowly through narrow defiles, destroying the defenses that had been set up astride the mountain roads.

The Seventh pushed on. The prisoner take grew larger, and the Germans' attitude lapsed to that of defense only. Little aggressive action was encountered, but there was never a decrease in the intensity of the fighting. There always seemed to be ample manpower, ample armor, ample everything. It was readily apparent that original estimates of 100,000 troops in the pocket was low; the Seventh alone took over 45,000 prisoners while engaged in this operation.

In order to gain deception and to utilize more suitable terrain, the division changed direction to the north as the attack progressed. On April 14, CC A fought its way into Hemer, and freed 23,000 former Allied soldiers, mostly Russian, from one of the largest prison camps to be overrun in the war by any force. The deplorable conditions that existed in that camp brought harshly to mind the brutality of the enemy that the Seventh was fighting.

The eastern part of the pocket collapsed when early on the morning of the 16th, a German representative came into lines of the 38th Armored Infantry Battalion, west of Menden, stating that he wished to discuss terms of surrender. In order to save time in effecting the surrender, Col. John L. Ryan, Jr., Seventh Armored Division Chief of Staff, went to an enemy Corps Command Post behind the enemy lines as a representative of General Hasbrouck. There Col. Ryan told the commander of the Corps (LIII) that the Seventh was poised for the attack, delivered the unconditional surrender terms, and gave the Nazi commanders 15 minutes to arrive at a decision. Within seven minutes the terms were accepted, bringing a complete collapse to the eastern half of the Ruhr pocket.

As a result of this negotiation, which entailed the surrender of the LIII Corps — including the 116th Panzer Division, 180th Infantry Division, 190th Infantry Division, the remnants of the Ninth Panzer Division and the Corps staff, 20,302 prisoners were taken into custody by the Seventh Armored Division on that eventful day of April 16.

As troops of "Lucky Seventh" approach Eisborn, Germany, Nazi soldiers come forward to surrender. April 1945. (Signal Corps Photo)

Pfc. Ives A. Herbert of Ville Platte, LA in a foxhole on alert for enemy movement near Schmallenberg, Germany, April 8, 1945. (Signal Corps Photo)

Knocked-out German Tank Destroyer and a Mark V tank knocked-out by the forward elements of the "Lucky Seventh" near Niedersfied, Germany, April 1945. (Signal Corps Photo)

"Lucky Seventh" infantrymen rush into woods near Maina, Germany, to route Nazi snipers 30 March, 1945. (Signal Corps Photo)

General Hasbrouck in jeep getting out his K-ration. April 1945.

Lt. Joe M. Valentine, 7th Armored Division, greets Allied POW airmen at PW camp "Dulag-Luft." He was one of the first Americans to enter the camp to arrange for their evacuation. (Signal Corps Photo)

"Old Glory" raised over the Edersee Dam by the 31st Tank Bn.

Pvt. Julius A. Simak of the "Lucky Seventh" fries a slice of ham over a gas burner on top of an armored car, April 1945. (Signal Corps Photo)

Medical Section, 434th Armored Field Artillery Bn. Capt. Ozamoto, Bn. Surgeon, Kneeling right.

You could call this "Sweet Revenge." Date 16 April, 1945 near Mendon, Germany. This is a picture of William C. Arthur's M-8 which was used to accompany Col. Jack Ryan, Chief of Staff, to accept the surrender of the German LIII Panzer Corps which included the 116th Panzer Div. which had given the "Lucky Seventh" considerable trouble during the Battle of the Bulge. The white flag was used by pre-arrangement to give "safe passage" through the German lines. The weapons were stacked by the German Hq. guards.

Platoon of Company A, 814th TD Bn.

Knocked-out German Tiger Tank somewhere in the Ruhr Pocket, April 1945. (Signal Corps Photo)

Rifle Squad (unit and names not available).

A rare instance — three brothers in the 814 Tank Destroyer Bn. Pfc. Leon A. Ostler in center is flanked by twins Pvt. Robert R. Ostler and Pvt. Roland Ostler. Berghasen, Germany, April 1945. (Signal Corps Photo)

M-8 Armored Car crew of 814th Tank Destroyer Bn take a break. L-R: Miller, Boykin, James and Reich, Germany 1945.

105 Howitzer crew of C Battery, 434th Armored Artillery Bn.

Medics of 31st Tank Bn. lift a wounded buddy and bring him to their litter jeep for evacuation to the Aid Station near Deekenbach, Germany. (Signal Corps Photo)

Col. Haskell, C.O. CCB, issues order to unit commander, April 1945.

One of three German anti-aircraft guns captured intact by the "Lucky Seventh" on the outskirts of Edensee, Germany. Pfc. Austin McGarrh and Pvt. Irwin Waxman, 165th Photo Co., attached to the 7th Armored Division, examine the piece.

General Hasbrouck munching on "K-Rations" for lunch, April 1945.

Staff, 17th Tank Bn. 1945. From L to R. Bottom Row: Lt. Col. John P. Wemple, C.O. Maj. Thomas W. Dailey, Maj. Theodore White. Top Row: Capt. John Black, Capt. Bruce Harrison, Capt. Jak Howison, Capt. Schroeder.

Taking prisoners.

Soldiers of the "Lucky Seventh" inspect a German Tiger Tank knocked-out by CCR near Mahmecke, Germany, April 11, 1945. (Signal Corps Photo)

Camouflaged German plane caught on the ground by the advancing "Lucky Seventh" near Ober Ofleiden, Germany. (Signal Corps Photo)

Pvt. Earl S. Switt, Jr., Pvt. James C. Ponticos and Pfc. John B. Jackson, 48th AIB, in the cockpit of their half track at Edersee, Germany, March 1945.

Entire unit surrenders.

Germans surrendering near Hodheim, Germany. (Signal Corps Photo)

A German officer following his surrender to the "Lucky Seventh" says goodbye to a German nurse as he prepares to leave for POW camp.

Lt. John M. Schwarz of the 7th Armored Division questions captured German Col. Helmuth Zollenkoph, 9th Panzer Division and Lt. Gen. Fritz Bayerlein, Commander of the 53rd Panzer Corps near Menden, Germany, April 1945. (Signal Corps Photo)

German 380 mm Assault Howitzer captured in the Ruhr Pocket. Sgt. Gritis on left, Lt. Yess on right.

Men of 48th AIB examine a German Mark IV tank knocked-out by the "Lucky Seventh" as it entered Oberkirchen, Germany, April, 1945. (Signal Corps Photo)

Pfc. Harley D. Wilson, 38th AIB, questions an 18 year old German prisoner who held the Nazi Iron Cross for bravery in the Battle of the Bulge, April 1945. (Signal Corps Photo)

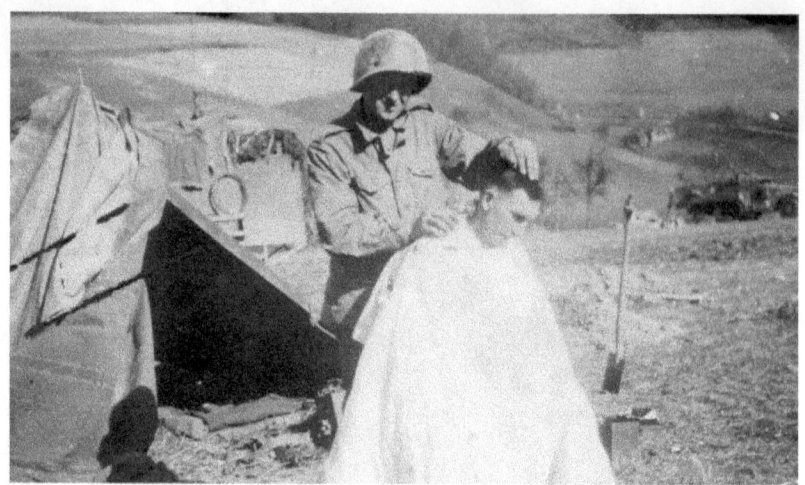

Barber of Battery C, 434th Armored Field Artillery Bn. in action.

Prisoner of War Camp "Dulag-Luft" for allied airmen near Wetzler, Germany, which was by-passed by the "Lucky Seventh" forcing the Germans to retreat without taking the allied prisoners with them. April 1945. (Signal Corps Photo)

German prisoners arrive on horse-back at "Lucky Seventh" POW cage. April 1945. (Signal Corps Photo)

S-4 Section, 48th AIB near Kassel, Germany April 1945.

German officers are lined up by their vehicles in a field at Menden, Germany, after their surrender to the 7th Armored Division. April 1945. (Signal Corps Photo)

Lt. Edward Horn and Lt. Joe Swader, Co. D, 40th Tank Bn., in front of light tank, Schweinberg, Germany.

Col. Rosebaum and a German general and his staff discuss surrender terms.

Germans surrender to 203rd AAA Bn. at Edersee Dam.

Uniformed Wehrmacht women telephone operators are among 400 prisoners taken by the "Lucky Seventh" at Deckenbach, Germany, April 1945. (Signal Corps Photo)

C Battery, 434th Armored Field Artillery Bn. in firing position in the Ruhr Pocket.

The Leica Camera Plant in Wetzler, Germany, which fell to the advancing "Lucky Seventh" March 1945. (Signal Corps Photo)

Part of 53rd German Corps after its surrender to the "Lucky Seventh" April 1945.

Lt. Col. Ted King, EXO, CCA and Lt. Col John Wemple, CO 17th Tank Bn.

T/4 Ralph J. Aofrate pointing to mark on German Tiger Tank made by a U.S. 90mm round. April 1945. (Signal Corps Photo)

German soldiers taken prisoners at Edersee, Germany.

Captured railway gun at Schmittlotheim, Germany, March 1945.

High ranking German officers captured by the "Lucky Seventh" near Menden, Germany, April 1945. (Signal Corps Photo)

More German prisoners.

Typical terrain in the Ruhr Pocket.

The "Ole Man" (as military commanders are affectionately called by their men) Major General Robert C. Hasbrouck.

German weapons and equipment captured in Iserlohn, Germany, April 1945. (Signal Corps Photo)

Trucks of the 17th Tank Bn. crossing the Elbe River in the advance to the Baltic Sea.

On the way to the Baltic Sea.

17th Tank Bn. in advance to the Baltic Sea.

# ADVANCE TO THE BALTIC
(April 18-May 9, 1945)

When all German resistance in Northwest Germany came to an end, the Seventh Armored found itself in the big middle of its very happening, speeding the collapse with its power and aggression.

It all came about after the division had a rest in the vicinity of Gottingen, and was working under the XVIII Corps (Airborne), only US formation committed with the British Second Army for operation north of the Elbe River. CC B, attached to the 82nd Airborne Division, was the first element to see action in this last stage battle, racing for 33 miles eastward from a bridgehead over the Elbe to the city of Ludwigslust, spearheading the Airborne Division's drive. The speed and power of the attack completely demoralized the already disorganized enemy, and his garrison of 5,000 troops surrendered after offering only negligible resistance.

It was from Ludwigslust that Lt. William Knowlton took his Troop B, 87th Cavalry Reconnaissance Squadron (Mechanized), to meet the Russians. The troops traveled east, spending 24 hours within the German lines, surrounded by SS units, before the Russians were contacted at 0925 on May 3. An element of the Seventh Armored made first contact with the Russians for the British Second Army.

It was also on May 3 that CC A and CC R drove north from the Elbe to reach the Baltic Sea, the first American troops to reach that body of water. In this operation, there was little need for the crushing power that the Seventh had at its command. The Germans that were encountered were those surrendering — and they were numerous, very numerous. There were more than 51,000 prisoners herded into division cages as a result of that final dash, bringing the total for nine months of combat to 113,041. Vast quantities of equipment were also taken on that day, including three airfields which were overrun — one a naval seaplane base.

And so ended the combat course of the Seventh Armored Division that had extended from Normandy to the North German coastline.

Column halted on the way to the Baltic Sea.

British Army takes over the clean-up at Belsen.

German Mark IV tank captured intact.

Entrance to Belsen Concentration Camp which was overrun by the flank guard of the 31st Tank Bn.

Unloading bodies found at Belsen Concentration Camp.

Sgt. Gritis and Pfc. Megna inspect unexploded bomb at Baltic Sea, May 1945.

Signs to be placed on graves at Belsen Concentration Camp, April 1945.

Germans mounted on horses surrender.

"Truck mounted troops" surrendering.

Mass grave at Belsen Concentration Camp.

B/87 troops with captured Germans in Parchim, Germany.

"Bicycle troops" surrendering.

Temporary halt on the way to the Baltic Sea.

"Vehicle mounted troops" surrendering. (original Volkswagon German Jeep)

A common scene in Germany on the way to the Baltic Sea.

Surrendering German soldiers passing the 31st Tank Bn. at Ludwiglust, Germany.

German prisoners near Lubz, Germany, May 3, 1945, after B Troop, 87th Recon. mission to contact the Russians.

Lt. Harry J. Clark (B/87), third from right, and unidentified G.I. with Russian soldiers, May 1945.

Prisoners captured by the 17th Tank Bn. in the advance to the Baltic Sea.

Lt. Lee A. Mestas (A/87) with captured German armored cars, Lubeck, Germany, May 1945.

"Tank mounted troops" surrendering.

Prisoners captured by the 17th Tank Bn. enroute to the Baltic Sea.

Lubeck, Germany, May, 1945.

War is over for these German soldiers.

The last day of the war, May 9, 1945, Germans surrendering to "Lucky Seventh" units.

Capt. John Kennedy, CCA, on the Baltic Sea, May 1945.

New U.S. 90mm gun tank received in the division near the end of the war. Kothen Airfield, not far from the Elbe River.

Co. A, 814th TD Bn. crossing the Elbe River on pontoon bridge.

Headquarters Platoon (A/87), near Lubeck, Germany, May 1945.

"Horse drawn troops" surrendering.

Seventh Armored Division POW Camp at Rhena, Germany, May 1945.

Lt. Col. King, Executive Officer, CCA and Major Sorenson, S-2 with captured German plane at the Tarnewitz Air Base on the Baltic Sea, May 1945.

German prisoners coming out of the "Black Forest."

"The long walk to the rear" for these German prisoners.

Co. A, 814th TD Bn. crossing the Elbe River on pontoon bridge.

German troops surrendering to "Lucky Seventh" rather than to surrender to the Russians not far away.

"Dismounted troops" surrendering.

## Grinnell Boy In Fantastic Meeting With Russians

A story in the Reader's Digest entitled "Your Mission is to Contact the Russians" has particular interest to many people in Grinnell, for Pfc. Eugene Breiting was one of the men who participated in what has been called one of the most fantastic episodes of the war.

Pfc. Breiting's story, told in a letter to his wife, Mrs. Eugene Breiting, 1108 Summer Street, is an interesting supplement to the drama-packed story of American initiative and daring, recorded in the magazine of how a troop of less than 100 men, ordered to find the Russian Army shortly before V-E day, bluffed their way over 60 miles through the whole German 12th Army and succeeded in disarming 275,000 Germans, as well as in establishing contact with the Russians.

Breiting's platoon, commanded by Lt. Earl Harrell, was on another mission when the advance began but finally caught up with the advance troops, according to the story told in the magazine. In his letter, Pfc. Breiting wrote.

"One armored car motor was acting up, so I had to stay behind with the jeep while the rest of the platoon went ahead. After we got the car acting properly, we continued about half an hour behind the rest. We would stop and ask civilians what direction the others had gone. As we went through the towns, people who had heard the news from the rest who had gone ahead, threw flowers at us, and waved and cheered.

"I didn't realize until it was over the danger we were in. The roads were choked with German troops and their equipment streaming in to surrender. The great majority had no orders to lay down arms and were ready for action. They knew the end was near, and all of them wanted to surrender to the Americans instead of the Russians. All the way we had to crowd the Germans over so that we could get down the road. Sometimes the road would get blocked with a stalled vehicle and we would have to wait five or ten minutes. During this time we collected pistols and rifles from those who would give them up. If they wouldn't give them up, we didn't argue for we were in no position to start a rumpus.

"The civilians in some of the towns had no idea we were near and their eyes popped out and their mouths fell open when they saw us. Some would quickly ask who we were, and we could see the relief they felt when they found out we were Americans.

"We stayed in Lutz that night in the second floor of a building that reminded me of Circle Hall. The floor was covered with straw, having been used previous nights by German troops. When I was coming around the corner with my bed roll on my shoulder, I bumped into a Kraut with his rifle on his shoulder. We politely begged each other's pardon and went on our way. In the morning when we got up, there were G.I.'s and Jerries sleeping side by side. What a day and what a night! There never was one like it.

"Columns of German soldiers and civilians continued all that night and the next day. Then the Russians started coming through and their procession continued most of the night. We stayed at Lutz until early the morning of our second day, then reported back to our outfit."

## GI Prisoner Enjoys Free Feeling

Private First Class Marcil Paseka, brother of Don Paseka, 17 Fifth street south, is one of the first men from this vicinity to return to the United States and home after being held a prisoner of war by the Germans and he says "no words can express, the feeling of freedom."

Taken prisoner on December 22, 1944, during the "battle of the budge" he was among a group of about 175 when captured. About 1,000 Yanks were captured in all at St. Vith, Belgium, and the men were forced to dig trenches, work on farms, help on railroads and do other manual labor with only watered soup and a few pieces of black bread as food.

As the American troops drew closer to the enemy lines, the men were moved to a camp at Limburg where they remained only a short time before being herded into small box cars, 70 men to a car, and transported further into central Germany. Paseka tells of times when American planes attacked the train not knowing it contained prisoners of war and how the next day the men labeled the roofs of the cars so the Yank pilots would know and would not bomb or machinegun them again. The men were on the train seven days.

While in prison Paseka says he received no mail. When liberated, the men found the contents of Red Cross packages they were to have received in the homes of the families of German soldiers and German civilians.

In the first prison camp the guards were made up of SS members and Hitler Youth groups who were brutally rough with the Yanks, stealing their personal belongings and making the men sleep on hard cots or on the ground with no blankets and in 10 degree below zero weather.

After marching two days and one night the men were quartered in a barn in a small village and when a small Cub observation plane of the American Army was spotted by the prisoners they knew that their hour of liberation was near if the Germans did not kill them first.

Paseka and two buddies watched the woods and soon tanks of a United States armored division were spotted and the three men dashed to the woods to tell them of the rest of the men in the barn. The German guards had put down their weapons and were letting the prisoners go to meet their liberators.

While marching to field head and his two companions had gone ahead) met four German soldiers who wished to surrender. The four Germans explained that there were more men in the woods who also wanted to give up to the Americans so the three Yank ex-prisoners of war, without weapons and with only a lot of nerve, went with the Germans to the woods where they found more than 150 German soldiers, still armed, who willingly became prisoners of the three Yanks.

Upon returning to the United States, Paseka says things moved so fast and so efficiently that three hours after arriving in Denver, Colo., he was home visiting with his wife and family who reside there.

Paseka will report to Hot Springs, Ark., at the completion of his furlough which will be about July 4.

President Truman awarding the Medal-of-Honor to Corporal Thomas J. Kelly, Co. C, 48th Armored Infantry Battalion United States Army.

Russian and American officers.

Dick Leathers (standing center) and men of Co. B, 38 AIB, in Ruksen, Germany, June 1945.

Crew of armored car "Babe," B Troop, 87th Cavalry Recon. Sqdn.

Meeting the Russians.

# VICTORY — OCCUPATION — DEACTIVATION

The Seventh Armored Division crossed the Elbe River on May 2, 1945 as part of the United States XVIII Airborne Corps, the only American unit attached to the British Second Army north of the Elbe. Combat Command "A" and "R" reached the Baltic Sea in the area between Lubeck and Wismar on May 3rd. Combat Command "B", which was attached to the 82nd Airborne Division, captured Ludwigslust on May 2nd. On that same day Lt. Bill Knowlton led "B" Troop of the 87th Cavalry Reconnaissance Squadron (Mechanized) from Ludwigslust through the German Twelfth Army to contact the Russian 191st Infantry Division at Reppetin, a distance of approximately sixty miles, at 0925 May 3rd. The last reported action probably occurred at Barnsdorf on May 5th where a Seventh Armored Division patrol killed the three-man SS garrison.

From May 4th to the 19th, the Seventh Armored Division was busily employed with the occupation and military government of that sector between Lubeck and Wismar, in the Province of Mecklenberg. At this time the division had control of 650 square miles, 90,000 German prisoners of war, 24,000 displaced persons and 170,000 German civilians.

As this area was in the British Zone, on May 20th the Seventh Armored Division moved south and east to a new security sector in the Provinces of Anhalt and Saxony, near Leipzig. The area was approximately 1,250 square miles, included the cities of Halle and Dessau, and was bounded on the east by the Mulde River, a tributary of the Elbe River. On May 30th, Memorial Day, services were held throughout the division to pay tribute to American soldiers killed in this and former wars.

During this time all of the men's clothing was cleaned, all 2,200 vehicles of the division were repainted, and a school for junior officers was conducted at a barracks at Kothen. On July 2nd, this area was turned over to the Russians and the Seventh Armored Division moved to its final place of occupation in the Landkreis of Buchen, situated about thirty miles east and a little north of Heidelberg.

During combat, the Seventh Armored Division had undergone a very large percentage in turnover of personnel, particularly in the combat arms units. The division that came out of the Ardennes in January 1945 was vastly different in personnel than the division that had landed in France some six months earlier. The operational statistics for the division indicate over 10,500 casualties, most of which resulted from the fighting at Metz, in Holland and in the Ardennes. To this day, General Bill Knowlton speaks of there being two "B" Troops of the 87th Cavalry Squadron; the one composed of those men who served prior to the battle of St. Vith, and the second "B" Troop made up of replacements for the losses sustained in the fighting of December 17th to the 23rd, 1944.

On July 11th the peacetime attrition of the Seventh Armored Division started. On that date 4,000 men of the division with less than 85 discharge points were transferred to units headed for the Pacific Theater of Operations. This change of personnel, based upon the discharge criteria, continued until the Seventh Armored Division returned to the United States where it was deactivated on October 9, 1945, at Camp Patrick Henry, Virginia.

434th Armored Field Artillery Bn., Medical Det., Capt. L. Osomoto, Bn. Surgeon, center.

"Motor stables" in Germany.

Sgt. Leonard Swida (147-Sig), with Russian soldier near Jena, Germany, June 1945.

Russians waiting to take over positions from Lucky Seventh, 1 July 1945.

Driver's nightmare! Enroute to Adelsheim, Germany, July 2, 1945.

Germany 1945, 48th Armd. Inf. Bn. Staff & C.O. L to R, back row: Joe Reddy, S-1, Liaison Officer (unknown), Elmer Morgan, Communications, Walter Pennino, S-4, Andrews Allen, Asst. S-3, Bob Heintzleman, S-2, Sid Frazier, S-3, Lynn Carlson, Exec., Richard D. Chappuis, C.O.

Lts. Jack Bray (L) and Charles Amos (R), Co. C, 23 AIB, at Hohenpriesnitz, Germany, 1945.

Sgt. Pete Gritis (L) and Sgt. Ronald Polomski (R) in front of Hq. 48 AIB, Roitzsch, Germany, June 14, 1945.

T/Sgt Elvin H. Saxberg (R), Co. C, 23 AIB, recovering in a U.S. Army General Hospital in England, June 1945.

Robert Blake, B/87, with captured German plane.

Near 48th AIB Command Post in Germany, L to R: Brig. Gen. Bruce Clark, Col. James Haskell and Lt. Col. Richard Chappuis, C.O. 48th AIB and CCB staff officer.

Lt. Col. John Wemple, 2nd from right, C.O. 17 Tank Bn., June 12, 1945.

L to R: Sgts. Krantz and Wiley, Lt. Swader, Lt. Horn, Capt. Bain, Co. D, 40 Tank Bn., Hardheim, Germany, August 1945.

3rd Platoon Machine Gun Squad, Co. A, 38 AIB.

An American flag, made by German women, at the request of Co. B, 17 Tank Bn., is flown in N. Germany. The red material came from a German flag, the blue from a bed spread and the white from a tablecloth.

Men of the Lucky Seventh relaxing on the banks of the Elbe River, Germany.

Lucky Seventh Band in formation, June 1, 1945.

A Russian general arrives at Halle, Germany.

V.E. Day parade by units of Lucky Seventh.

Complicated apparatus used to convert gasoline powered vehicles to wood burning.

V.E. Day parade by units of Lucky Seventh.

Scene in the Russian sector.

German Mark IV tank on U.S. recovery vehicle of CCA Tank Range new Halle, Germany, 14 June, 1945.

31st Tank Bn. conducts V-E Day ceremony in Gadabush, Germany.

Jack Benny and troupe entertain men of the Lucky Seventh.

Ingrid Bergman and Maj. Berkenfield, Seventh Armored Division Special Service Officer, Buchen, Germany, July 31, 1945.

Airport at Halle, Germany, June 1945.

Damaged German "JV-88" plane.

Sign courtesy of the 33 Engineer Bn.

Wrecked German "Dornier" plane near Halle, Germany, June 1945.

Lucky Seventh road check point, Germany.

German half track on CCA tank range near Halle, June 14, 1945.

German "Heinkel 111" plane.

Disabled German tank ready to be used as a target on CCA Tank Range near Halle, 14 June 1945.

Ingrid Bergman visits Lucky Seventh at Buchen, Germany, 31 July 1945.

Jack Benny, Ingrid Bergman, Martha Tilton, and Larry Adler entertain troops.

Radio Maintenance Section of the 147th Armored Signal Co. Front row: unknown, Elvan Lanham, Hubert Fuller, Robert James, Walter Erdman, James Sprague. Kneeling: Kaufman, Dale Harrell, Geoffrey Contillo, Emmett Harris, Herman Roecker, Joseph Vergona, Alvin Emrick. Standing: Lt. Davis, Earl Ripley, Frederick, John Harnevious, Boice Creasman, Paul Hadle, Clifford Koebel, Mr. George Brooks.

Jack Benny arrives at Buchen, Germany, to entertain troops, 31 July 1945.

CCA Commander and staff at Zschortau, Germany, June 1945. L to R: Capt. Kennedy, S-3; Dr. Bernard, Surgeon; Lt. Col. King, Executive Officer; Col. W. S. Triplett, Commanding; Maj. Gruen, S-4; and Maj. Sorenson, S-2.

31st Tank Bn. truck entering a Russian camp with civilian laborers.

Singer Martha Tilton at Buchen, Germany, to entertain troops of the Lucky Seventh, 31 July 1945.

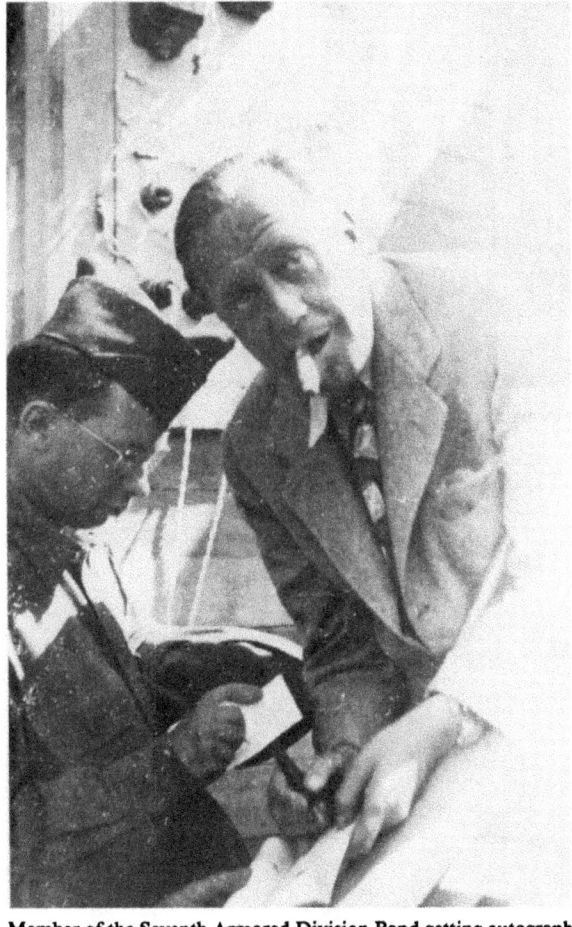
Member of the Seventh Armored Division Band getting autograph from Jack Benny.

Refugees at end of the war.

One of our Observation Cub planes is damaged in accident near Zimmern, Germany, July 1945.

Headquarters Company, CCA, and the Division Band, Zschortau, Germany, July 1945.

Captured bicycles!

General Hasbrouck speaking to troops in formation.

Col. Ryan, Chief of Staff, bids farewell to General Hasbrouck (standing in command car) and aides, Germany, 1945.

General Hasbrouck and Col. Jones, C.O. 814th TD Bn., reviewing troops, May 1945.

Bridge at Halle, Germany, destroyed by our air corps just prior to War's end.

General Hasbrouck's command car.

General Hasbrouck bids farewell to a light tank crew.

Seventh Armored Division Headquarters at Halle, Germany, June 1945.

General Hasbrouck bidding farewell to a load of 7th Armored GI's as their 2½ ton truck pulls out to take them to other divisions they are transferring to as Army of Occupation troops.

A Russian road block near the Baltic Sea area where war ended for the 7th Armored.

Sgt. Calvin C. Boykin, 814th Tank Destroyer Bn. in Germany after V-E Day.

Refugees.

# 7th Arm'd 'Ghost' Division Fought With Eight Corps In Four Armies

WITH THE 7TH ARMORED DIVISION OF THE 7TH ARMY, in Germany. — After 10 months, the 7th Armored (Ghost) Division, which "haunted" the enemy from Normandy to the shores of the Baltic, awaits its redeployment in the semi-nostalgic state which exists wherever soon-to-be-parted veterans assemble.

Its commanding general, Maj. Gen. R.W. Hasbrouck, its officers and its men can reminisce on a broad scope encompassing everything from classic armored drives to bitter unarmored-like defenses such as that at St. Vith.

Veterans they are, as the Tommy who watched them barrel down from northern Germany to meet Rundstedt testified.

"There's the bloody 7th," he said, almost unconcerned, to a small group of GIs looking for a morale booster. "They'll stop the bloody b----ds. They're the bloody veterans. We were with them in Holland, you know."

### Here, There, Everywhere

The words, "with them in Holland," were the key. The division was always with someone, some place, first with one, then another. The "Ghost" was wont to appear almost anywhere it was not expected. It fought with eight different corps in four different armies.

Offensively, it battered its way over mountains and through forests, as well as over plains against defenders who had the advantage of well-prepared positions. Defensively? Well, it is credited with two of the great stands of the war. And, that, even though armor was never intended to be a holding or defensive arm, snow and St. Vith and von Rundstedt with the pick of the German army, panzers and panzer grenadiers and planes and tanks.

Ordered to hold for two days, the 7th dug in and slugged it out for five, blunting the impetus of the foe's push for Liege and breaking the continuity of his drive. After a short rest came the retaking of St. Vith.

Then, as part of the 1st Army, the division raced out of the Remagen bridgehead and tore German resistance to shreds; covering 140 miles in four days. The dash ended with the capture of the great Eder See dam, largest water capacity dam in Europe.

### Makes German Panzers Quit

Afterward came reduction of the Ruhr pocket, which it had helped encircle. Slowly, then faster, it advanced. Resistance weakened, crumbled, ceased to exist. On April 16 negotiations were completed for the surrender of a German panzer corps, resulting in the complete collapse of the eastern sector of the pocket.

Into division enclosures, as a result of the surrender, came 20,302 prisoners, bringing to 37,383 the number taken out of the pocket by the division.

In northern Germany, again with the British 2nd Army, the 7th crossed the Elbe and swept to the Baltic Sea and a meeting with the Russians. On V-E Day it was processing prisoners of war. On that last dash the greatest need was for traffic control over thousands of prisoners streaming along the roads.

### Heroic 'Box Score'

On its combat route map is the "box score" which gives the results, the job done, but leaves out the play-by-play account.

The statistician says the division traveled 2260 miles, destroyed 2653 miscellaneous enemy vehicles, capturing 3517. It used 3,127,151 gallons of fuel.

Division 105s expended 350,027 rounds; 76s, 19,208, and 75s, 48,724. Nine DSC's were awarded members of the division; 351 Silver Stars and 888 Bronze Stars for heroic service and 1047 more for meritorious service.

A captured German officer summed it up from his place in a PW enclosure.

"We consider the American 7th Armored one of the five best American divisions — perhaps the best," he said.

The finest of the German Army and the worst of nature never dimmed its spirit or stunted its power.

In a combat life which ran from Aug. 10, 1944, to V-E Day, May 9, 1945, the 7th, among other things, took 113,041 prisoners, destroyed 621 armored vehicles and captured 89 more, destroyed 583 field pieces larger than 50 millimeter and captured 361.

The number of enemy dead and wounded it left on its trail cannot be estimated.

A look at the combat route map of the division shows it went virtually from cellar to garret and back again.

### Joins Patton's 3rd Army

After it landed at Omaha and Utah beaches, the division joined the 3rd Army. General Patton rolled the big "Seven" across the fields of France after the St. Lo breakthrough.

The cathedral city of Chartres fell and then Melun on the Seine river. Chateau-Thierry was freed. Rheims was liberated by encirclement and steel columns cut into Verdun, using the last gasoline to complete the sweep of France.

In 21 days the 7th, not as yet given the name "Ghost Division" by the Germans, clipped off 620 combat miles, spearheading the drive of the XX Corps and Patton's 3rd Army.

Refueled, the division struck for Metz to establish a bridgehead over the Moselle river and for two weeks fought against select enemy forces before it was called to Holland.

In the muck of the Lowlands, the 7th was assigned the mission of protecting the 2nd British Army supply lines and the right flank of the 21st Army Group engaged in clearing southern Holland and the Scheldt approaches to Antwerp.

### 20-Mile Defensive Front

The division was on a defensive front extending more than 20 miles when the German army threw a greater counter-drive at Meijel. Against odds of three to one, the 7th denied the enemy roads from Meijel to Asten and Liesel. It was credited with saving the campaign to clear the approaches to Antwerp.

Then came a brief stay with the 9th Army; then Christmas

*Article in ARMY TIMES, August 4, 1945*

---

## What They Did: Gas Shortage Hit 7th Armored

*By NEA Service*

In nine months of action, from August 1944, to May 1945, the Seventh Armored (Lucky Seventh) Division used up more than three million gallons of gas — an average of well over 10,000 gallons a day. And at that, it ran out of gas.

In its first 21 days in Europe, the Lucky Seventh covered 620 miles, passing through Reins, Melun and Chateau Thierry on the way. In its rampaging race through the continent the Seventh traveled nearly 2000 miles and served under four armies and eight corps. After being refueled at Verdun, where it had run out of gas, the Seventh headed for Metz, slugging away at that Nazi bastion along with doughs of the Fifth Infantry. Then the division was transferred to Holland, under the British Second Army.

After the Battle of the Bulge, the Lucky Seventh was given a brief rest, and came back to the front late in March. Breaking out into Germany after crossing the Rhine at Remagen, the division roamed unchecked in enemy territory, ultimately being assigned the task of reducing the Ruhr pocket.

The Germans tried to make the job as tough as they could but the Lucky Seventh could not be denied. On April 16 it forced the surrender of an entire Panzer corps.

From the Ruhr, the Seventh went on the move again, and this time it made a specialty of collecting prisoners. By the war's end, its total bag of captured Nazis totaled 113,042.

*Reprinted from The Stars and Stripes, Nov. 6, 1944.*

*Article in THE STARS AND STRIPES, November 6, 1944*

---

## 7th Tankmen Claim Fastest Sweep of War

By Marshall Morgan
Stars and Stripes Special Writer.

WITH THE SEVENTH ARMORED DIVISION, Nov. 5. — If it wasn't the fastest military sweep on record, then the "Lucky Seventh" Armored Division invites unofficial correspondence to the contrary.

Six hundred miles in 21 days — that's the fighting mileage clicked off by cyclometers of Maj. Gen. Lindsay McDonald Silvester's fighting armor as it spearheaded the Allied drive to the German border. The record advance for any one day was 65 miles.

In addition, from Aug. 10, when the division's first tanks rolled ashore in France, through Aug. 31, end of the 21-day period, the Seventh Armored liberated approximately 150 towns with an aggregate population of 350,000.

Brightest feathers in the Seventh's cap are the historic cities of Chartres, Chateau-Thierry, Rheims and Verdun. Major battles were fought at Chartres and Chateau-Thierry. At Melun, on the Seine, the Seventh encountered and overcame that bugaboo of all tactical problems: a river-crossing under fire.

More than 5,900 prisoners were scooped up during the drive, and an unestimated number of Nazi dead marked its path.

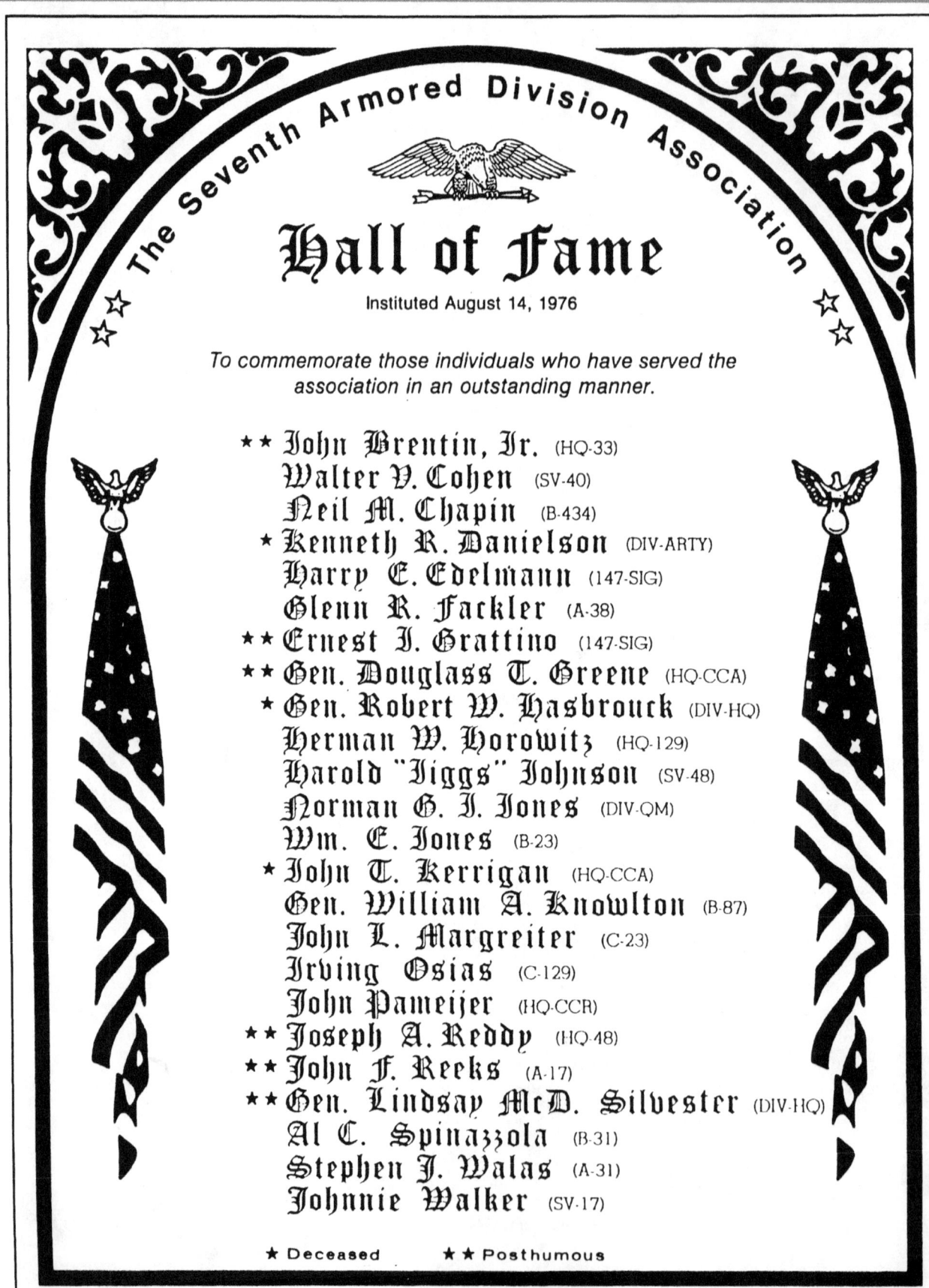

# The Seventh Armored Division Association
# Hall of Fame
### Instituted August 14, 1976

*To commemorate those individuals who have served the association in an outstanding manner.*

- ★★ John Brentin, Jr. (HQ-33)
- Walter V. Cohen (SV-40)
- Neil M. Chapin (B-434)
- ★ Kenneth R. Danielson (DIV-ARTY)
- Harry E. Edelmann (147-SIG)
- Glenn R. Fackler (A-38)
- ★★ Ernest J. Grattino (147-SIG)
- ★★ Gen. Douglass T. Greene (HQ-CCA)
- ★ Gen. Robert W. Hasbrouck (DIV-HQ)
- Herman W. Horowitz (HQ-129)
- Harold "Jiggs" Johnson (SV-48)
- Norman G. J. Jones (DIV-QM)
- Wm. E. Jones (B-23)
- ★ John T. Kerrigan (HQ-CCA)
- Gen. William A. Knowlton (B-87)
- John L. Margreiter (C-23)
- Irving Osias (C-129)
- John Pameijer (HQ-CCR)
- ★★ Joseph A. Reddy (HQ-48)
- ★★ John F. Reeks (A-17)
- ★★ Gen. Lindsay McD. Silvester (DIV-HQ)
- Al C. Spinazzola (B-31)
- Stephen J. Walas (A-31)
- Johnnie Walker (SV-17)

★ Deceased ★★ Posthumous

# THE SEVENTH ARMORED DIVISION ASSOCIATION

This is the continuing "success story" of the Seventh Armored Division Association from the time of editing the first volume of THE LUCKY SEVENTH in the fall of 1982, until the editing of this second volume four years later.

In any success story the elements of "luck" and "talent" are involved. By our very name we are termed "lucky," and for good reason. Just as the Seventh Armored Division was lucky to have excellent leadership during the War, so too has the Association been lucky in the talents of those people who have served the organization so well. Not only are we lucky in those perennial talents such as the Editor of WORKSHOP NEWS, Gene Jones (B/23), Treasurer Johnnie Walker (SV/17), and National Secretary Glenn Fackler (A/38); but also with those whose contributions to the success story, while not perennial, have been exceptional.

Our elected presidents fall into the exceptional category. At the time of the publication of the first volume of the Division History, Kenneth R. Danielson (DIV/ARTY) was the Association President. He was followed by Leon J. Minvielle (HQ/31), and our present President, Carl K. Mattocks (HQ/38). All have made significant contributions during their terms in office.

The 1982 reunion was held in New Orleans, Louisiana; 1983 in Boston, Massachusetts; 1984 in Winston-Salem, North Carolina; 1985 in Cincinnati, Ohio; and the 1986 "40th Anniversary Reunion" in Harrisburg, Pennsylvania. Each reunion was a success. While much is made of our "luck," good reunions are the result of good planning and a lot of hard work. The "hard workers" for our reunions have names like Steve Walas, Libro "Al" Spinazzola, Glenn and Dorothy Fackler, Gene Jones, John Martin, Bud Edelmann, Leonard Sudenfield, and most certainly their wives — and the members of the "Tar Heel" Chapter who planned and ran the Winston-Salem reunion such as Ray Wall, Jim Kiger, Gray Casstevens, Al Jenkins, Carl Calloway, Darwin Hastings, and Bob Idol; and for the record-setting Harrisburg reunion, Dave Buskey, Aaron Cohen, and many others.

An apology is extended to any person whose name is inadvertently missing. Suffice it to say that regardless of how able or dedicated the efforts of a few, the success that the Seventh Armored Division Association has achieved has been a total effort. For the main ingredient in the "success story" of the Association is the general membership that supports the efforts of the leadership.

The Association has continued a zealous Memorialization Program in the past four years. Names to be remembered with this effort are General Hasbrouck, General Knowlton, General Adams, General Clarke, Neil Chapin, Johnnie Walker, Ken Danielson, Steve Walas, Chewning Watkins, Leon Minvielle, Hy Horowitz, Ray and Virginia Willett, Norm Jones, Dr. Jan Pameijer, Dr. Maurice Delaval, Koenraad Molenaar, Peter Wampers — and again, the general membership for financial and team effort. In Harrisburg the retiring Memorilization Chairman was congratulated on the success of that committee. He observed that no one had ever said "no" to him when he had asked for help. Details of the Memorialization Program will be covered further in this volume.

While our continuing success is stressed, the past four years have inflicted losses. Among the many members who have passed away are General Hasbrouck, Ken Danielson, and our friend at Fort Polk, George Hammerschmidt, the Director of the Military Museum. Despite the losses, due to the efforts of our Association Secretary, Glenn Fackler, life memberships and members in the Association are at an all-time high. Secretary Fackler would agree that the vitality of the Association as reflected in WORKSHOP NEWS, reunions, memorializations, and the exceptional publicity program headed by James E. Hopkins (Div/Hq) have been helpful.

In these past four years the Association has been served by Reverend John W. Cermak (HQ/23) as Chaplain and Ben R. Freeman (HQ/48) as Judge Advocate. Ben Freeman took over as Judge Advocate following the death of Jack Kerrigan (HQ/CCA), who was another perennial asset of the Association.

The past four years have seen an increase in chapter and unit mini-reunions and functions, with activities being held by the Tar Heel, Chesapeake, and New York chapters and a new mid-West group (Illinois-Indiana-Iowa-Wisconsin) being active. Among the units the 17th Tank, 23rd Infantry, and 334rd Engineers hold annual functions. No doubt there are many other units and groups meeting and socializing, the newest being the "Desert" chapter headed by Colonel Sam Sharp (HQ/48), which held its initial meeting last year in Tuscson, Arizona

Three new members have been placed in the Seventh Armored Division "Hall of Fame": Colonel Neil M. Chapin (B/434), during the Boston reunion; Harold "Jiggs" Johnson (SV/48), during the Winston-Salem reunion; and Dr. John L. Margreiter (C/23), at Cincinnati.

The Association has continued as a member in the Armored Divisions Council since it was organized in 1981. Glenn Fackler, Frank Wickerham, Bud Edelmann and others have attended the annual meetings. Much of the information concerning items of general information for associations such as ours is made known and discussed; for example, the Armored Force Monument Committee. This committee, originally chaired by General Bruce Clarke (HQ/CCB), is seeking the placing of a monument to honor all armored units (divisions, tank destroyers, cavalry, etc.) in the Arlington, Virginia, area. Our Association has contributed funds in support of this project.

Another item of significant interest to our Association is the "Armor Memorial Park", Patton Museum of Cavalry and Armor, Fort Knox, Kentucky. This will be dealt with in the portion of the article dealing with "Memorialization."

The publication and distribution of our history, THE LUCKY SEV-

ENTH, came about in late 1982 and early 1983. It was well received by the members and all those who were presented complimentary copies. Copies were presented to the libraries of U.S. Army Military History Institute, Carlisle Barracks; The Infantry School and National Infantry Museum, Fort Benning; The Armor School and the Patton Museum, Fort Knox; The Fort Polk Military Museum; U.S. Military Academy West Point; The Artillery School, Fort Sill; The Quartermaster School, Fort Lee; The Signal School, Fort Gordon; The Engineer School, Fort Belvoir; National Defense University (formerly the National War College); Command and General Staff College; Training and Doctrine Command, Fort Monroe; The Army Library, the Pentagon; The National Archives; U.S. Army Chief of Military History; The Eisenhower Library Headquarters of the American Legion; Headquarters Veterans of Foreign Wars; Headquarters Disabled American Veterans; The Veterans of the Battle of the Bulge; the Imperial War Museum, London; The Overloon War Museum, Netherlands; Tidworth Barracks, England; Chartres and Verdun, France; and Vielsalm and St. Vith, Belgium. A copy presented to General Bruce Clarke was donated to the reading room of the Engineer School library, and Ken Danielson presented a copy to Third Army Headquarters Fort McPherson. Copies of THE LUCKY SEVENTH history have also been presented to foreign dignitaries during trips to Belgium, France, and the Netherlands by Seventh Armored Division members.

The New Orleans reunion in 1982 was a record breaker with 635 members registered, and there were many significant events. Among notable guests for the banquet were Mr. and Mrs. George Hammerschmidt, Director of the Fort Polk Military Museum. The music of Gus and Joyce Bortz (HQ/87) enlivened the C.P. and banquet. A very solemn and impressive memorial service was conducted by Chaplain Cermak who was assisted by Gene Sheehan and Ken Danielson, both of DIVARTY. As the names of each units' deceased during the preceding year were read, a candle was extinguished and a rose was placed in a bud vase.

During the New Orleans reunion, Carl and Betty Mattocks (HQ/38), Al and Ruth Spinazzola (B/31) and Gene Jones (B/23) drove to Magnolia, Mississippi, to attend a memorial service at the grave of former Association President, Alvie Davis (HQ/38). They were joined by the mayor, town officials, clergy, representatives of veterans groups, and the family and friends of Alvie who was one of the most respected members of the Magnolia community.

In the spring of 1982 a news item appeared in many of the U.S. veterans publications. It stated that in order to celebrate two hundred years of diplomatic relations between the United States and Holland, the Netherlands/USA Association wished to invite 75 American veterans who had been wounded in the liberation for a two-week sojourn in the Netherlands at their expense. Each American could bring one companion, and the selection process was to be coordinated by the Headquarters of the Disabled American Veterans. Six American divisions had fought in the Netherlands; the 82nd and 101st Airborne; the 30th and 104th Infantry, and the Second and Seventh Armored Divisions. As events transpired, only 57 men made the trip. Eight were from the Seventh Armored: Dr. John Margreiter, Jack Bray, Dan Gordesky, Dr. Maurice Lonsway and Elvin Saxberg (all of C/23rd AIB); Gordon Moore (HQ 434th/AAB); Robert Scrusa and D.E. Ike. These men were treated like royalty for two weeks by the Dutch hosts; two highlights being a reception with Prince Bernhard at the Royal Palace and participating (marching in a column of fours with the American flag out in front) in the annual Airborne march which honors those who fell in the Battle of Arnheim. A further extension of this event was the awarding of the Netherlands Resistance Cross to the Seventh Armored Division which was received by President Ken Danielson and Honorary President General William A. Knowlton in ceremonies held at American DAV Headquarters, Washington, DC, on the 6th of October, 1982. (See THE LUCKY SEVENTH first edition, page 326.)

On the 6th of August, 1982, General and Mrs. Hasbrouck celebrated their 50th wedding anniversary. To show its affection and regard, the Association made a $500 donation to the West Point Fund. General Hasbrouck graduated from West Point in August, 1917.

Seventh Armored Division Association members have been active in other veterans organizations; many serving as post and district commanders in the American Legion, Veterans of Foreign Wars, Disabled American Veterans, etc. Harvey Thiede (B/48) served several terms as President of the Military Order of the Purple Heart, and Tom Kelly (Med/48) as President of the Congressional Medal of Honor Society.

The Association learned that a black and white, 58-minute video tape on "The Battle of St. Vith," made in 1965, is available. The notice for it states: "These three days of heroic resistance captured the attention and the admiration of the entire world." Beginning with footage that describes the Nazis' "CONQUER OR BE CONQUERED" strategy for their winter offensive in

President Leon Minvielle (Hq/31) expresses appreciation to Dr. John Pameijer (CCR), The Hague, Netherlands; Konrad Molenaar (DIV/HQ), St. Denis, France; and Peter Wampers (D/17), Maasmrchelen, Belgium for their assistance in our European memorialization projects.

the Ardennes, this is the dauntless story of how the American GIs from the Seventh Armored and 106th "Golden Lion" Divisions, fighting against unbelievable odds, broke the back of the German offensive. Identified as C.M.I. Videotape No. 105, "The Battle of St. Vith" is sold by the Fairfield Book Company, Box 289, Fairfield Center, Connecticut 06805 (phone 800/243-1318).

During the 1984 reunion a number of gifts and letters from European communities relevant to the Seventh Armored Division's combat history were displayed. The gifts and complimentary letters were sent to the Association by the communities as a result of being informed of our 38th reunion which occurred during the time of the celebrations of the 40th anniversary of the "Liberation of Europe." Hy Horowitz (HQ/129), past President, had written these communities in the early part of the year and their responses to his initiative were very gracious. Letters of congratulations were usually written on the date when a particular community was liberated. This was especially so with letters from France. Letters were received from the following communities (some accompanied by gifts): Sprimont, Bovigny, and LaRoche, Belgium; Weert, Venlo, Nederweert, Overloon and Meijel, Netherlands; and Arpajon, Epernon, Suippes, Melun, Souilly, Fismes, Epernay, Bellot, Beton-Bazoche, Digny, Condie-en-Brie, Nogent L'Artraud, Marolles-en-Hure-Poix, and Chezy-ur Marne, France. Venlo had extended an invitation for a reunion of all veterans who had fought in that area; the reunion to be held on the 6th of June, 1984. Overloon also extended an invitation for a reunion of veterans to be held from the 11th to the 14th of October. Hy Horowitz attended this event, and as a representative of the Association presented a "Freedom Bell" plaque to the community of Nederweert. Hy presented the plaque at his own expense. Nederweert had sent, along with their letter, a book titled THE HEART OF THE PEEL. This was a pictorial book that showed the marshes which made armored operations so difficult. Nederweert also sent along pictures of the restored ancient church whose steeple is a part of the history of the Seventh Armored Division. It was here that Lt. Bill Knowlton, John "The Dutchman" Pameijer, and a one-legged priest made their reconnaissance on a dark, rainy night to gain the steeple which was so important as an observation post during combat of the fall of 1944.

Due to the fact that the Seventh Armored Division's action in France had to do with the liberation of many towns and cities, the French letters were particularly gracious and sentimental. In many cases the letters had been signed by all members of the town council and by everyone in a small village.

The French gifts included three pictures of the Seventh Armored Division passing through Arpajon in August, 1944. Epernon presented a "town medal" which was embossed to note the liberators of their community and the date it was liberated, August 16, 1944. Suippes sent an embroidered "Coat of Arms" and pictures of the town. Fismes sent a "Message of Gratitude" written on the date the city was liberated in 1944, making mention of the liberation "just as the brave soldiers of the (Meadville) Pennsylvania Regiment liberated it in 1918 after furious combat." Bellot sent pictures of General Silvester at the time of its liberation. Beton-Bazoche sent "Rose of Provins," a candy specialty of the area, photographs from the time of their liberation, and a letter from the town council. The town of Digny indicated that on the 15th of August, 1984, the anniversary of their liberation, the church service would be directed toward the "dead of the Seventh Armored Division, as well as their survivors and families," and that on the commemoration of their Memorial Day, 11th of November, 1984 (Armistice Day), "We will link together the names of your dead with ours, near the Monument to the War Dead in the town square, and further, it will be proposed to the council that a street in Digny be named "7th Armored Division Street." Conde-en-Brie sent a ten-inch commemorative ceramic plate. Souilly sent a congratulatory resolution signed by the mayor and each member of the town council. Marolles-en-Hurepoix struck a "medal of honor" conferred upon the Seventh Armored Division, along with a presentation certificate. Chezy-ur-Marne sent two gifts — a bronze plaque made at a local foundry in a relief reproduction of the letter the mayor of Chezy-ur-Marne wrote to the Seventh Armored Division on the 5th of September, 1944, as a testimony of the gratitude of the inhabitants of that village for their liberation. The second gift was the street sign from the "Avenue of the Liberation," which had for 40 years reminded passersby that it was by that road that the American soldiers of General Patton's Seventh Armored Division arrived. Further, that a new street sign would be inaugurated with a parade of vehicles which will follow the Seventh Armored Division route by which it entered into the Department of Aisne. The new street sign will also carry the dates, 27 August 1944 — 27 August 1984. The letter from Chezy-ur-Marne ended with this sentiment, which seems to indicate the feelings of all the above-noted letters and gifts, "In this way we shall render homage to all your soldiers who have given their lives for our liberty, and shall say to the survivors, THANK YOU FOR HAVING COME TO OUR AID AND HAVING BROUGHT BACK THE JOY OF LIVING IN FREEDOM." Joining with Hy Horowitz in this project were General Knowlton and his daughter, Holly, who translated the letters.

Colonel John Wempel, C.O. 17th Tank Bn., is recognized at the Harrisburg reunion for his long-term support and contributions to the Association.

The 40th anniversary of "D Day and the Liberation of Europe" inspired many other events pertinent to the Seventh Armored Division Association. A request for historical information from the Regimental Historian of the Military Police Regiment, Fort McClellan, Alabama, was satisfied due to the cooperation of Henry Lougee, Alfred F. Overling, and H. Edward Kennedy of the Military Police Platoon. Thus, the Seventh Armored Division Military Police are a part of the "History of Military Police Units in World War II."

Tom Kelly (MED/48), our surviving Medal of Honor recipient, was invited to Gelnhausen, Germany, by Colonel Waldo D. Freeman, Jr., Commander of the 2nd Brigade, 3rd Armored Division, to attend the dedication of an athletic facility named in honor of Kelly. Tom Kelly's outfit, the 48th AIB, is now the 1st Battalion, 48th Infantry of the 2nd Brigade. Tom was surprised and happy to receive the invitation and responded with the following words. "I will be happy to attend your dedication ceremony on 30-31 August. While I am personally proud, I am more pleased that the 48th Infantry is being recognized. My time in the Army had little meaning until I was assigned to the 48th as a Combat Medic. When I saved my first wounded comrade, I knew there was no better duty than to do God's work in a very hostile atmosphere. I was sustained in the belief that greater love hath no man than to be willing to give up his life for a friend, and all the men in the 48th were my friends."

It was also during the year of the 40th anniversary of "D Day" that other very significant memorial events were planned and came about. In 1976, General Bruce Clarke had obtained an M4 Sherman Tank to be used as a memorial for the Battle of St. Vith. From that date until early 1984, he had worked on having it moved from Grafenwoehr, Germany, to Vielsalm, Belgium. General Knowlton and our Association, with the help of the military services of the United States, Belgium, and Germany — and General Clarke, finally saw the tank on the concrete base built and provided by the town of Vielsalm, Belgium, in the spring of 1984. The Association provided the plaque that was to be placed on the tank, and dedication ceremonies were arranged with the town of Vielsalm, for the 16th of September, 1984. The Association also desired to have a memorial to signify the part of the Seventh Armored Division role in the Liberation of France. Utilizing the invaluable aid of the American Battle Monuments Commission, Koenraad S. Molenaar (DIV/HQ) of St. Denis, France; Dr. Delaval and the Municipal Authorities of Vielsalm, Peter Wampers (D/17) of Maasmechelen, Belgium; Mayor Georges Lemoine, authorities and the community of Chartres, France; the French Veterans of the Order of "Rhin et Danube", plans for both ceremonies were finalized. The Chartres Plaque was to be dedicated in the "Garden of the Bishop" at the rear of the great Cathedral of Chartres on the 21st of September, 1984. The dates were coordinated with a tour which members of our Association were taking.

Through Koenraad S. Molenaar, a third event came to be known to the Association. This was an annual ceremony that he participated in as a veteran of the Seventh Armored Division at the "American Eagle Monument" at Rambouillet, France. This monument had been built in June, 1947, by the Union of French Veterans on the spot where seven American soldiers had been killed on the 16th of August, 1944. The names or units of the seven Americans were unknown. The monument was dedicated on the 1st of June, 1947, by the President of France, Mr. Vincent Auriol, and the American Ambassador, Mr. Jefferson Caffery. Knowing that the Seventh Armored Division had seen action at Rambouillet, Koenraad Molenaar sought the Association's assistance in attempting to identify the names of the men killed on the 16th of August, 1944. Though unsuccessful in finding the names of those seven, the Association, in cooperation with Colonel John Wemple, Colonel (then Lt.) Vernon Files, and Captain Al Neil, of the 17th Tank Battalion, and Calvin Boykin, Recon Platoon/814 TD, did establish that Lt. Charles E. Fairweather (D/17) was killed at Rambouillet, France, on the 18th of August, 1944. Eventually the Association was able to find Lt. Fairweather's next of kin, Mrs. Lela Carson of Waverly, Illinois, and inform her of the details of her brother's death and that his sacrifice would be remembered at each ceremony at Rambouillet.

Note: (Please see the section on "Memorialization" for a detailed account of the ceremonies at Vielsalm, Belgium, and Chartres, France).

The book, A TIME FOR TRUMPETS, written by Charles B. MacDonald and published by William Morrow and Company, was on the readers' market around the time of the 40th anniversary of the Battle of the Ardennes. Subtitled THE UNKNOWN STORY OF THE BATTLE OF THE BULGE, contains much information on the actions of the Seventh Armored Division at St. Vith, Baraque-de-Fraiture (Parkers Cross-Roads), LaRoche, Samree, Manhay and the fighting following the halting of the German offensive when the "Bulge" was eliminated.

Raymond E. Michel (B/129) has a responsible position with the American Legion Headquarters at Indianapolis, Indiana. Ray, in conjunction with Thomas A. Hull, Curator of the Emil A. Blackmore Museum at the Legion Headquarters, made possible a display in the Museum of the Seventh Armored Division Combat Generals. The portraits of Major General Robert W. Hasbrouck, General Bruce C. Clarke, General William A. Knowlton, Lt. General John Ryan, Major General Andrew J. Adams, Major General Lindsay McDonald Silvester, and Brigadier General John B. Thompson make up the display.

On the 40th anniversary of "V-E Day," 8 May 1985, General and Mrs.

The American Monument at Rambouillet, France, where each year the U.S. servicemen who gave their lives in the liberation of Rambouillet are honored.

Knowlton represented the Association at a ceremony at Fort Myer, Virginia. This event was hosted by Caspar Weinberger, Secretary of Defense. Many miles removed and some hours later, Dr. Shoichi Asahina (MED/87) and Major Bruce Mosely, USA Ret. (HQ/31) represented the Association at Chiriaco Summit, California. In addition to the ceremonies linked to "V-E Day," the occasion marked the dedication of the site as the future "General George S. Patton Memorial." Chiriaco Summit is the location of Camp Young, Headquarters of the Desert Training Center which General Patton instituted in 1942. Camp Coxcomb, where the Seventh Armored Division trained in 1943, was part of the California-Arizona maneuver area. Over 400 people attended the ceremony with veterans from the 2nd, 3rd, 4th, 6th and our 7th Armored Divisions. The following year our Association donated $250 to the memorial by purchasing a "Founders Brick" which will be placed in a museum pathway or courtyard wall. Our "Founders Brick" will be inscribed to show that the Seventh Armored Division trained at Camp Coxcomb, California, and served in four campaigns in the ETO.

On the 30th of April, 1985, Association President Leon Minvielle and his wife, Irene, flew to Amsterdam as guests of the Netherlands-American Foundation, also to represent the Association for eight days of ceremonies marking the liberation of the Netherlands in 1945, by American, British and Canadian troops. The "red carpet" treatment was extended to the veterans by the Dutch people. All the highest dignitaries in the Netherlands and those of the American, British, and Canadian embassies were present for the functions. At the very first one Leon Minvielle saw a man with a Seventh Armored Division "bolo"; it was Koenraad Molenaar, the Dutch patriot, who is a member of our Association and active in our European memorial events. Koenraad and his wife, Mies, were at the reception as supporters of the Netherlands-American Foundation. During the trip, Leon and Irene were guests of Dr. Jan and Mies Pameijer who also took them to the town of Tiel, where a memorial service was held in the ancient St. Maartens Church, built in 1400. During the eight days of formalities that included a ceremony at the American Cemetery at Margraten, the city hall of Maastrich and Veghel, where the 101st Airborne Division made its "drop" in September, 1944, Leon presented a Seventh Armored Division "History" to Princess Irene for her father, Prince Bernhard, who was ill. The final event was a "farewell" at Keukenhof, the largest flower park in Europe. Symbolically, a blazing "orange tulip" was christened "Liberty" in honor of the 40th anniversary of the liberation of the Netherlands.

One of the Association's finest reunions was held in Cincinnati, Ohio, in September of 1985. We had a fine hotel, great weather, a great attendance that included Dr. Jan Pameijer (HQ/CCR) from the Netherlands, Peter Wampers (D/17) from Belgium, and Koenraad Molenaar (DIV/HQ) from France. All three were presented with Presidential Awards for working on memorialization events in Europe. A memorable event was a trip to Riverfront Stadium, home of the Cincinnati Reds, on the night that Pete Rose broke Ty Cobb's hitting record. Before Pete Rose broke that record the huge scoreboard welcomed the Seventh Armored Division as the "Heroes of the Battle of the Bulge," and requested everyone to sing our theme song, "Roll Out the Barrel." Despite the festivities, a solemn memorial service reminded those in attendance that we had lost many members, two of whom had made an indelible impression on our Association; General Hasbrouck and past President Kenneth R. Danielson.

General Hasbrouck had been able to attend the last few reunions only because his friend and nurse, Joan Beavers, accompanied him. It was appropriate that at Cincinnati the Seventh Armored Division Association made Joan Beavers an Honorary Member.

On the 10th of April, 1986, a framed "First Day of Issue General Adna Chaffee Commemorative Eagle Print" was presented to the United States Military Academy at West Point, New York. Lt. General Willard W. Scott, Jr., Superintendent of West Point, accepted the print from President Carl Mattocks, with Robert W. Hasbrouck, Jr., standing with him to make the presentation. The framed print bears a brass plate that reads, "Presented to the United States Military Academy, in memory of Major General Robert W. Hasbrouck, by the Seventh Armored Division Association." The presentation was made in the great Awards Room of the Administration Building. Representing the Association were Carl and Betty Mattocks, Robert and Astrid Hasbrouck, Jr., and daughter Melinda, Mrs. Hasbrouck's mother, Mrs. Frieda Scheerbarth, of Fulda, Germany, and Norman Jones.

Carl K. Mattocks (HQ/38) became President in 1985 at Cincinnati and immediately started to prove he was short on speeches but long on effort. One of Carl's first moves was the acquisition of an IBM Computer for National Secretary Glenn Fackler. Thus, in the winter of 1985-86, the Seventh Armored Division Association became computerized. Carl had always been one to put his means to

Veterans of the U.S. Army Divisions who participated in the liberation of Holland return as guest of the Stiching Nederland-Amerika Foundation to commemorate the 42nd anniversary of the liberation of S.E. Holland. Lucky Seventh members are: Standing extreme left, Glenn Fackler; third from left, Col. Sam Sharp; third from left kneeling, John Flanagan. September 1986.

any venture in which the Association was involved, and through his well-directed efforts with the Reunion Planning Committee, the Association was headed for another record-breaking reunion at Harrisburg, Pennsylvania

The Harrisburg 40th Anniversary Reunion was held on the 29th of August through the 1st of September, at the Harrisburg Marriott Hotel Pennsylvania. It was an all-time record-setting reunion with 776 in attendance. Among those were Mr. and Mrs. Robert Hasbrouck, Jr. Our late Commander's son indicated that the Hasbrouck close ties to the Seventh Armored Division Association will continue.

Presidential awards were given to John Flanagan, Dale Harrell and Max Steinbaum in recognition of 40 years' perfect attendance.

Other Presidential Awards were made to Dorothy Fackler, Mary Walas, Thelma Martin, Frances May, Ruth Spinazzola, Dave Buskey, Aaron Cohen, James Hopkins and Frank Wickerham for exceptional service(s) rendered to our Association. Also honored were outgoing Memorialization Chairman, Norman G.J Jones (DIV/QM) and Colonel John P. Wemple, Commanding Officer of the 17th Tank Battalion, who has vigorously supported the Association and continues to be an inspiration to the men of the 17th Tank Battalion.

Another distinguished member to visit the Association during the 1986 reunion was General Bruce C. Clarke, who had commanded Combat Command "B" during the defense and recapture of St. Vith. Though not as vigorous as he had been remembered by the men who had served under him, his recollections and mental ability were amazing, a particular quality that seems common to the great leaders of World War II. General Hasbrouck had it, as did Winston Churchill and most of the other great men of that period. During a luncheon hosted by President Carl Mattocks and the men familiar to General Clarke and St. Vith, Belgium, General Clarke told of his appreciation of the ability of General Hasbrouck during those days. He related many of his experiences on a command level in World War II, Korea, and as an advisor during the Vietnam War. Of particular interest was his recounting of the political influences he had to abide during the building of the Berlin Wall during the period when he was Commander-in-Chief, U.S. Army Europe and Commander of NATO Central Army Group.

At the end of his talk, this old and distinguished soldier made a point that I believe was one of the reasons he made the tiring trip to be with the men of the Seventh Armored Division Association. General Clarke stated: "At the time the 4th Armored Division formed their association, I was a member of that group, and in the company of General Clarence Huebner who had commanded the 1st Infantry Division on "D Day" and later the United States V Corps. General Huebner looked at me and said, 'General Clarke, if this association lasts thirty years, it will indicate it was a great division.'" General Clarke then looked at the men seated around him and repeated for emphasis, "If this Association lasts for thirty years it will indicate it was a great division." He said this with the realization that the Seventh Armored Division was now having its 40th reunion, and plans to have its 41st in St. Louis, Missouri, in 1987.

On September 16, 1986, immediately following the Harrisburg reunion, John Flanagan (C/129), Colonel Sam Sharp (HQ/48) and Glenn Fackler (A/38) departed for the Netherlands as guests of the Stiching Nederland-American Foundation. Once again our members were treated royally by the Dutch officials and people. A highlight of the trip was the presentation of the Seventh Armored Division Flag at the Overloon War Museum.

Norman G. J. Jones
For the History Book Committee

The "First Day Issue of the General Adna Chaffee Commemorative Eagle Print" is presented to the U.S. Military Academy, West Point, NY, in memory of Major General Robert Hasbrouck on April 10, 1986. L to R: Betty Mattocks, President Carl Mattocks, Norman Jones, Lt. General Willard W. Scott, Jr., Superintendent of the Military Academy, Robert Hasbrouck, Jr., Astrid Hasbrouck, daughter Melinda and Mrs. Hasbrouck's mother, Mrs. Freida Scheerbarth of Fulda, Germany.

Glenn Fackler, Sr., in Amsterdam, Netherlands on the occasion of the 42nd anniversary of the liberation of S.E. Holland. September 1986.

Lt. Charles E. Fairweather (D/17), killed at Rambouillet, France on August 18, 1944. His sacrifice is remembered each year during the Liberation Day Ceremony at the American Monument built by the French Veterans at Rambouillet.

Pictorial book from Nederweert, Netherlands.

## MEMORIES OF A BATTALION SURGEON

By: Wendell H. Cook, Captain, M.C.,
Medical Detachment,
129th Ordnance Maintenance Battalion

I spent my entire World War II career of three and one-half years in the 7th Armored Division. For most of that time I was the Battalion Surgeon for the 129th Ordnance Maintenance Battalion. It has been over 40 years since World War II ended, but I still carry many memories from that time, some of which are as vivid today as they were then. I reported for duty at Camp Polk, Louisiana, the night of October 5, 1942. The next night I slept on the ground out in the field with my unit, which was then on maneuvers with the Division. So the change from a comfortable civilian life in Gulfport, Mississippi, to bivouac in the field was an abrupt one.

From Camp Polk we moved to Camp Coxcomb, California, for desert training. From a medical standpoint one of the biggest concerns we had was the threat of an epidemic. We had no sewerage system at Camp Coxcomb. Instead, we treated the sewage with liquid chemicals. We had lots of flies which could carry disease among the troops. Someone had predicted to the Division Surgeon that it was just a matter of time before some fly-borne epidemic would break out. The Division Surgeon instituted one of the strictest sanitation measures ever taken. Inspections of the kitchens and mess tents were so intense that no scrap of food could ever be found on the ground. So we managed to get through our desert training without experiencing any large-scale medical problems.

From Camp Coxcomb we moved back south to Fort Benning, Georgia. My duties at Fort Benning were mostly routine. I ran the dispensary for the 129th Ordnance Maintenance Battalion and treated the men and officers of the Battalion while we continued our training in preparation for movement overseas. I remember one day at Benning, the Division Surgeon summoned all of the medical officers of the Division to his office. He asked for volunteers to join an Infantry Division which was slated for early movement overseas. No one volunteered. The officers with the least amount of service were then selected. Captain Hackett, from New Jersey, walked into the meeting late. Hackett was asked if he would volunteer, and he replied, "I will go if you send me, but I will not volunteer." The Division Surgeon allowed Captain Hackett to remain with the 7th Armored Division, and Hackett was later killed in action near Metz, France, by enemy machine gun fire. He was the only medical officer of the Division to lose his life during the War.

We left Benning in April of 1944, and by August 11, 1944, our ships were lodged on the sandy beaches of Normandy. My Medical Detachment vehicles were tied down on the deck of our landing ship. I got into my jeep and rolled off the ship onto Utah Beach without even getting my feet wet. After all our vehicles were unloaded and assembled we started off down the dirt road into France.

Shortly thereafter the 7th Armored Division participated in the breakout from the Normandy Beachhead and the dramatic dash across France. I remember that as soon as we left La Haye du Puits, France, we began to encounter crowds of Frenchmen, greeting and cheering us along the road. We were the first Americans a lot of these French people had seen, since the Division was at the point of the drive across France. During the first night of our first long march, my jeep took the wrong road at an intersection in a French village. Not knowing we were lost, we proceeded in blackout in convoy with an Infantry Division until dawn the next day. When I discovered the mistake, we left the convoy and traveled alone on side roads trying to find the 7th Armored route. As we were driving along, suddenly a P-47 fighter appeared and started on a dive toward our jeep. I was flying the Geneva flag on the front of the jeep. No one said anything except my driver, Corporal Upchurch from Jonesboro, Illinois. He said, "Well, Captain, this is it." We thought we were going to be strafed, but at the last moment the pilot veered off. Apparently he thought we were Germans trying to escape from the Falaise-Argentan rocket in a captured vehicle, but on seeing the Geneva flag, held his fire.

I remember when we paused in the French towns, people of all ages crowded around our vehicles, shaking hands, kissing us and holding up pitchers filled with what they called cognac. It was actually cider. But they were all well repaid with cigarettes and chocolate bars. This was a great holiday for the French. After long years of German occupation, at last — liberation.

A few days later some soldiers came into my station suffering from combat exhaustion. It was called "shell shock" in the first World War. They were in bad shape. I had learned in my military psychiatry course how to best deal with combat exhaustion. The procedure was to give the men rest and food and something to make them sleep, and then to send them back to the front again. We had been told that the quicker we treated such cases and returned the men to their units, the better off they were. The farther away they got from the front, the worse they would break. So I gave these men a good meal and a good rest and the next thing I knew they were ready to return to their unit. They wanted to go back. These were the first combat exhaustion cases I had seen.

An incident I remember from these early days happened when a soldier was rolled between a truck and a tree. I arrived on the scene just after the accident, and we picked him up and took him immediately to a Field Hospital (now called a Mobile Army Surgical Hospital, or M.A.S.H.) which was adjacent to our bivouac area. This was a tent hospital. Surgery was started immediately. The man was opened up by the surgical team and was found to have a ruptured liver with profuse bleeding. I was on hand and assisted. My job was to give the blood transfusions, and I was running one unit of blood after another into the man. Finally the surgeon in charge of the operation ordered the transfusions to stop, believing that it was hopeless. I pretended not to hear him and continued to give the soldier blood. After a while the surgeon again ordered the transfusions stopped. I could not ignore him any longer, and I said, "Do you want it stopped?" His reply was "Yes, please!" So we packed the liver with surgical packs in a feeble attempt to stop the bleeding and left the wound open with a portion of the surgical pack protruding for later removal. Anyway, the War moved on, and we moved our separate ways. But I found out later that this man lived. I never learned his name.

One humorous incident I remember occurred near the town of Fismes, which one of my men called "Fizzmezz." Corporal Upchurch and I were driving in to see the famous Cathedral at Reims, France. At Fismes we were directed down the wrong road by a Frenchman. We had gone about four or five miles when suddenly some French farmers ran a steamroller across the road to stop us. They all pointed toward a wooded area, not far away, and were yelling "les Boches, les Boches." There were Germans in the wooded area, and these farmers saved us from certain ambush. Corporal Upchurch wheeled that jeep around and shot down the road so fast that I didn't even have time to say thank you. Upchurch's unforgettable remark was "Hell, I can come back and see Reims Cathedral after the War."

The Division was able to race across France, without too much opposition, until it reached Metz in eastern France. At Metz we hit a stone wall. Metz was one of the bloodiest battles of the War for the 7th Armored. At one time combat commanders were lost at a rate of three a day. I remember Colonel Rosebro, a young aggressive officer who was our Trains Commander was ordered up to the front to take one of the commands. Colonel Rosebro gave his very fine camera to his driver just before his departure, saying, "You can have this camera. I will not be needing it where I'm going." He was killed later that day at the front. My unit was stationed at Mars-la-Tours. Across the road a Field Hospital was set up. Terrible casualties streamed in at all hours of the day, and surgical teams worked day and night without rest. It was at this station that the body of Captain Hackett was brought in. Hackett had started across a field to pick up a man who he thought was wounded. He was caught by German machine gun fire, and killed instantly. The man he had gone to rescue was dead.

From Metz the Division was transferred north into Holland, where it engaged in another intensive battle. Yet, despite all of the hardships of the War, the men of the 7th Armored always managed to retain their sense of humor. While in Holland the Division was assigned briefly to the British Second Army. The 129th Ordnance Maintenance Battalion contained a few tank recovery vehicles, also called prime movers, which carried disabled tanks. These were awesome vehicles. One day a British Major, upon seeing one of our prime movers, exclaimed in dismay, "Christ, what will you blooming Yanks be doing next, running locomotives up our highways?" Sergeant Lonnie Dangerfield from Texas said, "Aw shucks, Major, this ain't nothin'. You should see the one we brought this one up on." The British Major's mouth fell open, speechless.

Finally, we were ordered into reserve for a well-deserved rest. It was while we were in reserve that the Battle of the Bulge began. The Division was ordered south immediately to St. Vith, and it was at St. Vith that the Division earned its greatest glory. Ordinarily my unit, which was part of Division Trains, was one of the rear echelon units, but the Battle of the Bulge was so chaotic that Division Trains found itself facing German troops for a period of time. During this time we were bivouacked in the little town of Beausante, Belgium, and it looked as if the Germans were going to come in on us one night. So that afternoon, my good friend, Captain Shelby Howell, a Texan, who was the Company Commander of Headquarters Company of the 129th, assembled his men in the courtyard with their arms and ammunition and gave them a pep talk. As best I remember the talk, it went like this:

> Now, men, the Germans are coming in on us tonight. They are going to get us, but we are going to fight. Now they may take us, but we want them to know they've been in a fight [the implication being that we would fight to the last man]. Now, you've got nothing to worry about. We'll have

Capt. Wendell H. Cook, MC, Bn. Surgeon, 129th Ordnance Bn., Leipzig, Germany, June 1945.

roadblocks out, and we've even got the medics here with us.

I doubt if the men were comforted by Howell's statement that the medics were there, especially since these men would be manning the roadblocks. Howell, of course, was serious, because it was a serious situation. But in retrospect I have projected humor into this speech because I have likened Howell to Colonel Travis of the Alamo speaking to his men. Of course, the Germans did not come in that night, and the story of the epic stand of the 7th Armored in the Battle of the Bulge is well known.

Another incident that I remember in the Bulge area occurred on Christmas Day, 1944. This was the first day in a long time that dawned bright with sunshine and unlimited visibility in the sky. Our fighter planes were out in great strength, and the sky was filled with thousands of our bombers headed for Germany. About noon, while I was out on a visit to one of the other Companies in my Battalion, I saw a most terrifying sight. High above one of our bomber formations two German Messerschmidts started an attack, and I saw five of our bombers shot down. One of the German fighters was shot down, and the pilot bailed out. He was captured and brought into my aid station, where he had the audacity to state that he had been attacked by the bomber formation. One of my men wanted to kill him right on the spot and had to be restrained.

In the spring of 1945 the 7th Armored participated in the Conquest of Germany. As we crossed the Elbe River, deep in Germany, we came upon one of the most amazing and dramatic scenes of this or any other War. Bearing down upon us, just as we crossed the river, were masses of dazed German soldiers — on foot, in wagons, on bicycles, in trucks, in carts, and every other conceivable form of transportation. They came in hordes, completely choking the roads, streaming by our stalled vehicles. They didn't look to the right or the left. They didn't seem to notice our forces. Some were old, white-bearded men, 70 years of age or more; some were young boys — all in the green uniforms of the German Army. We were observing the death of the once-invincible Germany Army. These men only wanted to reach the safety of our lines and escape from the Russians. There was no longer any fight left in them. As we continued along this road for a few miles we saw thousands of German soldiers sitting and standing out in the fields where improvised prisoner of war compounds had been set up. There was only a tank here or there guarding them. One night my unit bivouacked across the road from one of these compounds, and I was called upon to go in to treat a German soldier. But I soon had so many soldiers applying to me for treatment that I had to leave. I also remember being sought out to examine a young girl occupying a small German civilian sedan that approached our roadblock. An old German doctor was driving the car, and he stated that the girl was sick with diphtheria and he needed a pass from a doctor to get her through the American lines to a hospital. I suspected that they were just trying to escape the Russians, but I could do no more than check the girl's temperature. When I found it was 105° Fahrenheit I wrote the pass, and they continued their flight to the West. After the War for a brief period of time, our Battalion was stationed at an old Luftwaffe base in Kothen, Germany. While we were there, American Army trucks brought in thousands of displaced persons and lodged them in barracks on the base. These people were mostly Slavic peoples, from Russia and the east European countries. The Allies were moving them back to their homelands. I had occasion to go into the barracks to treat some of the sick children, and I remember that the adults were always playing musical instruments and engaging in folk dances. On the whole they seemed to be a happy, irresponsible people. However, there were some who were terrified at the idea of returning to Russia. For example, one day a Russian man was brought into my dispensary. He had just hanged himself and was dead. He couldn't face what lay ahead of him back in his homeland. As for us, we were glad that the War was over and were anxious to get back home. It was not until the fall of 1945, however, before we were able to return home.

The greatest memories I have of the 7th Armored Division are not of the epic events in which it was involved, but of the everyday, ordinary happenings in the life of the Division. The 7th Armored was truly a great Division, even in the day of its earliest training at Camp Polk. The efficiency and discipline of the Division were not that of a green Division, but had the unmistakable mark of a professional organization. During the War the Division had participated in the campaigns of Northern France, the Ardennes, the Rhineland, the Battle of Germany, and Central Europe, and had gained distinction in all of them. Approximately 18,000 men and officers went to War. How many we left in Europe I have never known. Many of my friends, officers and enlisted, were killed in battle. Great credit must be given to General Silvester, who trained and inspired the Division so well, and to his successor, General Hasbrouck, who proved himself so well in the epic Battle of the Bulge.

As for my Detachment — from Fort Benning days on until the end of the War — we lived as one close-knit family through many ordeals of battle and under adverse field conditions of rain, mud, and severe cold. But there was an esprit de corps that the civilian never knows. I never would have been willing to rotate back to a rear hospital for easier living, but preferred to stay with the Division wherever it went. The officers in my unit were Captain Henry Herzog, MC, of Lockport, New York, and Lieutenant Tindall, MSC, of Des Plaines, Illinois. My enlisted men were Staff Sergeant Joseph Garrett of Greenville, Mississippi; Sergeant Raymond Rust of Lawton, Oklahoma; Sergeant Frank Theiss of Anna, Illinois; Corporal Upchurch of Jonesboro, Illinois; Corporal Burns of Philadelphia, Pennsylvania; Corporal Boyer of East St. Louis, Illinois; Corporal Oliver of Detroit, Michigan; and Corporal Ed Ringer of Cohoes, New York.

The greatest gain for me was the comradeship I enjoyed with the officers and enlisted men, who were my friends and patients. I knew and respected men from many ethnic origins who made up the Battalion. I found that the boys of Brooklyn were not any different from the boys of the rural South and West. This comradeship was my greatest experience, a comradeship which still exists over 40 years later among the members of the 7th Armored Division Association.

Wendell H. Cook, M.D.
Meridian, Mississippi
October 3, 1986

Officers and men, Medical Det., 129th Ordnance Maintenance Bn.: Front row L to R, Sgt. Raymond Rust, Lawton, Okla; Cpl. Boyer, East St. Louis, Ill; Cpl. Ed Ringer, Cohoes, NY; unidentified; S/Sgt. Joseph Garrett, Greenville, Miss. Back row L to R, 1st Lt. Tindall, Des Plains, Ill; Sgt. Frank Theiss, Anna, Ill; Louis Vincent, Belgian civilian; Capt. Wendell H. Cook, Philadelphia, Miss; Cpl. Burns, Philadelphia, Pa.

# Our General Bob

(Gene Jones)

General Robert W. Hasbrouck was a soldier, leader, statesman, gentleman and a friend. In our imagination we can see this young man — already a soldier in his heart — as he left his home in Kingston, N.Y. to enter the United States Military Academy on the first step of preparing himself for a most worthy lifetime career.

The training experience, his ability and the character displayed by this young Cadet then — officer later — as he merited recognition along the route toward maturity placed him in the position of great responsibility and leadership and whatever the order of assignment may have been throughout the years of his service to his country, it was carried out in first class military form which proved him to be the soldier he was and the leader he became.

With the many qualities he possessed and the experience gained, General Hasbrouck proved to be a statesman. His broad views and knowledge of public affairs gave him the ability to deal with questions and problems concerning the activities, not only of our country, but the nation.

General Hasbrouck was a man of compassion, a man of love whose lifestyle displayed these wonderful qualities. We recall the many enjoyable conversations, welcomed letters and the many telephone calls exchanged over the years and how he always expressed himself of the concern of his family's well being and of our family. He had become acquainted with our family over the years of reunioning and he enjoyed telling us of the progress of his flowers and yard each season that he admired so much.

He was always interested in the welfare of the men and families of the Seventh Armored Division and often mentioned them, especially of something directly involved with these people. We remember so well how he felt when his daughter Margie and her family moved to Paris to make their home. He expressed his feelings on how much he was going to miss those grandchildren whom he loved so much, and the joy he had when he and Mrs. Hasbrouck made their first trip to see them. What a thrill! Then immediately on their return home he informed us of the great pleasure and happiness they had on the visit and the thrill of that super jet trip.

Yes, General Hasbrouck was a distinguished soldier, an outstanding and courageous leader, a fine statesman, a respected gentleman and a wonderful friend. The Seventh Armored people will always cherish the memory of "Our General Bob."

General Hasbrouck's tombstone, West Point, NY.

General Hasbrouck's funeral U.S. Military Academy, West Point, NY. August 1985.

Medallion from Epernon, France.

Commemorative plate from Conde-en-Brie, France.

Armored Infantry moving through Arpajon, France.

# Farmington Observer

Old photos, a division patch and notes to home were among the items Glenn Fackler received in the mail. The message scrawled on the $10 bill gave Fackler the clue he needed to find the owner of the items.

RANDY BORST/staff photographer

## Super sleuth
### $10 bill helps solve a WW II puzzle

By Casey Hans
staff writer

It's a present-day war story about courage, honesty and a soldier's never-ending mental conflict.

**Glenn Fackler**

Farmington Hills resident Glenn Fackler, secretary for the Seventh Armored Division Association from World War II, hopes his actions last week ease the mind of an anonymous soldier and a self-proclaimed "living coward."

The soldier wrote Fackler an anonymous letter, seeking a man who "half dragged me, half carried me" to safety, saving his life during World War II's Battle of the Bulge in the Ardennes Forest of Belgium. He enclosed some war mementoes and photos found in the man's field

> 'Whoever and wherever the "living coward" is, I hope he's got the peace of mind now that he's done this (sent the war memorabilia).'
> — Glenn Fackler
> Hills resident

jacket, which was left to shelter him. All he knew, according to his letter to Fackler, was that the man was from Philadelphia.

Fackler found the man's Philadelphia savior last week after two days of hard work and some good luck.

Fackler gets requests regularly to find soldiers locally, but, he said, "this is the most satisfying thing I've done in 40 years."

THE ANONYMOUS soldier had haunting memories of a December day in 1944 at St. Vith, Belgium, as a member of the 106th Infantry Division in World War II. That frontline division, never having seen a German soldier, was the first to be hit by the Germans at the start of the Battle of the Bulge Dec. 16.

The anonymous soldier talked of his fright and desperation when his division was hit.

"I got hit very bad; I was near a railroad tunnel and this soldier found me," the "living coward" wrote. "I was almost gone. He took his field jacket and put it on me. I was so cold I was blue."

The "coward" made it safely to England, where he spent three months in the hospital, leaving behind the lifesaving stranger from Philadelphia without a field jacket. The stranger stayed at the front line.

"The valor this soldier showed — not just for me but the seven men he went back for," the soldier's anonymous letter said. "It's been 42 years, and I never went to bed not thinking of this soldier."

Please turn to Page 4

# Hills resident unravels WWII mystery

A letter home, rolled up and placed inside a German rifle shell, describes a battle that took place with German soldiers. The bullets were intended as souvenirs of the war.

Continued from Page 1

THE FIELD jacket contained the war mementoes of Charles Atkinson of Philadelphia, formerly of Fackler's 7th Armored Division. It included letters to his wife, Mary, scribbled on remnants of paper in the heat of fighting, a Nazi lapel pin, two German-made armor-piercing shells and a photo of his child.

"He had remembered everything in his pocket," Fackler said, after speaking with Atkinson.

Atkinson's jacket pocket also held a $10 bill, carried since the day he enlisted Feb. 10, 1942, which was the key to "detective" Fackler's finding him.

On the bill was the notation that "McCormick had died Dec. 21, 1944," Fackler said. Checking the list of those killed and interred overseas, he discovered a Robert McCormick killed in action Dec. 23. He was a member of the 33rd Engineers.

A call to 33rd Engineer Grover Raymond in Livonia substantiated the fact that a now-deceased McCormick served in the 33rd. Checking another list, Fackler found only one man from the 33rd in the Philadelphia area — Charles Atkinson.

FACKLER WAS happy to find Mary Atkinson also alive. "She will cherish these things with him," he said.

Whoever and wherever the "living coward" is, "I hope he's got the peace of mind now that he's done this (sent the war memorabilia)," Fackler said.

"It took a lot of guts to do this — he's honest."

Secretary Glenn Fackler, Sr. at the Lucky Seventh IBM computer.

Ralph N. Fackler, Sr., age 9 months, August 1944.

SEVENTH ARMORED DIVISION Association

"From The Beaches to The Baltic"

MAJOR GENERAL ANDREW J. ADAMS

U.S. Army Photograph

# MAJOR GENERAL
# ANDREW J. ADAMS
## SECRETARY, AMERICAN BATTLE MONUMENTS COMMISSION, APPOINTED JUNE 1967

Andrew Joseph Adams was born in Andalusia, Alabama, on August 29, 1909. After graduation from the United States Military Academy in 1931, he was commissioned a second lieutenant. He has also attended the Infantry School (1938), the Command and General Staff College (1946), the Air Command and Staff College (1947), the Army Language School (1949), the Industrial College of the Armed Forces (1953), and was awarded the educational equivalent to the Armed Forces Staff College.

During World War II, he served as Trains Commander, Chief of Staff, and Combat Command Commander with the 7th Armored Division in the European Theater.

General Adams returned to the United States in 1945, and in March 1946 became an instructor at the Air Command and Staff College, Air University, Maxwell Air Force Base, Alabama.

After holding this position until July 1949, he studied six months at the Presidio Language School in Monterey, California, and then, in December, went to Lima, Peru, as Deputy Chief of the Army Mission and Advisor to the Peruvian Army. He left in July of 1952 to return to Washington to attend the Industrial College of the Armed Forces.

General Adams was named Assistant Chief, Management Division, in the Office of the Comptroller of the Army, Washington, in July 1953.

He became Commanding Officer, 23rd Infantry, 2nd Infantry Division, U.S. Army Far East Command in December 1953. In September of the following year, he became Senior Advisor to the Commanding General, Second Republic of Korea Army, and Commanding Officer, Detachment "R", Korean Military Advisory Group.

In July 1955, he was named as Director of Personnel, Office of the Deputy Chief of Staff for Logistics, in Washington, D.C. In October 1957, he became Director of Supply Operations in that same office. He was designated Deputy Chief of Staff, Logistics, Headquarters, United States Army, Europe, in July 1959. In March 1961, he was named Commanding General of the Seventh Army Support Command with additional duties as Commander of Mobile Land Forces, Allied Command Europe, and Deputy Commander of Seventh Army.

General Adams returned to the United States in November 1962 to assume command of Fort Chafee, Arkansas, and the XIX U.S. Army Corps. He was assigned to Headquarters, U.S. Army, Pacific, as Assistant Chief of Staff, G-4 (Logistics), effective September 1963. Assigned Fort Monroe, Virginia, as Deputy Chief of Staff for Logistics, Headquarters U.S. Continental Army Command, June 1966.

His decorations include: Distinguished Service Medal, Silver Star, Legion of Merit (1st Oak Leaf Cluster), Bronze Star Medal, Army Commendation Medal (1st Oak Leaf Cluster), Legion d'Honneur (France), Croix de Guerre avec Palm (France), Ulchi with Gold Star (Korea), European-African-Middle Eastern Campaign Medal with four Bronze Service Stars, National Defense Service Medal (1st Oak Leaf Cluster), Korean Service Medal, United Nations Service Medal, General Staff Identification Badge, Order Militar de Ayacucho (Peru)

Memorial Day, 1986, Fort Polk, LA. Harold "Jiggs" Johnson (HQ/48), places wreath at the Seventh Armored Division Monument.

# MEMORIALIZATION

The first volume of THE LUCKY SEVENTH described the memorials of the Seventh Armored Division that had materialized prior to its publication in 1982. What follows are the memorial events since then, what is currently being accomplished, and what is planned to further commemorate the Seventh Armored Division and its members.

While this report is written over the name of the Memorialization Chairman for that committee, it is again emphasized that all memorials have come about through the efforts and cooperation of many other people; none more so than Major General Andrew J. Adams and the members of the American Battle Monuments Commission, of which General Adams is the Secretary. The American Battle Monuments Commission is that agency of the United States government responsible to the people of the United States for the construction and permanent maintenance of military cemeteries and memorials on foreign soil, as well as for certain memorials on American soil. Under U.S. law, no memorial can be placed overseas without the approval of the American Battle Monuments Commission and the Fine Arts Commission.

During World War II, then Colonel Adams, was G-4, Chief of Staff, Commander of CCB, CCA, CCR and Trains. He held every colonel's position in the Seventh Armored Division with the exception of artillery commander. His skillful command of the Seventh Armored Division Trains in the Battle of the Ardennes is reported on page 105 of the first volume of THE LUCKY SEVENTH. As of this time General Adams has seen 55 years of active duty and is probably the only general officer on active duty that served in World War II. Though required to retire in 1967, he was recalled on his retirement by President Johnson for continued service with the American Battle Monuments Commission.

Through the years, Association member General Adams has had our memorials checked for condition and appearance. In 1972 he submitted a list to the Association of the Seventh Armored Division's dead, either buried or remembered on the Walls of the Missing, in American overseas cemeteries. That list indicated 6 in Cambridge, England; 3 in Normandy, 40 in Brittany, 39 in Epinal, 114 in Lorraine, all in France; 164 in Margraten, Netherlands; 37 in Ardennes and 168 in Henri-Chapelle, Belgium; and 35 in Hamm, Luxembourg.

Since the placement of the Vielsalm and Chartres plaques, the Association has arranged to place wreaths on Memorial Day at the Seventh Armored Division monuments at Fort Benning, Georgia, and Fort Polk, Louisiana, and once each year at the plaques in Europe. At Chartres, France, this is done during its Liberation Day ceremonies in August, in conjunction with the total ceremonies honoring the French Veterans and Resistance. On each occasion when our wreath was placed by either Koenraad Molenaar or Peter Wampers, the Mayor of Chartres placed the wreath of the community of Chartres, as he indicated would be done when our plaque was dedicated on the 21st of September, 1984.

At Vielsalm, Belgium, Peter Wampers has placed, or arranged for the placement of, our wreaths at the Tank and the Seventh Armored Division Monument, as does that community by Deputy Mayor Gilson and Major Paquay of the 3rd Chasseurs Ardennais, both of whom played a large part in our dedication ceremonies in 1984. Also, the town of Vielsalm is supplied with American and division flags by our Association to be flown at the monuments during ceremonies. In the Netherlands Dr. Jan Pameijer continues to place our wreaths at Margraten Cemetery at each Memorial Day Ceremony.

This past year at Fort Benning, Hubert Martin (HQ/48), Arthur Farrel (C/48), and Paul Massengill (SERV/48) were in attendance as Colonel Fred O. Jackson (DIV/HQ) placed the wreath on Memorial Day at the Seventh Armored Division Monument. The 69th Armor provided an Honor Guard for this ceremony. All arrangements for the Association were made by Dick Grube, Director of the National Infantry

Memorial Day, 1986, Fort Benning, GA. L to R: Arthur Farrell (C/48), Col. Fred Jackson, Ret. (DIV/HQ), Warrant Officer-4 Paul Massengill, Ret. (SVC/48), Hubert Martin (HQ/48), and Col. Dick Grube, Ret., Director of the Fort Benning National Infantry Museum, after the Seventh Armored Division wreath had been placed at the monument.

Museum at Fort Benning.

At Fort Polk, Harold "Jiggs" Johnson (HQ/48) placed our wreath which was in the form of our division patch. The staff of the Fort Polk Military Museum arranged this ceremony. "Jiggs" has been provided with a set of Seventh Armored Division Heraldry posters to give to the 40th Armor stationed at Fort Polk. It is hoped that this present day unit which, in army lineage, is the 40th Tank Battalion of the Seventh Armored Division, will be a part of coming Memorial Day ceremonies at the Seventh Armored Division Monument at the fort. In the future we look for more of our local Seventh Armored Division Association members to attend our memorial ceremonies at both Fort Benning and Fort Polk.

To those new members of the Association it may not be known that Fort Polk was declared the "home station" for the Seventh Armored Division in 1972, and it is there our Division Flag with Battle Streamers is officially placed. The Seventh Armored Division display in the Fort Polk Military Museum is the largest; and even though the museum, which is housed in an old World War II barrack, is short of space, it has recently accepted the "pinks and greens" of our late General Hasbrouck. The uniform, complete and correct as to decorations and division patch, was donated by Robert W. Hasbrouck, Jr.

At the Harrisburg reunion the Association approved the placement of a Division Obelisk at the Armor Memorial Park, Patton Museum, Fort Knox, Kentucky. The granite, four-sided obelisk is 64 inches high, with a bronze plaque on each side. A photograph of our obelisk appears in this section.

During the 1984 trip to Belgium and France to dedicate the Seventh

The Seventh Armored Division Obelisk with First, Sixth and Twelfth Division Obelisks in the background, Fort Knox, KY.

The great Chartres Cathedral where the Seventh Armored Division Plaque was placed in the "Garden of the Bishop" in September 1984.

Staff Sergeant Robert H. Dietz, 38th Armored Infantry Battalion, awarded the Congressional Medal of Honor posthumously.

The Seventh Armored Division Obelisk at the Armor Memorial Park, Patton Museum, Fort Knox, NY.

Armored Division Plaques, Carl and Betty Mattocks, Dr. John and Carol Margreiter, and Al and Ruth Spinazzola visited the "EXPOSITION PERMANENTE DU DEBARQUEMENT" (The Invasion Museum) at Arromanches, Normandy France. They recommended to the Association that our division flag be sent there to be displayed with the other flags of the divisions that arrived on the continent over those shores. The next year this was done, and the Curator, Mr. Jean Noel, has promised a picture of our flag in place when an enlargement to the museum is finished. We have also arranged for a Division History to be presented to the museum.

There are also plans to have a division flag placed in the area of Melun, France, where the Seventh Armored Division crossed the Seine River on the 23rd of August, 1944. There is a marker at that crossing site indicating another division crossed there first. The Association feels this matter should be clarified, and while we can hardly demand the removal of the erroneous marker, we do plan to have the accurate historical facts made known and request that our division flag be placed in a suitable place as a reminder of that historic event.

In addition to having a flag placed at Melun, we feel it would be appropriate for the Association to place a flag in a suitable place to signify the brutal combat in which the Seventh Armored Division was involved from the 6th of September to the 23rd of September, 1944, in the vicinity of Metz. During this time the division advanced from the area east of Verdun to the crossings of the Moselle River and fought to the Seille River. This was Fortress Metz, and during the time noted, the Seventh Armored Division, in frontal assaults against stubbornly defended and wellI-fortified positions, suffered losses of 47 medium and 8 light tanks, plus 469 men dead or missing and 737 wounded. Combat Command "R" had eight different commanders from the 1st to the 21st of September, most of whom became battle casualties, and on the 19th of September on the edge of Sillegny, the 38th Armored Infantry Battalion had its Commanding Officer, LTC Rosebro, mortally wounded. The Executive Officer, Major Rankin, was killed, and the next senior officer to take command, Major Wells, was killed. LTC King, who was sent forward from Division Headquarters to take command, was wounded and replaced by LTC Rhea. In a period of less than a day, the 38th had five different commanders.

Should it come about that the Association is able to have a division flag placed at Melun and one at an appropriate place in the area of "Fortress Metz," our goal to have each location of historical significance to the Seventh Armored Division recognized with a memorial or flag will have been achieved.

Norman G. J. Jones
Past Memorialization Chairman

## DEDICATION OF THE SEVENTH ARMORED DIVISION PLAQUES AT VIELSALM, BELGIUM, AND CHARTRES, FRANCE

The following is the personal account of Norman G. J. Jones, past Memorialization Chairman, of the dedications of the plaques on the Sherman M-4 Tank at Vielsalm, Belgium on September 16, 1984 and at Chartres, France on September 21, 1984. Both of these events have been mentioned briefly in the foregoing sections of this volume. Because of the paramount significance of these events in the Association's overall memorialization program and the large number of Association members who participated, these ceremonies are described by Norman Jones in some detail.

At Vielsalm on September 16th there were actually four different ceremonies in which our members were a part: At 9:30 AM a mass was held at the Vielsalm Church; at 10:45 there was the Ceremony of the Secret Army at the church; at 11:05 AM there was a ceremony at the Monument of the Seventh Armored Division (known as the Bruce Clark Monument); and at 11:40 AM the ceremony at the Sherman M-4 Tank was conducted. Space limitations will permit recounting the Sherman Tank ceremony only, which was the most significant of the day for the Seventh Armored Division Association; however, photographs show all four ceremonies.

FIRST CEREMONY — at the Monument of the "Secret Army" (UNDERGROUND), located at the Church in Vielsalm, Belgium.

The President of the association of the "Secret Army" delivers the address at the opening of the ceremony.

Peter Wampers (D/17) and the Mayor of Salmchateau have placed the wreaths at the Monument of the Secret Army, and the salute is presented.

Peter Wampers (D/17) with the "UNDERGROUND ARMY INSIGNIA" on left sleeve; and Mr. Siquet, Mayor of Salmchateau, place the association and community wreaths. Battle Flags of the Veterans of the Brigade Piron, and other organizations are in a "lowered" position. (Salmchateau is where the units retreated across the last bridge over the Salm River on the 23 of December 1944. The "Brigade Piron" was attached to the Seventh Armored Division during the fighting in the Peel Marshes in the Fall of 1944.)

SECOND CEREMONY — at the Seventh Armored Division Monument, General Bruce Clarke Square, Vielsalm, Belgium.

THIRD CEREMONY — at the Monument of the Vielsalm War Dead of World War I and World War II, located in the Vielsalm Cemetery.

Dr. Jan Pameijer (HQ/CCR), citizen of Vielsalm, and members of the Belgian Military, and Gendarmes — stand at attention and salute monument with wreaths in place. Dr. Pameijer placed the Seventh Armored Division Association floral piece.

Colonel Sam Sharp (HQ/48), center, reads General Hasbrouck's message to those assembled for the ceremony. Koenraad Molenaar (DIV/HQ), translates the message standing on Colonel Sharp's left, while Norman Jones (DIV/QM) standing on Colonel Sharp's right, coordinates the ceremony.

Base of Monument showing wreaths in place, with Seventh Armored Division Association at right. (Point of interest — the Commander of the 3rd Chasseur Ardenais Troops, for the four ceremonies was a Maj. Paquay. M. Paquay, fifth name from top, is memorialized under 1914-1918 on left of monument.)

The assembled organizations, bands, and veteran's groups in place around Seventh Armored Division Monument.

Deputy Mayor Gilson of Vielsalm, James Feldhusen (HQ/129) and Carl Little (B/38) stand at attention, after placing wreaths at Seventh Armored Division Monument.

Top portion of Monument of Belgian War Dead, showing fallen soldier.

# CEREMONY AT THE SHERMAN M-4 TANK
## VIELSALM, BELGIUM, SEPTEMBER 16, 1984

As previously noted the TANK is on a full concrete base, on a triangular shaped plot that is landscaped, and is walled and hedged. Opposite the Police Barracks, it is on the road that Combat Command "B" took to Poteau and St. Vith on 17 December 1944. The procession was placed with Seventh Armored people on the apex of the triangular plot facing the Tank, which was flanked with the Guard of Honor, at the rear of the Tank was the Battle Flags of the Belgian, and of course, the Seventh Armored Division Veterans. Along with the Seventh Armored contingent the Pompiers, School Children, Municipal Authorities, Patriotic Associations, and Bands flanked both sides of the plot on the long side — so as to be able to observe the ceremony.

The first speech was made by Mr. Gilson, a deputy mayor, who, acting as representative of the mayor, told of the history of the warfare around Vielsalm in World War II. He told how the 3rd Chasseurs Ardennais fought a hard and gallant delaying action against the blitzkrieging Panzer Army in 1940. How in September of 1944 the First United States Army liberated that portion of Belgium, only to have the December Offensive again see Vielsalm under the Nazi yoke — despite the heroic efforts of the Seventh Armored Division. He also told of the American counter offensive — that saw the final liberation of Vielsalm.

Mr. Gilson went on to tell of the efforts to have the Tank placed at Vielsalm (it is a story in it's own right); how General Clarke obtained the tank and for six years, along with Dr. Delaval, worked without being discouraged to have the tank finally placed in February of 1984. Mr. Gilson also mentioned the efforts of our Association to do all it could to have the tank placed. He told of the efforts of the American, Belgian, and German armed forces to transport the Tank to Vielsalm. How a German Leopard tank was used to pull the M4 on to the transporter, of the long journey that required roads to be blocked off so the transport vehicle had the right of way required. How it was an effort made by the present day Allies of American, Belgian and German armed forces. It is ironic that in the last leg of the journey to Vielsalm, the Tank passed through St. Vith.

When Mr. Gilson finished his speech, Koenraad Molenaar (Div/HQ), who acted as our interpreter at all the ceremonies at Vielsalm and Chartres, and I stepped to the microphone to dedicate the Seventh Armored Division plaque.

I recognized the officials of Vielsalm, Colonel Duysen of the Belgian Army, Lt. Col. Mathen of the 3rd Chasseurs Ardennais, Lt. Col. Painter US Army — who represented the United States Embassy, the religious authorities, the Honor Guard, the Veterans of Colonel Piron's Belgian Brigade, and those in attendance.

On behalf of the Association I expressed our gratitude to the munic-

FOURTH CEREMONY — at the M4 Sherman Tank located opposite the Vielsalm Police Barracks, on the road Combat Command "B" took to Poteau and St. Vith on the 17th of December 1944.

Group of Seventh Armored Division Association people in front of Tank after the conclusion of the ceremony. Mr. and Mrs. Peter Wampers (D/17), Dr. John Margreiter (C/23), who read the Division's Battle Awards during the ceremony, Norman Jones, the Memorialization Chairman, Jany Delaval, Carole Margreiter, Dr. Maurice Delaval, Betty Mattocks looking toward Carl Mattocks (HQ/38) who has back to camera, and who uncovered the Plaque during the ceremony of dedication.

Peter Wampers (D/17), Norman Jones (Div/QM), Honor Guard from the Vielsalm based 3rd Chasseurs Ardennais (Hunter) Unit, Robert Owens (HQ/23) reading all the Seventh Armored Division and Attached Units that fought in the Battle of St. Vith, Koenraad Molenaar interpreting into French for the reading of the Units. Koenraad Molenaar served with Civ/HQ.

Left — William Raab (C/87) and William Cohan (HQ/48) have just placed the association wreath in front of the M4 Tank, and stand with their hands over their hearts as the "Star Spangled Banner" is being played.

Right — Honor Guard from 3rd Chasseurs Ardennais (Hunter Regiment), at "Present Arms" after wreaths have been placed in front of Tank and "Star Spangled Banner" is being played.

ipality and people of Vielsalm, General Clarke, The American Army, The American Battle Monuments Commission, and the 3rd Chasseurs Ardennais for the placing of the Tank and our plaque.

In abbreviated detail I related the events of the Battle of St. Vith, naming General Hasbrouck, General Clarke, General Hoge of Combat Command "B" of the 9th Armored Division, and Colonel Adams of the Division Trains.

To recognize the part played by the units that fought with the Seventh Armored Division at St. Vith, we had Mr. Robert Owens (HQ/23) read all the units recommended by General Hasbrouck for the Presidential Unit Citation. This included the various units of Combat Command "B" 9th Armored Division, the 424th and 112th Infantry regiments, the 275th Armored Field Artillery Battalion, down to the separate platoons from odd units.

At this point Carl Mattocks (HQ/38) came to the Tank and removed the cover (made by Peter Wampers) of Armored Force Green — from our plaque. I explained the wording — "LE CHAR INVINCIBLE" — THE INVINCIBLE TANK, REFLECTS ON THE TANK, — WHICH IS THE MONUMENT, AND THE PART IT PLAYED IN THE BATTLE. "LE COURAGE INVINCIBLE" — THE INVINCIBLE COURAGE, REFLECTS ON THE BRAVERY OF THE MEN WHO FOUGHT AT ST. VITH. I ADDED THAT IT TOOK INVINCIBLE COURAGE TO FACE THE GERMAN TANKS, FOR THEY WERE, DUE TO THEIR GREATER ARMOR AND FIRE POWER, MORE FORMIDABLE THAN THE AMERICAN TANKS.

THE INSCRIPTION READS: "THE AMERICAN SEVENTH ARMORED DIVISION AND ATTACHED UNITS HEADQUARTERED IN VIELSALM DURING THE CRUCIAL PERIOD OF THE GERMAN OFFENSIVE IN THE ARDENNES IN 1944 — HELD THE IMPORTANT CENTER OF ST. VITH — PREVENTING ANY ADVANCE AND ANY EXPLOITATION ON THIS MAIN LINE — THUS FRUSTRATING THE GERMAN OFFENSIVE — BY ITS SACRIFICE PERMITTING THE LAUNCHING OF THE ALLIED COUNTER OFFENSIVE."

I explained the seven stars and insignia represent the Seventh Armored Division, the appropriate dates are indicated, and the phrase of dedication reads: "PRESENTED BY THE SEVENTH ARMORED DIVISION ASSOCIATION IN HONOR OF ALL WHO FOUGHT SO VALIANTLY AT ST. VITH."

I ended my speech by noting that on the 23rd of January 1945, the Seventh Armored Division took St. Vith back from the enemy.

At this point Mr. Gilson came back to the Tank and uncovered the two Seventh Armored Division insignia attached to each side of the turret. These insignia were made up by a Vielsalm artist by the name of Mr. Renard

At this point William Raab (C/87) and William J. Cohan (HQ/48) came forward to place our wreath, along with the wreaths of the other principals. The "LAST POST" (Equivalent of the American "TAPS") was played, the Star Spangled Banner, and the Belgian National Anthem. The Seventh Armored Division people were each presented flowers and serenaded with American Music. The ceremonies had ended. The procession then moved to the Officers Mess of the Vielsalm Garrison, there we were accorded a Wine of Honor, that was generous to the extreme with Champagne.

# CEREMONY AT CHARTRES, FRANCE, SEPTEMBER 21, 1984

The ceremonies at Chartres were in three parts preceded by a luncheon hosted by the Mayor of Chartres, Mr. Georges Lemoine, for the principals, and followed by a Wine of Honor for all principals and visiting veterans and wives of the Seventh Armored Division Association. The Wine of Honor was also hosted by Mr. Lemoine, who in addition to being Mayor, holds the cabinet post of the Secretary of the Interior for France.

The three ceremonies were the dedication of the monument to Field Marshal Jean de Lattre de Tassigny, the dedication of the Seventh Armored Division Plaque, and the service in the Great Cathedral of Chartres, the "Te Deum," which is a concert of sacred music.

In all three ceremonies, the French Veterans organization, "Rhine et Danube" and the Seventh Armored Division Association took part. Again, I must emphasize the welcome put forth to our Association by Mr. Lemoine and the municipality of Chartres. As at Vielsalm, it was sincere and the generosity of both places was beyond any expectation we had envisioned when arranging the ceremonies.

Again, because of space limitation we can cover only the dedication of the Seventh Armored Division Plaque in the Garden of the Bishop and the service in the Great Cathedral following the dedication ceremony. Photographs show the dedication of the monument to Field Marshal Jean de Lattre de Tassigny.

FIRST CEREMONY — the dedication of the monument to the French Field Marshall Jean de Lattre de Tassigny, who had commanded the First French Army during the invasion of Southern France in mid-August of 1944. For this ceremony the Seventh Armored Division Association joined with the French Veterans Organization named "Rhin et Danube" (Rhine and Danube), for their ceremony in dedication the monument to the French Field Marshal. Following this ceremony, the French Veterans and all participants, joined with our association in the dedication of the Seventh Armored Division Plaque.

Near to the end of the dedication of the monument to Marshal Jean de Lattre de Tassigny, all present are saluting — or at attention — as the "Marseillaise" is being played. Facing the monument from the left are the Senior Military Officer, Mr. Georges Lemoine, Mayor of Chartres; the widow of Marshal Jean de Lattre de Tassigny, two officials of the French Veterans organizations, William Renner (C/203) and Grover Ponder (C/48) who had placed the Seventh Armored Division Association wreath, and Walter Keely (C/23) holding the American Flag.

Norman Jones (Div/QM) introduces Colonel Sam Sharp (HQ/48), who is standing at his left, to read General Knowlton's letter to the dedication of the monument to French Field Marshal Jean de Lattre de Tassigny. To the right, Koenraad Molenaar is prepared to do the translation to French. The ceremony took place in a park on the Boulevard Chasles, Chartres, France.

Colonel Sam Sharp (HQ/48) reading General Knowlton's message, with Koenraad Molenaar (Div/HQ) doing the interpreting on his left. On Sam Sharp's right is Norman Jones (Div/QM) who has introduced Colonel Sharp. Over Jone's right shoulder is the widow of Field Marshal Jean de Lattre de Tassigny, who is standing with the group of officers from the French Veteran's organization of "Rhin et Danube." Walter Keely (C/23) stands with the American Flag, with the bearer of the Flag of France in the forefront of the French and American veterans. Directly to the rear of the monument, William Cohan (HQ/48) carries the Seventh Armored Division Flag.

View from the rear of the monument being dedicated to the Field Marshal Jean de Lattre de Tassigny, on the Boulevard Chasles in Chartres, France. Picture taken while Colonel Sam Sharp (HQ/48) is delivering General Knowlton's message, and shows the crowd through the battle flags of the French veterans organization of "Rhin et Danube."

## DEDICATION OF THE PLAQUE IN THE GARDEN OF THE BISHOP

Mr. Goupillon, the Chief of Protocal for Chartres, indicated to the assembly to form the parade to the Garden of the Bishop for the dedication of the Seventh Armored Division Plaque. The order of the parade was the Military Band, the Flags, the Civilian Authorities, the Military Delegation, the French Veterans of "Rhine and Danube," and the Seventh Armored Division Delegation. The parade led from the Boulevard Chasles to the Cathedral, about a fifteen minute walk, led by the Military Band that played martial music — along streets that were closed off to the public. Arriving at the Cathedral the parade passed on the north side to the rear of the edifice to the Jardin de l'Eveche (Garden of the Bishop). This garden is a four level terraced garden about the size of a football field, as expected, it is immaculately landscaped and walled. Our plaque is on the south side on the second level. The different organizations were placed with the principals in the ceremony being on the same level as the plaque, along with those placing the wreaths. The Seventh Armored delegation on the level above the plaque, "Rhine and Danube" veterans formed a perimeter at right angles to the Seventh Armored Division delegation. The battle flags were on the level below the plaque, with the American and Seventh Armored Division Flags to the front. The Guard of Honor and the Military Band formed the angle to finish the squared formation, which put the plaque in the focal point along the wall. When all were in place, the Guard of Honor saluted.

When all the units were in place, Mr. Goupillon, the Chief of Protocol, indicated to Koenraad Molenaar that the ceremony could begin. Koenraad again introduced me as the Memorialization Chairman of the Association and that the ceremony was to dedicate the Seventh Armored Division Plaque. I recognized the principals, expressed our gratitude to the Mayor and City of Chartres, and to the American Battle Monuments Commission. I expressed our pleasure that the plaque is near the Cathedral, in the serenity of the Garden. I recognized the French martyr, Jean Moulin, who had been the prefect of Chartres and had been tortured to death by the Germans, after organizing all the French Resistance in France, doing this after he had parachuted back into France after escaping to England. During the speech the French Military Mission to the Seventh Armored Division was related, including their losses of seven killed in action, three wounded, and thirteen missing in action. That in France our division was commanded by Major General Lindsay Macdonald Silvester, who had fought with distinction in World War I. That Chartres was the first major engagement for the Seventh Armored Division and it was a difficult fight because no artillery was used in order to spare the Cathedral, that the armor was confined in the narrow streets that there was particularly hard fighting at the airport and railroad station. Also, that in the latter stages of the fighting the 5th Infantry Division was committed. That the French Military Mission served with our division until the end of the War, that the French citizens, Free French Forces of the Interior, and the Resistance did all they could to aid in our liberating actions in France, some of whom joined the French Military Mission, one example being Nick Daniloff.

The memorials that exist in Chartres to the French Patriots were noted, and recognized.

At this point I explained the design of the plaque. "VIVE L'AMERIQUE" (LONG LIVE AMERICA), "VIVE LA FRANCE" (LONG LIVE FRANCE), "VIVE LA LIBERTE" (LONG LIVE LIBERTY) was taken from letters written by liberated communities to the Division Commander. The reproduction of General Walker's letter authenticates the part the Seventh Armored Division played in the liberation of France. The letter written under the letterhead of the 20th Corps, dated 19 September 1944, reads: "TO THE SEVENTH ARMORED DIVISION . . . DURING THE DRIVE FROM LE MANS TO METZ, THE TWENTIETH CORPS, GENERALLY WITH THE SEVENTH ARMORED DIVISION IN THE LEAD, WAS THE SPEARHEAD OF THE ALLIED ARMIES. THE EVENTH ARMORED DIVISION CAPTURED CHARTRES, MELUN, CHATEAU THIERRY, REIMS AND VERDUN, OPENING THE WAY FOR SUCCESSFUL CROSSINGS OF THE SEINE, THE MARNE, THE VESLE, THE AISNE AND THE MEUSE RIVERS, THUS LIBERATING LARGE AREAS AND INNUMERABLE VILLAGES OF FRANCE. SOLDIERS OF THE SEVENTH ARMORED DIVISION, I CONGRATULATE YOU ON YOUR ACHIEVEMENTS. SIGNED . . . WALTON H. WALKER, MAJOR GENERAL, COMMANDING.

In order that those assembled should know of our division, Dr. John Margreiter (C/23) came to the microphone and read the Seventh Armored Division's Battle Honors and commendations. We announced that Mr. John Eckerman (B/17) would uncover the plaque, and that our wreath will be placed by Mr. Harry Garren (A/87) and Libro "Al" Spinazzola (B/31). As soon as John Eckerman moved to uncover the plaque the military commander called all the military to "Present Arms." When the plaque was uncovered the members of the Fire Department of Chartres assisted in the placing of the wreaths of the Seventh Armored Division, "Rhine and Danube," Mayor Lemoine's, and the Prefect of the district of Eure and Loire. With the wreaths in place, the Commander of the Guard of Honor called the "Present Arms," the last Post (Taps) was played, followed by a minute of silence, the band played the Star Spangled Banner and the Marseillaise. All the military, including Mayor Lemoine and the Madame le Marechal de Lattre came up to a position before the plaque and stood at attention. The military stood and rendered a salute. The ceremony dedicating the Seventh Armored Division Plaque had ended.

SECOND CEREMONY — the dedication of the Seventh Armored Division Plaque in the Garden of the Bishop to the rear of the Cathedral at Chartres, France.

Harry Garren (A/87), who along with Libro "Al" Spinazzola (B/31) placed the Seventh Armored Division wreath, the two Gendarmes who stood attention on each side of the Plaque for the entire ceremony, and John Eckerman (B/17) who uncovered the plaque. The four wreaths placed show the white wreath from our association directly under the plaque and up against the wall, in front of our wreaths are the ones placed by "Rhin et Danub" on the left, and the two others from the City of Chartres and the District of Eure et Loire.

The participating units have marched from the park on the Boulevard Chasles, where the Seventh Armored Division veterans joined with the French veterans of the order of "Rhin et Danub" to dedicate the monument to the French Field Marshal Jean de Lattre de Tassigny, — to the rear of Chartres Cathedral (Garden of the Bishop) to dedicate the Seventh Armored Division Plaque. Mr. Goupillon, Chief of Technical Services and Protocol for the city of Chartres, has formed the assembly for the ceremony on the tiered levels of the "Garden."

Norman Jones (Div/QM) with Koenraad Molenaar (Div/HQ) translating, have told the reason and design of the plaque, John Margreiter (C/23) has read the Division's Combat Awards, and John Eckerman (B/17) has uncovered the Plaque. From the left the dignitaries — that include from the top of the picture, the two senior military commanders, Mayor Goerges Lemoine of Chartres, Madame "Le Marechal" de Lattre de Tassigny, Mayor Thompson — the military representative of the American Embassy, and a French official. On the steps, with the metal helmets, are the members of the Chartres fire fighters with the wreaths. Harry Garren (A/87) and Libro "Al" Spinoza (B/31) stand ready to place the wreaths; below, in front of the flag bearers of the French Veterans are Walter Keely (C/23) with the American Flag and William Cohan (HQ/48) with the flag of the Seventh Armored Division.

Following the dedication of the Seventh Armored Division Plaque in the Garden of the Bishop at Chartres Cathedral, France, members of the association pause to have their picture taken at the plaque. John Margreiter (C/23) who read the Seventh Armored Division Battle Awards, Colonel Sam Sharp (HQ/48) who read General Knowlton's message at the dedication of the monument to Field Marshal Jean de Lattre de Tassigny, Koenraad Molenaar (DIV/HQ) who did the translating at the ceremonies, Libro "Al" Spinoza (B/31) who with Harry Garren (A/87) placed the Seventh Armored Division Association wreath at the plaque, Norman Jones (DIV/QM) association Memorialization Chairman, and the French Gendarmes that remained at attention through and after the dedication ceremony.

Following the "Te Deum" service in the cathedral, the Flag Bearers, Bands, Guard of Honor were led out of the Cathedral first, so that they could form a cordon to the City Hall of Chartres. All the members attending the ceremonies were marched through that cordon to attend a "Wine of Honor" hosted by Mayor Georges Lemoine, at extreme right. Madame Le Marechal stops to shake hands with William Cohan (HQ/48) holding the Division Flag and Walter Keely (C/23) the American Flag.

## SERVICE IN THE CATHEDRAL OF CHARTES

Following the plaque dedication, the assembly was led by the flag bearers, out of the terraced garden to the front of the Cathedral, and made a special entry through the Royal Doors (it was told to us at the meeting that these doors are usually opened only twice a year). It was significant, that on the low altar, though our ceremonies had been to the French Field Marshal and the Seventh Armored Division, the only two flags on the low altar were the American and Seventh Armored Division Flags. The rest of the Battle Flags were below the altar which faced the congregation. With all of the principals and attending public in place the Abbe (Abbot or Priest) Hercouet, assisted by three other priests in the vestments of their calling, sang a Te Deum Service. A Te Deum interprets into a "Thanks be to God," sung in latin, it was accompanied by the organ. Chartres Cathedral is believed by many to be the most impressive of all, unlike the flat topped spires of Notre Dame in Paris and Reims, the spires of Chartres Cathedral soar to a height of 112 meters, the one a filigreed gothic style started in the year 1134. One cannot write of Cathedrals without mentioning the magnificent stained glass windows, especially the round ones known as "Rose" windows. The "Te Deum," sung in the atmosphere of that historic edifice with the sun's rays occasionally coloring the stained glass windows, and Walter Keely (C/23) holding the American Flag and Bill Cohan (HQ/48) — the division flag on the raised altar was an impressive experience. When the "Te Deum" was ended the clergy led the Flag bearers to the Royal Doors and greeted the assembly as they filed out of the Cathedral.

Following the service in the Cathedral, the procession was then led to the City Hall where Mayor Lemoine hosted a "Wine of Honor." Mayor Lemoine welcomed the Seventh Armored Division guests and made a sincere speech to emphasize the significance of the day's ceremonies. He also directed remarks to Madame le Marechal de Lattre on the ceremony honoring her husband; he ended his remarks by presenting the "Medaille D'Honneur De La Ville-Chartres" — (The Medal of Honor of the City of Chartres) to the Association, and promising that each year, on the day Chartres was liberated, flowers would be placed at the Seventh Armored Division Plaque. He then presented an English version book on the Chartres Cathedral to the Seventh Armored Division, and a souvenir folder containing a transparency of the North Rose Window, to all the Seventh Armored Division guests. We had Roland B. Prieur, Superintendent of Suresnes American Cemetery, do the instantaneous translation for Mr. Lemoine's speech. We then read President Kenneth R. Danielson's message, which briefly told the circumstances of the fighting at Chartres, reiterated our gratitude for the placing of the plaque, that the plaque symbolized what the sacrifices of War had been — and the hopes that future generations would be reminded that Freedom is always threatened — and that seeing the plaque would be the reminder.

The Association then presented a Division History to Mr. Lemoine and Madame de Marechal de Lattre, a Seventh Armored Commemorative Plate to Mr. Paoli, the Secretary General of "Rhine and Danube," and to Mr. Grima, of the Chartres French Forces of the Interior. Koenraad Molenaar presented a framed Seventh Armored Division Box Score and a copy of the letter written by the Mayor of Senonches, France to General Silvester. (Mr. Grima is the regional President of "Rhine and Danube," and is also the present day Mayor of Senonches, which was liberated by the Seventh Armored Division on the 14th of August 1944.) A Seventh Armored Division Bolo was presented to Colonel Jacrot, Chief of the Military District of Eure et Loire. The presentation of a plaque was made on behalf of the Seventh Armored Division members on the Galaxy Tour by William Raab (C/87) and Lee Mestas (A/87), to Mr. Lemoine — who said it would be placed in his office. Mr. Goupillon, Chief of Protocol, was also presented a Seventh Armored Division Commemorative Plate. The formalities had ended and the champagne was poured, a Frenchman wearing a worn Seventh Armored Division patch on his coat made himself known as one who had served with the Seventh while it was in this area. Carl Mattocks gave him a Division History that he had carried along as an extra, it was an overwhelming gift. The City of Chartres had a pictorial display of the Seventh Armored Division, taken in 1944, on exhibit at the entrance to the Grand Salon where the "Wine of Honor" was held.

The Memorialization Committee would like to express its gratitude to Koenraad S. Molenaar (Div/HQ) for his invaluable help in arranging the ceremonies and acting as interpreter at Chartres. The Committee would also like to recognize the members of the Association who traveled with the Galaxy Tour, and those other Association members who traveled by separate means to attend and take part in the day's events. It was a tiring day, followed by an early flight home for those on the bus. We hope their hardship was compensated by the ceremonies.

For the Memorialization Committee:
Norman G. J. Jones, Chairman

Seventh Armored Division Association members at the American Cemetary at Hamm, Luxembourg. The cross indicates General Patton's grave, in the immediate foreground.

General Patton's grave at the American Overseas Cemetery at Hamm, Luxembourg.

Inside of Patton Museum, Luxembourg.

William Renner (C/203) stands along side of road signs indicating some historical places in the Battle of the Ardennes. Located at the General Bruce Clarke Square, Vielsalm, Belgium, the Malmedy-St. Vith sign hides the Seventh Armored Division Monument, which is in front of the building with the American and Belgian Flags. The "Galaxy Tours Operation Friendly Invasion" bus can be seen parked, with members of the Seventh Armored Division Association standing outside.

# BIOGRAPHICAL SKETCHES
# OF
# MEMBERS OF THE ASSOCIATION

All the biographical sketches were written and submitted by individual members, relatives, or close friends. The facts as they appear are the best recollection of the writers and the Seventh Armored Division Association has not endeavored to research or edit the material. In most instances, the stories appear as they were originally written.

## HUBERT L. ANDREW

Born November 6, 1925 in Gravious Mills, Missouri. He was inducted into the Army in April of 1944. Basic training took place at Ft. Knox, Kentucky. They sailed from New York to South Hampton, England where they were bombed so their ship, the USS General Brooks, pulled back out to sea and docked at Le Havre, France. From there they went to Lilie, France and worked their way into Liege, Belgium. He served as a first scout in B Troop, 87th Mechanized Cavalry under (then) Lt. William A. Knowlton. His most memorable part of the war was his trip to meet the Russians, which took place 55 kilometers inside the German lines at Lubz, Germany, which might have turned out very differently had it not been for the wittiness, craftiness and determination of Lt. Knowlton which resulted in the surrender of more than 3000 German troops to their small band of 65 men. While in Arlington, Virginia in March of 1983, he contacted General Knowlton and was happily surprised that he remembered him as well as several other men he had served with during that time. Hubert married Ruth Stromire in Idaho in 1945, and they have two sons who have given them three granddaughters and one grandson as well as two great-grandsons. He retired in 1980 after having worked over 30 years for the J.R. Simplot Company, a major potato processing firm in Idaho. Since retirement he has lived in the small mountain town of Albion, Idaho. His hobbies are hunting, fishing and enjoying his grandkids.

Hubert L. Andrew

## CHARLES H. ATKINSON

Born December 31, 1916 in Philadelphia. Inducted into the army February 10, 1942. Trained at Camp Polk, Louisiana. Six months of desert training, back to Ft. Benning, Georgia. He was with the 7th Armored Division from the start till the finish.

Received the Bronze Star in the Battle of the Bulge. Discharged August 22, 1945.

Retired in 1970, and enjoying every day of it. Married in Leeville, Louisiana in 1942. Has two boys and one girl and

Charles H. Atkinson

five grandchildren as well as one great-grandchild. He wishes he could talk to and see everyone from Co. B, 33rd Eng Bn. They were the best bunch of guys just to be with. They all made history.

## GEORGE M. AUSTIN

Born April 25, 1920, and raised in Cleveland, Ohio. He was inducted into the United States Army in February, 1942, and took basic training at Camp Polk, Louisiana. After basic, he spent time in the California Desert on maneuvers, followed by additional training at Ft. Benning, Georgia. On June 6, 1944 (D-Day), he embarked from New York for Europe as part of the "Lucky Seventh." In the following year, the 7th Armored Division engaged in battles and campaigns in Northern France, Belgium and Central Europe. They were credited with five campaigns. In December, 1944, during the Battle of the Bulge in Belgium, George was wounded and earned The Purple Heart. He was discharged from the U.S. Army on July 4, 1945, as Staff Sergeant, 7th Armored Division.

George M. Austin

In 1951, George went to work for General Motors, using his training and experience with tanks, in the Testing and Development Department at the Allison Tank Plant in Brookpark, Ohio. He retired in 1981, after 30 years with General Motors.

George and Sybil, his wife of over 40 years, now reside in Westlake, Ohio. They have two grown daughters and three grandchildren.

## JOHN G. AVAU

Born June 24, 1917, in Charleroi, Pennsylvania. Graduated from Charleroi High School in 1936. Worked at Pittsburgh Steel Company until entering the army on February 23, 1942 at New Cumberland, Pennsylvania. Was sent to the 3rd Armored Division at Camp Polk, Louisiana for basic training. From the 3rd Armored Division, he was transferred to Co A of the 77th Medical Battalion of the 7th Armored Division. Spent five months on maneuvers in the California desert. From there, sent to Ft. Benning, Georgia. While at Ft. Benning, was sent to Ft. Knox, Kentucky to Radio Operators School where he spent about three months. From Ft. Benning went overseas to the European Theater of Operations and was engaged in battles in Ardennes, Central Europe, etc. After the surrender of Germany, he was returned to Indiantown Gap, Pennsylvania where he was discharged on October 16, 1945, after spending 44 months in the service.

John G. Avau

Returned to his job at the Pittsburgh Steel Company from which he retired in January, 1978. Married and has two sons and four grandchildren.

## RAYMOND H. AYERS

Born February 4, 1917, in Bel Air, Maryland, and graduated from high school there in 1935. Entered the Army in March, 1941, and was sent to the 47th Coast Artillery at Ft. Monroe, Virginia for basic training. Received extra training after basic in the Norfolk, Virginia area. Was sent on cadre as a platoon sergeant to Ft. Bliss, Texas, to help form the

Raymond H. Ayers

203rd AA Battalion. After this he finished training at Ft. Bliss and moved to Louisiana for maneuvers. Sailed from New York in February of 1944 for England and received more training. Arrived in Cherbourg, France in June, 1944, and later joined the 7th Armo Red Division. He remained with them until the end of the war in Europe.

He returned home and was discharged September 15, 1945 with five campaign stars, the Bronze Star, and the Purple Heart. Returned to work at his previous job two days after returning home, and worked there until 1966. He worked 28 years for this company, then decided to go to work for the Federal Government at Aberdeen Proving Ground. Retired from Federal Service in February, 1979. He feels very proud to have served his country in this way.

## HARRISON L. BARDEN

Born March 13, 1920, in Richmond, Massachusetts and was raised in East Chatham, New York. Following induction into the Army on February 12, 1942, at Camp Upton, New York, he was sent to Camp Polk, Louisiana for basic training with the 3rd Armored Division. Upon completion of basic training, he served with the 440th Field Artillery, seeing action in Northern France, Rhineland, Central Europe, and at St. Vith in the Ardennes during the Battle of the Bulge. When the break-up occurred, he was transferred back to the 3rd Armored Division, then to the 272nd Field Artillery. Received his discharge on November 30, 1945 at Camp Dix, New Jersey.

Harrison L. Barden

After the Army he went back to East Chatham, New York where he farmed, then took employment as a truck driver. Seeking a change of scenery, in 1969, he took a driving job in the Salt Lake City area and has been there ever since. He has been married for over 40 years to the same woman and has three daughters and two grandchildren.

## VERNON "SAM" BASS

Born 30 July, 1921, Greenville, South Carolina. Enlisted in US Army 10 March, 1942, Ft. Bragg, North Carolina. Assigned to Seventh Armored Division, Camp Polk, Louisiana, March, 1942. Underwent training in Louisiana, Texas, California desert, and Georgia. Embarkation for Europe on the Queen Mary, June, 1944. Debarkation, Scotland, then to Tidworth, So. England for final vehicle and equipment preparation prior to channel crossing. Landed in Normandy, August, 1944. Remained with "Lucky Seventh" from Normandy to Baltic Sea, participating in all division campaigns.

Vernon "Sam" Bass

Following WW II, continued military service until November, 1967. Eighteen months with 3rd Infantry Division in the Korean Conflict. Retired November, 1967 in grade of Command Sergeant Major, E9, with 26 and ½ years service.

Following military retirement, assumed 14 years employment with a manufacturing firm in Colorado. Retired March, 1983.

Today: fully retired, active trout fisherman, and maker of hunter-type knives. Married, 1948, to Maria K. Gulde. Three sons, all Viet Nam veterans. Five grandchildren (three girls, two boys). Life membership: Seventh Armored Division Association, Veterans of the Battle of the Bulge Association, Veterans of Foreign Wars, and Disabled American Veterans.

## RICHARD TROY BEAMAN

Born November 9, 1919, Greene County, Snow Hill, North Carolina. Graduated from Snow Hill High School, married a local Greene County girl, Addie Elizabeth Clark. They have two sons, Rick and Jeff and four grandchildren, Nancy, Barbara, Ricky, and Kelly.

He was inducted in the Army in March, 1944 at Ft. Bragg, North Carolina and took basic training at Camp Wheeler, Macon, Georgia. After an eleven day leave, he boarded the Ile de France

Richard Troy Beaman

in New York City on August 17, 1944 and arrived at Glasgow, Scotland a couple of weeks later. From Glasgow, they went to Southampton, England and crossed the English Channel to Omaha Beach. He joined the 7th Armored Division near Metz, France. From Metz, their line of duty took them through Marche, Weert, Overloon, Meijee Liesel, Heerlen and Aachen, into the Battle of the Bulge at St. Vith and other points. He was at Lubeck on the Baltic Sea when the war ended and left Marseille, France for home in December, 1945. He was discharged when he arrived in North Carolina that month.

After the war, he was relocated in Dover, Delaware, where he accepted a job with a civilian contractor at Dover Air Force Base where he was an electrician on the C-138 aircraft. At the end of that contract, he began working with The General Foods Corporation in Dover, and worked there 18 years. He has been enjoying his retirement since 1982 just taking life easy, gardening, and being with his family, all here in Dover.

## JOHN J. BESHADA, JR.

Born April 18, 1926 in Du Bois, Pennsylvania. He entered the army on June 16, 1944 at New Cumberland, Pennsylvania. He received his training at Ft. Knox, Kentucky. He became part of the

John J. Beshada, Jr.

7th Armored Division, 87 Rcn. Sq., Troop B in December, 1944. He engaged in three battles and campaigns: Ardennes, Rhineland, and Central Europe. An article of their mission to contact the Russians was put in the Readers Digest by General Knowlton. General Knowlton was their Company Commander at that time. John served as a tank gunner with the 7th Armored Division, returned to the states and was discharged on June 16, 1946.

He worked for Speer Carbon Company and now works for Jensen Speaker Company as an industrial engineer. He married his wife, Helen, in 1951 and has four lovely daughters and two grandchildren.

## WILLIAM GORDON BLACK

Born July 1, 1917. Raised in Ringgold, Catoosa County, Georgia. Graduated from Ringgold High School in 1935. Upon entering the U.S. Army, was County Supervisor of the County Agriculture Adjustment Program of Catoosa County, Georgia. Was inducted January 6, 1942 at Ft. McPherson, Georgia. Took his basic training at Ft. Belvoir, Virginia. After basic training, was sent to Camp Polk, Louisiana to Co E, 3rd Armored Division. Was a part of a cadre forming the 7th Armored Division as a member of Co E, 33rd Armored Engineer Battalion. Remaining with Co E, 33rd Engineers until the Division was transferred to Ft. Benning, Georgia. Was then transferred to Hq 33rd Engineer Battalion, then Co. E formed the 991st Engineer Treadway Bridge Co. Was with Hq 33rd Engineers until about one week after arriving in France, then was sent to one of the tank battalions with truck as a truck driver. Was often sent to front lines with ammunition. After some time was released and was headed back to rear echelon to the 33rd Hq. On the way back, he met Capt. David Van Winkle. He needed a truck, and somehow he managed to keep me with the Division PX. July 2, 1945, he had an accident on the autobohn highway near Rena, Germany. During his stay in the hospital was in about seven hospitals in Germany and France. September 3, 1945 was transferred to Baty General Hospital, Rome, Georgia. November 11, 1945 was transferred to Northington General Hospital, Alabama until the day of his discharge, February 14, 1945. Was in four battles and campaigns and received three decorations and citations.

After discharge, worked in supervision in three carpet mills in Ringgold and Dalton. Worked as a guard for the Catoosa County Commission of Roads and Revenue, Ringgold, Catoosa County, Georgia. Retired May 27, 1982.

## JAMES Q. BLALOCK

James Q. Blalock

## WARREN RALPH BRADSHAW

Joined the Army, November, 1940. Training at Ft. Benning, Georgia with the 2nd Armored Division; General Patton, commander. Went to Ft. Knox, Kentucky to school then to Camp Polk, Louisiana with the 3rd Division and from the 3rd to help form the 7th. Went from Camp Polk to desert maneuvers in California, then back to Ft. Benning, Georgia, then to port of embarkation. Went on the Queen Mary to England, then to France to the 3rd Army commanded by General Patton.

Left the army October, 1945 and went to work for Union Carbide Corporation, Oak Ridge Gaseous Diffusion Plant in Oak Ridge, Tennessee, May, 1946. Retired March, 1982. Married Ruth Grimes, August 10, 1946. They have three children, two sons, Horace and Larry, and one daughter, Karen Gray. Now lives at Ft 4, Callaway Road, Box 282, Loudon, Tennessee 37774.

## EUGENE R. BREITING

Drafted June, 1944, Grinnell, Iowa — age 31 — married eight years with three small children. Basic training at armored school, Ft. Knox, Kentucky and spent Christmas, 1944, on a Liberty Ship in New York harbor on which he volunteered to assist the meat cutter on ship enroute to Europe. He had five years experience cutting meat. Joined B Troop, 87th Recon. in January, 1945, and was assigned to drive a jeep for a mortar team. Bernard Hansen (Iowa City, Iowa) was the mortar man. In a few days he found Donald Pederson (Grinnell, Iowa), radio man, B Troop, 87th. Pederson and he had been inducted same day, same place, but arrived to B Troop by different routes. B Troop was being rebuilt.

Eugene R. Breiting

His first impression — buzz bombs, frozen German soldiers, sleeping on the snow covered ground in vacated artillery dugouts, cold feet, warming his hands in armored car exhaust, motorized night patrol. Then building corduroy roads through heavily forested areas with German 88's screaming overhead. How could accordian music played by Lt. Knowlton be enjoyed so much when in the pitch dark outside, rifle fire could be heard, and when you knew soon it was your turn to go out on guard? Somewhere they inherited an enormous quantity of canned sardines. They lasted for weeks and tasted great with K ration crackers and "liberated" Schnapps. Warm weather came early and they quickly moved to Bad Godesberg. From the west bank of the Rhine they could watch the fireworks

William Gordon Black

Warren Ralph Bradshaw

opposite as their artillery did its thing. Then came the pontoon bridge crossing at Remagen and the dash through the Ruhr Valley ending at Ludwigslust. From there he accompanied Lt. Knowlton's group to Lutz. His version of the "Mission," written in a letter to his wife was published in his hometown newspaper, August 2, 1945.

After the war, he assisted Lt. Harold Kavalaris (HQ) supervising German civilians who repainted all 7th AD vehicles at the Linder AG factory at Ammendorf of Halle. August to November was spent in Zellendorf of Berlin at the motor pool for OMGUS, Group CC, under Maj. Mike Greene and Lt. Kavalaris. This command was taken over later by Bill Knowlton. Eugene shared living quarters at this time with Ernie Harris and frequently saw Carrol LaMarque and Edmund Ruschkewiez and his dog. He left Berlin October 15, and was discharged from Camp Grant in Illinois, November 26, 1945.

The next years were spent as a civilian and he retired from Amana Refrigeration October 31, 1977. In 1986 he visited with Ernie Harris (Tampa), Paul Senne and Donald Helgeson (North Dakota). Also he sees Donald Pederson who lives on the same street, three blocks away.

## VICTOR CALDWELL BURDEN

Born on November 13, 1918, near Goodman, Mississippi. Graduated from Camden High School, Camden, Mississippi, in 1939. Inducted into the service on February 6, 1942 at Camp Shelby, Mississippi. Basic training with the 3rd Armored Division at Camp Polk, Leesville, Louisiana. Made cadre to the 7th Armored Division, Co D, 17th Tank Bn. Was on maneuvers in the Mojave Desert in California, then to Ft. Benning, Georgia, to Camp Myles Standish, Massachusetts, to Camp Shanks, New York. Left New York on June 6, 1944 aboard the Queen Mary to Glasgow, Scotland, then on to Tidworth Barracks in Wiltshire, England. Crossed the English Channel from Southampton to Omaha Beach at Normandy. Was in combat in Lemans as tank driver, technician 5th, in Patton's 3rd Army until Metz, then transferred back to 3rd Army and down to St. Vith, Belgium and the Battle of the Bulge. Was wounded in chest with shrapnel on December 23, 1944. Operated on at Field Hospital in Liege, Belgium then was transferred to Army Hospital near London, England until March 1, 1945. Was assigned back to France on limited service, but requested to go back to his old company, D. Rejoined Co D latter part of March, 1945, near the Remagen Bridge and served until the Baltic Sea. Army occupation until discharged October 17, 1945, from Camp Shelby, Mississippi. Received the Purple Heart and battle stars.

Returned home and married Eloise Parks, October 25, 1947 and they have one daughter, Vicki. Presently retired from Mississippi Forestry Commission with 26 years service. Devoting his time now to hunting and gardening.

## MORRIS W. CALLAHAN

Born October 7, 1916 in Theirot, Louisiana. Was educated in Houma, Louisiana and entered the service on November 27, 1942. Trained at Camp Polk, Louisiana for three months and was sent to the Mojave Desert in California where he stayed for five months. Then went to Camp Shanks, New York, where he boarded the Queen Mary and went to England. They then liberated 150 towns in France. He had eleven and one half months of combat, fought all during the Belgium Bulge, and was wounded in Meigel, Holland. Received the Purple Heart, the Good Conduct Medal, and the Bronze Star in 1944. On October 19, 1945, was separated from the army at Camp Shelby, Mississippi. Returned home to Houma, Louisiana and married Geraldine M. Walker. Now in cattle ranching and rental houses.

Victor Caldwell Burden

Morris W. Callahan

## DANIEL W. CANTWELL

Born September 6, 1922 at Lawrence, Pennsylvania. (Pittsburgh) Was raised in Detroit, Michigan. Worked for General Motors for 40 years. He started in Detroit and retired as Purchasing Agent at the Fisher Body Plant in Columbus, Ohio.

Daniel W. Cantwell

Entered the army at Camp Custer, Michigan March 12, 1943. Basic training with the 106th Division at Ft. Jackson, South Carolina. Later accepted as an Aviation Cadet, but because of D-Day had to return to ground forces at Ft. Jackson. Joined the 87th Division until assignment for overseas duty. Joined the 7th Armored Division in the Met area as a Corporal with the Anti-tank platoon, Co A, 23rd Armored Infantry Battalion. Remembers Holland well, was active at St. Vith (Leaving and returning), was on site when the Remagen Bridge on the Rhine collapsed. Crossed the Rhine River up the Ruhr Pocket and finally to the Baltic Sea. At that time he was the Anti-tank platoon Sergeant (S/Sgt.).

After the war, he married Elizabeth (Betty) Cummings in Detroit, on September 21, 1946 and moved to Columbus, Ohio. They have a daughter, Colleen, who is a nurse at Hupp Hospital in Philadelphia, Pennsylvania. He and Betty have been happily retired since 1980.

## STEPHEN U.G. CASE

Born in Henderson County, North Carolina, February 9, 1917. Was brought up on a small farm and saw mill. It was steam powered and it was his job to keep the fire going. They hired two men to help with the logs and off-bearing the lumber. His dad sawed and kept the time and books but was injured and died from it in 1932. Stephen was in the seventh grade, but had to quit after he finished the year. He went to work in a hosiery mill to help his Mom keep the home together. You had to learn the trade on your own (You did not get paid to learn to knit, and they

Stephen U.G. Case

held back a week and paid every two weeks.) His first pay day was only $.64. He bought a 24 pound bag of flour with it and that was exactly what it cost at the A&P in 1933. His next paycheck was near $10.00 and in those days that was a fair amount for a beginner. He worked off and on with the mill until he got his greetings from Uncle Sam.

Was inducted at Ft. Bragg on March 13, 1942. Went to Camp Polk, took basic from there, then to the desert in California in March, 1943. Was in Co F, 48th AIB in Camp Polk, but volunteered for a trip as truck driver in Service Co where he was assigned to Service Co 48th until they were called to guard or work German POW's on the farms in SC. Was with HQ Co 48th at Spence Field, Georgia as truck driver on the detail. When they got back to Ft. Benning that fall, the 48th had been broken into four separate Bn. His Co was Ser. 38th. They maneuvered at Ft. Benning until spring when they went to Miles Standish. Left the outfit there, April 27. When new field jackets were being issued, notified to see doctor. Entered hospital for eye problems. Had five brain operations with 13 months hospitalization. Still there when the war was over in Germany. Celebrated there with the doctors and nurses and was discharged May 18, 1945. Sent to hospital in Atlanta and have been rated 100% disabled all the time.

## IRVIN CASH

Born April 8, 1923, in Fancy Farm, Kentucky where he attended school. Enlisted in January, 1942, and was inducted in East St. Louis, Illinois and had basic training with the 3rd Armored Division at Camp Polk, Louisiana. Was assigned to the cadre forming the 7th Armored Division. Received more training at Polk, the California desert, and Ft. Benning, Georgia. Boarded the Queen

Irvin Cash

Mary on June 6, 1944, landed in Scotland. Saw action in France, Holland, Belgium and was wounded April 9, 1945 at Smallenburg, Germany. He was hospitalized in a Paris hospital. Returned to the 77 Med. Bu. in August, 1945. Sent stateside and was discharged October 16, 1945.

While living in California during the 60's joined the 7th Armored Association, Western Chapter. In 1968, moved to Memphis, Tennessee. Resumed business as mail contractor with the Postal Service. In 1970 moved to Paducah, Kentucky, where he now resides with his wife of 40 years, Margaret. They have four sons, three daughters, four grandsons and one granddaughter. Retired in 1984 and enjoying every minute of it. He has attended ten 7th Armored reunions, where he is a life member and he eagerly looks forward to them each year.

## EDWARD L. CHARLTON

Born and raised in California, Pennsylvania. Before WW II, he attended art school in Pittsburgh and worked there as a commercial artist. He served with the 7th Armored from Camp Polk days, where he was one of the first to complete radio school, to the end of the war. He was known as "Charlie" to his buddies in the 7th. His final rank was Staff Sergeant and his "home" during the war was his half-track, the "Ruptured Duck."

Edward L. Charlton

He was awarded the Bronze Star for meritorious service. He remembered the fighting at Melun, where the Nazi Radio Paris was captured, and the defensive action in the Peel Swamps as being the toughest for him personally.

After the war, he worked for the coal division for J & L Steel, first as a miner and then as an engineer after he received his engineering degree. He supervised the construction of what was at that time, the longest underground coal conveyer belt system in the world at J & L Gateway Mine in Pennsylvania. He received his professional surveyors license and formed his own land and surveying company after his retirement from J & L.

Edward died in 1974 and is survived by his wife, Mildred; his son, Ronald, with his wife and two grandchildren; and his daughter, Kathy, with her husband and three grandchildren.

## FRANK T. CHISHOLM

Born February 27, 1916 in Everett, Massachusetts. Inducted into the Army at Ft. Devens, Massachusetts on February 16, 1942 and sent to Camp Polk, Louisiana for basic training with the 3rd Armored Division. He was then assigned to the cadre that formed the 7th Armored Division, as Tech Sgt., Medical Detachment, 40th Armored Regiment. Maneuvered through Louisiana, California desert, and Ft. Benning, Georgia. Before going overseas with the Division, was reassigned as 1st Sgt of Hq Co, 40th Tank Bn. Overseas to England, then on to combat on the French coast through Belgium, Holland and Germany. Received the Bronze Star for action in the Eder See Dam area. After the war ended, was transferred to the 1st Armored Division for Army of Occupation, August 1945, arrived back in the U.S.A. and discharged, November, 1945.

Frank T. Chisholm

Returned to work at Standard Duplicating Machines Corporation, Everett, Massachusetts as Traffic Manager. Retired after 43 years of service to Harwich Port, Massachusetts, and enjoys life with his wife, Alberta, on the sea coast of the Cape.

## NICK CHRISTIE

Born in Farrell, Pennsylvania on July 24, 1916. Educated in Farrell schools and graduated from Farrell High in 1935. Entered the service in May, 1942. Basic training at Ft. Knox, Kentucky. Sent to Camp Polk, Louisiana. Took part in the Louisiana Maneuvers with C-23 A.I.B. and sent to Desert Training. Sailed from New York on the Queen Mary, June 6, 1944, for England. Went to France in August, 1944. First action at Chartres and Melum, France. Wounded September 8, 1944 at Donat, near Metz, France. Rejoined the 7th in Holland in November, 1944. Received a three day pass to Paris, December 1st. Rode in the back of a G.I. truck from Holland to Paris on a cold December day, but it was worth it. Entered the hospital at Liege, Belgium, December 17th. Had his knee operated on for shrapnel. City was bombarded by V-2 bombs on Christmas Day and they had to be evacuated. Was sent to England by plane. Got back to the U.S.A. in August, 1945 and was discharged October 15, 1945.

Nick Christie

Worked at Sharon Steel Corporation for 32 years and retired in 1978.

## HAROLD H. COOPER

He was born in a sheep herders wagon in Idaho. His family moved to Chestertown, New York when he was five years old and he has been there in the Adirondack Mountains ever since except for the time that he spent in the Army.

He went into the Army in February, 1942, and was sent to Camp Polk, Louisiana, where he received basic training in the Third Armored Division. He trans-

Harold H. Cooper

ferred to Co. C, 77th Armored Medical Battalion in the 7th Armored Division when it was activated. He was sent to Billings General Hospital for special training and became a surgical technician, eventually reaching the rank of Technician 4th grade. He stayed with Co. C as the technician half of an ambulance team and went all the way to the Baltic Sea. There were many great moments but the greatest would be when Stanly Bond the ambulance driver and he went behind enemy lines at St. Vith to evacuate casualties from the 17th Tank Battalion.

After discharge in October, 1945, he became a woodland manager and logging contractor. He married Josephine Nisky of Baltimore, Maryland and has two sons and one daughter. They also bought a small farm in Bolton, New York, raised Alpine dairy goats and Araucana chickens for meat, eggs and milk.

He is now retired but still raises the chickens and is tracing his family history.

## HARM CREMER

Pvt. Harm Cremer helps a British soldier, Lance Bombardier Harry Frost at an American water point in Holland.

## ROBERT W. CUNNINGHAM

Born October 7, 1920 in St. Louis, Missouri. After graduation from Kirkwood (MO) High School, he went on to graduate from Virginia Tech, Blacksburg, Virginia in 1943. Became commissioned

Robert W. Cunningham

2nd Lieutenant, July, 1943, at the Ordnance O.C.S. Aberdeen Proving Ground.

Married Harriett Hausman July 5, 1943, and proceeded to Ft. Benning as a 2nd Lt. in Hq Co, 129th Ordnance Maintenance Battalion where he remained until the War ended. Was discharged in October, 1945, having gained a boost in discharge points (12) for a first child, Marian, for whom he named his jeep.

They settled in Portsmouth, Virginia for 11 years. While there, increased the family by three, Carol, Lucy and Joan. They then moved to Midland, Michigan to join Dow Chemical Company. He retired from Dow in December, 1983 while in Freeport, Texas. In retirement, they have relocated back in Virginia at Virginia Beach. It was wonderful renewing old acquaintances at the 7th Armored Division 40th reunion. Particularly his buddy, Will Wilken.

## EUGENE R. DALE

Born Camden, New York, February 4, 1924 and moved to Boonville, New York in September 1924 where he still resides. Attended Boonville High School, graduating in 1942, lettering in baseball, basketball, soccer and track and his .525 (1941) batting average is still a school record. He joined the U.S. Army in February, 1943 and was assigned to Co I, 6th Armored Regiment, 8th Armored Division, Camp Polk, Louisiana. Graduated from Ft. Knox Gunnery School in November and shipped to E.T.O. on the Queen Mary in May. Omaha Beach July 2 and was assigned to Co C, 31 Tank Battalion which he finally caught at Epernay. Tank gunner for Sgt. Al Ettinger, Capt. Flournoy and Capt. Swonger. After V.E.

Eugene R. Dale

Day, he pulled occupation duty with the 1st Armored and 36th Infantry Division embarking with them for home in November. Discharged December 24 and arrived home on Christmas Day, 1945.

Married in September, 1947 and raised a daughter and two sons who have blessed him with three grandsons and two granddaughters. He worked for the New York Central RR for nine years and then 27 for the Department of Defense USAF at Griffiss Air Force Base, retiring July, 1982.

Boonville Volunteer Fire Company, VFW and K of C, along with Little League and Babe Ruth have enriched his life for the last 40 years. Hobbies are hunting, fishing, and bowling. His wife died October 1, 1984 and he resides alone, operating a small painting and roofing business in the summer. He will cherish the memories of the men of the Lucky Seventh the rest of his life.

## WILLIAM (BILL) DASSINGER

William (Bill) Dassinger

## ANTHONY J. DILEO

Born in Glen Cove, Long Island, New York in 1918. The first twenty-four years of his life were uneventful until the greetings arrived and he was subject to the draft. The year was 1942 and he remembers how his father who couldn't read or write, had found the staging area that he would be leaving from on his way to the Wars. He was a man with strong feelings for his children and so he was there to see his son and probably praying that he would return.

Anthony J. DiLeo

Received basic training in Ft. Knox, Kentucky, Camp Polk, Louisiana and later out west for desert training in the Mojave desert with the 7th Armored Division. He remembers moving from Camp Miles Standish to Camp Shanks, in closed gate camp as they waited to move out on the Queen Mary to Glasgow, Scotland, and further on to England to pick up their equipment. While there they trained for the channel crossing in full field equipment. From the day they hit Utah Beach right to the Baltic, his job was in service to the B Co. of the Division. He operated a truck with trailer, moving ammo and field supplies to the company. The unpleasant part of the job was removing dead and wounded during the height of action. He knew our tanks were in trouble with the superior German machinery and that the 75's had to manage a direct hit broadside to stop the enemy tanks and he watched this happen many times. The ammo improved as the Division continued to press on to other battles.

He was once listed as missing in action during his truck breakdown and he joined another company temporarily. With their help he made it back to Co. B and just about the time the Capt. was sending out mail listing M.I.A.'s.

Of all the battle engagements (and he was with the Division from the beginning) Bastogne probably could be considered the worst and the toughest for all. He has nothing but praise for the men who took an active part in this campaign. There is one remembrance he has and that was a day that he ferried replacements for the Company. They came under such severe attack by the German tanks that they seemed to scatter in all directions but as it turned out they wound up in the same place huddled together with shells whistling overhead.

He has been a member of the Seventh Armored Division Association since it was formed and has attended some 35 reunions and looks forward to attending many more. He was extremely proud to serve with the "Lucky Seventh" in all of their bold moves and engagements with the enemy from Utah to the Baltic. He will continue to remember in his prayers those comrades of the Division who were not as fortunate and who still stand guard in places such as France, Belgium, Holland and Germany. Anthony J. DiLeo is retired and lives with his wife Angelina in the quaint town of Sea Cliff, Long Island, New York.

## ROBERT WILLIAM DOKOUPIL

Left Ft. Dix about March 25, loaded on the train and arrived at Ft. Jackson, South Carolina, received shots and quarantined for 14 days. Maj. Gen. Jones was the commander of the newly organized 106th Infantry Division (Division patch — gold lion head on blue field and a red, white and blue circle). Left Ft. Jackson, December, 1943 to go on maneuvers in Tennessee to March, 1944. Served with the 592nd F.A. Bn, C Battery. Went to Ft. Knox, slept in the field (concrete slabs). Continued in a northerly direction to Camp Atterbury, Indiana.

Robert William Dokoupil

Put in for overseas duty. Felt division would not see action until '45. Request was accepted and with regret. This was the time after Italy invasion and the Casino hold up. Sent to Ft. Meade, Maryland. Hung around during May. Got so bored, joined the Special Service, boxing weekly (undefeated).

June 6, 1944, was alerted and boarded a convoy, then orders cancelled. (D Day invasion going on). Left Meade on the 10th, shipped to Camp Kilmer, New Jersey. Left Kilmer and loaded on H.M.S. Aquatania troop transport, landed in Scotland, June 22, then transported to a replacement camp in Codford, England. Was an artillery man converted to infantry in 2 and ½ months. Landed on the continent in September, moved around France, then north to Belgium where joined the 7th Armored, then up to Maastricht, Holland and was assigned to the 38th Armored Infantry. December 17, got march orders, destination unknown. Travelled through the Sigfried Line into

Germany then back into Belgium to St. Vith. Everybody said "The refugees are coming." It wasn't until this year I remembered they were all old women (no small children or men). Missed Catholic mass, caught protestant mass. Dug in the 17th. First thing, saw the familiar Lion's Patch, my state-side outfit, the 106th. Had to leave under dark. Dug in that night. Dawn, first offensive. Arrived 3 p.m. The second offensive, he was the last to leave. Gave straffing fire so all could move back any that were left. Then "I bought it." Rest is history and recovery.

## JAMES R. DUFFY

Born January 30, 1916, in Kingston, Pennsylvania and graduated from St. Vincent's High School, Plymouth, Pennsylvania in June, 1934. Was inducted in January, 1942 at New Cumberland, Pennsylvania, and began his basic training at Camp Polk, Louisiana where he was on manuevers from September until December, 1942. From March until August, 1943, he spent more time on manuevers in the desert in California and in August, 1943, reported to Ft. Benning, Georgia for advanced training until April, 1944. On June 6, 1944, he left for Scotland on the Queen Mary and arrived there on June 15, 1944 and then proceeded to England. He engaged in battles and campaigns of Northern France, Ardennes, Rhineland and Central Europe and was awarded the Bronze Star, Purple Heart and the French Croix de Guerre with Palm. He completed his service as a Master Sergeant, 7th Armored Division, 48th Infantry. Was discharged at Indiantown Gap, Pennsylvania on October 22, 1945.

James R. Duffy

He returned to Kingston, Pennsylvania where he later worked at O'Neill Motors until 1962 when he took a job as executive staff analyst at Reedman Motors Corporation in Langhorne, Pennsylvania. He moved to Morrisville, Pennsylvania in 1962 where he resided until his death on June 9, 1986. He is survived by his wife and three children.

## JUSTICE CALL DUNLANEY

Born in Peola Mills in Madison County, Virginia in 1920. Graduated from Criglersville High School in June, 1937. Was always very talented in woodworking and, along with his father, made several pieces of furniture. Also worked on building the Lodge at Big Meadows on Skyline Drive in Virginia. Was doing defense work in Newport News, Virginia when he was inducted into the service in February, 1942 at Camp Lee, Virginia. He was then sent to Camp Polk, Louisiana for basic training with the 3rd Armored Division. He was with Training Co #1, Co C of the 23 Armored Engineers. Later, he was transferred to the 7th Armored Division, Co C of the 33 Armored Engineers. He was on manuevers in Louisiana, Texas and California. From the desert, he returned to Ft. Benning, Georgia. He went to Scotland on the Queen Mary. He was killed near Metz, France, on September 19, 1944, and is buried in Hamm Cemetery, Luxembourg. He is survived by his sister, Judith Blacklock, of Culpepper, Virginia, and two nephews.

Justice Call Dunlaney

## RAYMOND L. DYE

Born March 22, 1920, in Parsons, Kansas. Graduated from Parsons High School in 1938. Entered the Army at Ft. Leavenworth, January, 1942. Had his basic training at Ft. Sill, Oklahoma. Was assigned to the 814 TD Battalion as cook for Recon Co for almost two years in Camp Polk, Louisiana, and Camp Bowie and Ft. Hood, Texas. After that, assigned to 814 Medical Detachment to go overseas in January, 1944. Stationed in England until going to France. Was injured in England and did not join his unit till September of 1944 at Metz, France.

During the battle for Aston and Leesel, Holland, October 27-29, 1944, he was wounded and spent five months in hospitals in England and the U.S. Received the Silver Star and Purple Heart.

Was discharged from the Army on March 22, 1945 (birthday). After returning to civilian life, he owned restaurants until his retirement in 1980. Was married to Edith Steel in 1945 and has five children and three grandchildren.

## DEWEY DYER

Born April 25, 1924, Knoxville, Tennessee. During high school, acting Sgt. in R.O.T.C. Enlisted February 8, 1941, Ft. McPherson, Georgia, 2nd Armored Division, under Gen Patton. Advance Cadre to form the 3rd Armored Division, Camp Beauregard, Louisiana. The first to be in Camp Polk, Louisiana, Co C, 36th Infantry Armored Regiment. Later changed to the 36th Armored Infantry Battalion. (He has the history and pictorial review book of the 36th Armored Infantry Regiment, 8th Armored Division.) Trained the February and March recruits in 1942. Cadre to the 7th Armored Division, Co C, 38th Infantry Battalion, 57th Anti Tank Squad. Left the unit April 17, 1945 and was flown stateside, Thayer General Hospital, Nashville, Tennessee. Honorably discharged September 26, 1945.

Dewey Dyer

Worked at Oak Ridge, Tennessee, A.E.C. and U.S.E.D. under Gen Groves. Moved to Chicago, 1947 and worked for Signode Corporation. 1977 moved to Deerfield Beach, Florida. Remembers all the men and places: Ft. Benning, Georgia, Alexandria, Louisiana, Camp Polk, Louisiana, Camp Cockcomb, California,

Raymond L. Dye

the desert with all the goodies, Sylvinia, Georgia, guarding the P.O.W.s on the peanut farm, Boston, Massachusetts, England, Tidworth Barracks, the trip home. Treasures all the friendships of all and all the memories of long ago.

## DUANE K. ECKEL

Born September 4, 1925, Hadley, Michigan. Graduated Hadley High School, June, 1943. Inducted September 15, 1943, reported to Ft. Custer 21 days later. From there went to Ft. Knox, Kentucky for Basic and Tank Training. Then to Ft. Meade, Maryland where they were formed into an armored replacement package, then to Camp Shanks, New Jersey. Arrived in Liverpool, England on May 14, 1944. After attending the American School Center for eight weeks, went to France, then Holland where joined the 7th Armored Division, Co. B, 31st Tank Bn. in late September and remained with them until the end of the war in Europe. Shortly after, was transferred to the 817th T.D. Bn. where trained for Pacific warfare. Was ordered to LeHavre, France for shipping to the C.B.I. Theater direct from France, but before they could leave, the war with Japan was over. Sent back to Nuremberg, Germany where guarded railroad yards and trains. Returned to the States on March 16, 1946 and was discharged ten days later at Camp Atterbury, Indiana.

Duane K. Eckel

Retired September 1, 1982, after working for Buick Motor Division in Flint, Michigan for 3 and ½ years. Widower with five children and grandchildren.

## ANDREW R. ESPOLITA

Born November 30, 1908, Key West, Florida. Moved to Tampa, Florida in 1913. Raised there, married Lila Carrera, February 7, 1942.

Andrew R. Espolita

Inducted February 9, 1942 at Camp Blanding, Florida. Sent to Camp Polk, Louisiana. Arrived February 13, 1942 took basic training with the 3rd Armored Division. Became part of the cadre for the 7th Armored Division. Became part of Co A, 77 Med Bn. Maneuvered in Louisiana, Camp Coxcomb, California and Ft. Benning, Georgia and then went to Camp Miles Standish, Massachusetts for a week, then Camp Shanks, New Jersey P.O.E. Left for England June 7, 1944 and arrived in Scotland days later. Went to England, Tidworth Barracks. Four campaigns: Northern France, Ardennes, Alsace, Rhineland, Central Europe, Belgium, Fourrogere. Has a citation for Verdun, French medal, left Division at Bofshien, Germany August 12, 1945. Left Belgium September 21, 1945. Arrived Boston October 5, 1945. Discharged October 10, 1945, Camp Blanding, Florida.

Worked for one year for the Post Office, 1947; worked for the Tampa Recreation Department in 1950. Took leave of absence and went to Managua, Nicaragua. Was manager of the baseball team, came back in 1952. Worked for the Recreation Department until he retired January 7, 1975. The number 7 has been lucky for him, he's 77 years old.

## WILLIAM EDGER EVANS

Born June 29, 1921 in Kingston, Pennsylvania. Graduated from Kingston High School in June of 1941. Moved to Washington, D.C. and entered the Army at Ft. Meade, Maryland, on February 14, 1942. Was sent to the 3rd Armored Division for training at Camp Polk, and later was transferred to Co B, 48th Armored Infantry Bn, 7th Armored Division. Was a mail clerk for Co B. Was with Co B for training at Camp Polk, Camp Coxcomb, and Ft. Benning. Went overseas with the division on the Queen Mary and stayed with the division all through France, Belgium, Holland and Germany. Was with the 7th Armored Division in the Army of Occupation. Left the division in Germany and was discharged at Walter Reed Hospital in Washington, D.C. on December 11, 1945. Received the Combat Infantry Badge and all other medals due.

Was married at Walter Reed Chapel to Virginia Pierce on November 18, 1945, and in 1947 they moved to Wilson, North Carolina. They have two children, Cheryl and Billy, and five grandsons. Joined the Post Office in January, 1952, and spent the next 28 years as a letter carrier. Retired October 5, 1978.

## JOHN G. FARLEY, SR.

Born April 15, 1920 in Danbury, Connecticut. Graduated from Danbury High School in 1938. Enlisted February, 1942 and was sent to Camp Devens, Massachusetts for processing. Went to Camp Polk, Louisiana and was attached to the 3rd Armored Division as a recruit basic. Assigned to the 32nd Armored Regiment. When the 7th Armored Division was activated, became part of the cadre that formed the 31st Tank Battalion. Went into the Service Company. Went to the Mohave Desert, where his favorite memories are of the Ballroom at the Douglas Aircraft plant in Long Beach. Went to Ft. Benning, Georgia and then to Camp Shanks, New York. He clearly remembers the ferry ride and the long ladder climb onto the Queen Mary. What he remembers most about Tidworth Barracks, Scotland was clearing off the cosmoline from their equipment. They crossed the channel in their L.S.T. Was part of the liberation of Chartres, the crossing of France to the Moselle River, and the invasion of Holland. They had their hardest times at St. Vith, Belgium. Crossed the Rhine at Remagen, where he first saw jet aircraft. Took part in liberating a forced labor camp and his most striking memory of the end of the war was the stream of refugees passing them for two solid days.

William Edger Evans

John G. Farley, Sr.

After being promoted to W.O.J.G. was sent to Kothan Tech to learn how to become an officer. When the 7th disbanded, he was assigned to the 3rd Tank Battalion, 1st Armored Division in the Army of Occupation. Was detached from duty in December of 1945, and arrived home in Danbury just in time for Christmas.

Since the war, he has had a very happy and fulfilled life. Has just recently retired, after 35 years in the airline business. Worked for Eastern, Allegheny, and finally U.S. Air. Was assigned to many stations, including Daytona Beach, Miami, Pittsburgh, New Haven, Connecticut, Boston, Albany, and ended his career at Bradley Field, in Hartford, Connecticut. Has lived with his family in New Haven, Connecticut, for the last 30 years. His wife Leonora and he were married in 1948. They have raised seven children, two boys and five girls, who have rewarded them with 16 grandchildren, to date.

There is one person he would like to acknowledge: Lt. Col. Robert C. Erlenbusch, the Commanding Officer of the 31st Tank Battalion.

## JACK L. FAWBUSH

Born in Union County, Tennessee, on February 12, 1923. Attended school in a one room schoolhouse. Worked for the Ft. Wayne Wire Die for 44 years. His wife's name is Viola (Schaefer) and he has six daughters and one son.

Jack L. Fawbush

Went overseas in 1944 and joined the A38 and was wounded in Belgium on November 2. 1944. Was a German Interpreter in the front lines. After that, went with the 156 M.P. Outfit. For 15 months, he was a guard at a P.O.W. camp near Cherburg, France. The medals received were two battle stars and a Purple Heart.

## ALBERT FISCHER

Born May 4, 1919, Philadelphia, Pennsylvania. Graduated Frankford High School, 1938. Worked as a florist until drafted into the Army, February 21, 1942 from Bustleton. Went to Ft. Meade, Maryland, then on to Camp Polk for

Albert Fischer

basic training, 83rd Recon, B Troop. Became part of cadre of the 7th Armored Division, Headquarters and Service, 87th Recon. Bn. Drove supply truck and kitchen truck at Camp Polk and Camp Coxcomb. Assigned to Maintenance Half Track at Ft. Benning, Georgia. Went to Ft. Knox, Kentucky Wheeled Vehicle School; home on furlough, got married, returned to Ft. Benning. From Camp Shanks, left on the Queen Mary, arrived in Scotland June 13, 1944. Was with the 7th Armored Division until August 8, 1945. Discharged from Ft. Leonard Wood, Missouri, November 23, 1945.

Returned to being a florist until 1959 when he went to work for Plumb Tool, retiring in 1982. Went to Frankford Trust as a Security Officer then fully retired in 1985. Has two married sons, six grandchildren. Enjoys woodworking and gardening.

## JOHN W. FORD

John W. Ford

## JOSEPH F. FORD

Born, raised, schooled, and graduated college in Philadelphia, Pennsylvania. In 1941, received B.S. from Drexel University on June 16 and went to summer camp on the same day. Six weeks later, received gold bars. Three days later, had active duty orders and reported to the 40th A.R. — 3rd Armored Division on

Joseph F. Ford

August 13th. After a short tour as Officer's, Mess Officer and Morale Officer, was transferred to the 33rd Armored Regiment as platoon leader on January 1, 1942. On April 10, 1942, while on leave to marry Janet, was transferred to the 40th Armored Regiment, 7th Armored Division. Served in tank companies as platoon leader and company commander. In July, was made the Rcn. Co. Commander, and in December went up to Regimental Headquarters as S-2. When the regiments were converted, moved up to S-2 Combat Command A where served most of the war until February, 1945. Then was kicked upstairs, serving as Asst. G-2 of the Division. After VE Day, spent three months as S-1 of Camp Miami and two months with the I.G. Section of O.I.S. before leaving Europe for the U.S.A. on December 9, 1945.

After Christmas, started looking for a job and joined Drexel University as assistant professor in January, 1946. Forty years later, retired, having served as professor of accounting, departmental chairman, director of the M.B.A. program, and associate dean of the College of Business.

Remains active in the reserves, and after graduating from the Command and General Staff course, was with the Philadelphia U.S.A.R. School serving as instructor, department head (C&GS), and commandant. Had good credit for 23 years before retiring and now welcome the pension check each month.

As he looks back, believes that his best days in the service were as a company commander, but his best friends were made in C.C.A.

## JOSEPH E. FOREMAN

Born March 11, 1925 at Gloster, Mississippi. He was inducted at Camp Shelby, Mississippi, March, 1943. Took basic training at Ft. Bragg, North Carolina. He went to England in March, 1944 and landed on Utah Beach June 6, 1944 (D Day) about 3 p.m. Fought in Normandy until September when he joined A Co. 434th Battalion. Stayed with the 7th Armored Division until they met the Russians. Was sent back to the States on the point system and was discharged

Joseph E. Foreman

from Ft. Lewis, Washington after the Japanese surrendered.

Received five major battle stars, the Presidential Citation, and the Belgium Fourragere for the battle of St. Vith.

The thing he remembers most was all the snow (five feet or more) in Belgium with the temperature in the teens for days. They wrapped paper around their feet under their socks to keep them from freezing.

Moved to Texas in 1947 and married Mary Agnes Brown from Port Arthur. They have four children. Retired from Gulf States Utility Company in May, 1986, after 38 years of service. They divide their time between Hull, Texas and Gloster, Mississippi.

## CHARLES E. FUHS

Born January 16, 1925, in Lawrence, Kansas, and was inducted into the Army on June 19, 1943, at Ft. Leavenworth, Kansas. He received basic training at Camp Callen, California.

Charles E. Fuhs

He then went to Ft. Bliss, Texas, to Co. A, 583rd A.A.A. A.W. Bn for antiaircraft training, then to Camp Chaffee, Arkansas for infantry training for three months.

On August 17, 1944 he sailed from New York City on the Ille de France, landed in Glasgow, Scotland, traveled through England to South Hampton, crossed the English Channel and embarked onto Omaha Beach. He joined the 7th Armored Division, B Co. 23rd Armored Infantry Battalion at the Moselle River, near Metz, France, commanded by Capt. Dudley Britton. From there he went to Holland through the hell of swamps and canals with British 9th Army to Marche, Weert, Overloon, Meijel Liesel, Heerden, and Aachen. He fought in the Battle of the Bulge at St. Vith, Belgium and was taken prisoner December 23, 1944. He was in a work camp and was also at Stalag 12A at Limburg, Germany. He was put on a train for five or six days until stopped by American planes, was recaptured by the Sixth Army Division March 29, 1945. He was sent by air to the 217th General Hospital, Paris, France for a month then by air to the Zone of the Interior, May 1, 1945 to Winter General Hospital in Topeka, Kansas, for four months, then to Camp Carson Hospital Center for two months and was discharged October 31, 1945.

He retired in 1983 from McDonnell Douglas Aircraft after 27 years of service due to disability. He now resides in Long Beach, California with his wife. He has one daughter and two grandchildren.

## WILLIAM T. (ROLLIE) GILL

Born June 25, 1926 at Lakewood, Ohio. Abandoned school at 16 to work in a war plant. Two years later, volunteered for immediate induction, preference Marine Corps. Was quickly sworn in, right into the army, and on to Camp Fannin, Texas for I.R.T.C. training. Following a brief furlough at Christmas, it was on to the E.T.O. in late January, 1945, to join the 7th Armored in Belgium. Was one of those replacements for the casualties incurred during the Battle of the Bulge. Joined C Co, 48th A.I.B. and was given two bags of mortor shells, which he lugged all over Europe. Stayed into occupation until July, 1946. Came home and was discharged.

William T. (Rollie) Gill

Between jobs, joined the 52-20 Club. Married his high school sweetheart in 1947. Two sons came later. Began training at the Recordak Microfilm Lab in 1951. During WW II, Redordak invented and processed all the V mail. In 1957, Kodak, the mother company asked him to go to the new Hollywood branch. After 32 years, retired in 1983. Favorite activities: golf, photography, travel and sporting events with the four grandchildren.

## CYRIL H. GOETTEN

Born July 5, 1917 at Fieldon, Illinois and raised on a farm near Jerseyville, Illinois. He was inducted January 30, 1942, at Scott Field, Illinois and received basic training at Camp Polk, Louisiana with the 3rd Armored Division then went to the 7th Armored Division when activated.

Cyril H. Goetten

Had training and maneuvers with the 40th Tank Battalion in Louisiana and Texas, then to Camp Coxcomb, California for desert training; to Ft. Benning, Georgia for eight months; to Camp Miles Standish, Massachusetts; to Camp Shanks, New York; to the Queen Mary at midnight on June 6, 1944; to Scotland; and to Tidworth Barracks in England. He landed on Omaha Beach in August, 1944 with Service Company, 40th Tank Battalion as Parts Supply Sergeant.

His campaigns include Northern France, Ardennes, Rhineland, and Central Europe. Left Le Havre, France on November 18, 1945 on the ship SS Waterbury Victory, arrived in the United States November 27 at Camp Kilmer then to Camp Grant and was discharged December 2, 1945.

Married Margaret Pohlman in June, 1950. They have three sons, and three grandchildren. He is retired from Olin Corporation after 42 years of service and now resides on his farm.

## JOSEPH J. GORLESKY

Inducted into the army February 3, 1942. Shipped to Camp Polk, Louisiana and the 3rd Armored. Selected for Signal Company. Trained as high speed radio operator and then went to the 147th Armored Signal Company when the "Lucky Seventh" was formed. During his training, had a run-in with a non-com who caused him to pull other duties not

Joseph J. Gorlesky

related to his M.O. In the desert, he was assigned as driver of a half track crewed by other black sheep of the Signal Company. Overseas, was a radio operator with crews mostly assigned to combat commands. Loved the freedom there. Several close calls with shelling near Metz and the Battle of the Bulge. Discharged November 24, 1945.

Returned to his old position with ITT in New Jersey. After 28 years, rose to the position of supervisor. Had a bout with cancer and was laid off with no pension — little over one year too young. Joined Aero Mayflower at Indianapolis, Indiana, as an owner operator of an "18 wheeler." Hauled electronics and bedbugs for nine years all over the "good ole USA" and Canada. Met a good woman and retired at age 60.

## HOWARD N. GRIFFITH

Born April 11, 1917, in Gibraltar, Berks County, Pennsylvania. Entered the Army on March 11, 1942 at New Cumberland, Pennsylvania and was sent to Camp Polk, Louisiana. Assigned for basic training to Reconnaissance Co., 32nd Armored Regiment of the 3rd Armored Division. Shortly thereafter became a member of the newly formed 7th Armored Division. Took desert training in California. Returned to Ft. Benning, Georgia, where the 7th Armored Division was revised. Became a truck driver in Service Co., 31st Tank Bn. During the war hauled ammunition. Remained with the 7th Armored until the end of the war in Europe. Returned to the States on November 29, 1945. Discharged from Indiantown Gap, Pennsylvania on December 5, 1945.

Howard N. Griffith

Returned to old job in the steel industry. On March 1, 1951 started a career in the insurance industry. Retired May 1, 1982, as a property insurance specialist. He and his wife recently attended the 40th Annual Reunion of the Seventh Armored Division Association, held in Harrisburg, Pennsylvania. Also they celebrated their 45th wedding anniversary while there.

## JOHN GRITTER

Born June 29, 1917 in Grand Rapids, Michigan. Was inducted at Camp Custer, Michigan on June 14, 1941. Was sent to the 3rd Armored Division at Camp Polk, Louisiana for basic training. Then assigned to Ammunition Training, 67th Armed Field Artillery Battalion. After basic training, was sent to Radio Operators School at Ft. Knox, Kentucky. Then returned to Camp Polk and was placed on cadre to 7th Armored Division. Was assigned to Service Battery, 440th Armed Field Artillery Battalion. Later transferred to Hq. Battery. Went on maneuvers in Louisiana and Texas in 1942. Returned to North Camp Polk. Was sent on advance detail in February, 1943 to Camp Coxcomb. First week there it rained, the only time all summer. He left the desert in August and went to Ft. Benning, Georgia for further training and maneuvers. Spent two weeks at Camp Gordon, Georgia for Anti-Aircraft training.

John Gritter

Boarded the Queen Mary for overseas on June 5th. The three artillery battalions pulled the duty aboard ship, so were placed on A deck. The 440th field artillery were the M.P.s on the trip. Arrived in Scotland June 14, 1944, the third anniversary of his induction. Was sent to Tidworth Barracks for equipment and supplies, then in August, he went to France. He traveled with the Division to France, Holland, Belgium and to Germany and the Baltic Sea. After Victory in Europe Day, he was transferred to the 2nd Armored Division, 78th Armored Field Artillery Battalion. Went to Berlin with the 2nd Armored for the Potsdam Conference. Left Marseille, France on board the General Goethals, arrived in Boston on October 12, 1945. Was released from service on October 12, 1945.

Worked at Sears Roebuck in Grand Rapids for 33 years. Retired from Sears in April of 1981.

## FORREST L. GROBE

Born March 6, 1919 in Dixon, Illinois. Graduated from Dixon High School, 1938. Owned and operated a general trucking business before entering the service. Was inducted into the Army at Ft. Sheridan, Illinois, June, 1941. Sent to Camp Polk, Louisiana, to the 3rd Armored Division for basic training. Assigned to Barricade Headquarters as a truck driver. When the 7th Armored Division was activated in March, 1942, was part of the cadre assigned to Combat Command — B, Headquarters. Went through training and maneuvers at Camp Polk. April, 1943, went to Camp Coxcomb, California for desert training and maneuvers. Went to Ft. Benning, Georgia, August, 1943. Was a Sgt. and a tank commander. Left the States June 6, 1944 and arrived in England later that month. Left for France August 7th, and arrived there August 11. Engaged in battles and campaigns of Northern France, Ardennes, Rhineland and Central Germany. Was awarded the Silver Star August, 1944 in area of Chartres, France. Returned to the States, September, 1945, and was discharged.

Forrest L. Grobe

Worked for Northern Illinois Gas Company in Dixon, Illinois for 38 years. Retired March, 1984. Married and has four sons and four grandchildren.

## RALPH M. HAAG

Born in San Francisco, June 27, 1912. Attended Polytechnic High School. Was inducted in March of 1942 and took basic training at Camp Roberts, Califor-

Ralph M. Haag

nia. Joined the Seventh Armored Division, Headquarters Btry., 434th F.A. at Camp Polk, Louisiana. Attended Small Arms and Mechanics School, also Mine and Booby Trap School. Service overseas in a forward observation tank, until sent to the rear with frozen feet. Spent the next six months in various hospitals, and was finally given a medical discharge from Camp Carson Hospital, Colorado, in July of 1945.

Went to work as a salesman in the industrial line until 1953. Then went to work for the State of California in the Department of Corrections until retirement in 1976. He now lives with his wife in San Anselmo, California.

## NICHOLAS HALUSZKA

Born December 8, 1918, in Baudette, Minnesota and raised in Cleveland, Ohio. Married Ann Pavluk, March 5, 1942, and shortly thereafter was an inductee at Ft. Benjamin Harrison, Indiana March 27, 1942. Completed basic training at Ft. Knox, Kentucky and became part of the 7th Armored Division at Ft. Polk, Louisiana. Following training maneuvers with HQ/48 in Louisiana and the California desert, he was transferred to Co. B, 38th Armored Infantry Bn. when the division was streamlined at Ft. Benning, Georgia. Final preparations at Ft. Miles Standish and Camp Shanks, and they sailed for England's Tidworth Barracks on the Queen Mary, June 7, 1944.

Nicholas Haluszka

After the Omaha Beach landings in August, 1944, he was engaged in combat as a S/Sgt. in battles of the Northern France campaign lending an anti-tank gun squad. They advanced rapidly across France until they met a Waterloo of sorts: the battle of the fortress city of Metz. About Metz, with its many fortifications and the German well entrenched on the high ground, General George S. Patton said: "We're using Metz to blood the new divisions."

In spite of the German force, and General Patton, he recuperated in an English hospital and completed his tour overseas in Compiegne, France as part of a cadre training GI's for the infantry, and later in charge of a "call station" in Bremen, Germany.

He returned to the States on the Italian ship, the Vulcania, and was discharged at Indiantown Gap, Pennsylvania on December 10, 1945 and was awarded the Combat Infantry Badge and the Bronze Star with three campaign stars. He and Ann have three sons and three grandchildren and are retired from a self-employed grocery business in Parma, Ohio.

## WARREN P. HANSEN

Born April 28, 1918 in Lincoln, Nebraska. Inducted December 21, 1942 at Ft. Leavenworth, Kansas. Joined the Rec. Co. 814th T.D. Bn. at Camp Bowie, Texas. Sailed for E.T.O. February 14, 1944 on the Ile de France. Landed in France on Omaha Beach August 8. His platoon, operating with CCR of the 7th Armored Division, participated in the drive across France to Metz. September 24 they moved to Liesel, Holland and served as infantry during the counterattack at Meijel. He was awarded the Bronze Star for action near Someren, Holland. December 22, operating with Task Force Jones, they were trapped near Salmchateau, Belgium. Got out the night of December 23 and moved to Harze. He was promoted to S/Sgt. during the stay at Harze. Moved to the Rhine River and crossed at Remagen, March 24, 1945. His unit was dissolved after V.E. Day and he was transferred to another unit. Returned to the U.S. and discharged October 22, 1945.

Warren P. Hansen

He now lives in Columbus, Nebraska. He and his wife Marian were married September 18, 1947. They have three children and five grandchildren. He was Tooling and Production Manager at Dale Electronics Inc. and retired in 1983 after 27 years of service there.

## ARVILLE H. HARBIN

Born December 21, 1908 in Eldridge, Alabama. Went to school at Eldridge Baptist Academy and entered the Army on March 7, 1942 at Camp Shelby, Mississippi. Sent to Camp Polk, Louisiana and was trained with the 7th Armored Division. Was put in the 87th Recon. Squadron, stayed with the 87th until he was wounded on September 14, 1944. Stayed in the hospital until the war was over. Was an M 8 Recon car driver.

Arville H. Harbin

Married and has one daughter, three grandchildren and six great grandchildren. Retired as a salesman in 1973 and now lives in Trussville, Alabama.

## SIM A. HARDY

Charter member of the 147th Signal. Instructed throughout the division and had the unique experience of testing Gen. Sylvester's radio proficiency. He passed. During desert maneuvers, served on G-4 crew and received a Meritorious Service Commendation. In combat, served on various liaison crews including Division Ammo Officer, all three combat commands and the 102nd Infantry. During assignment to Col. King's jeep, made seven runs up to the lead tanks to find Col. Wemple. Each was adventurous, with the last one winding up in a head-on crash, in the dark, with another jeep. While running to get help, he tried to

Sim A. Hardy

wave down an approaching tank before it hit the wreckage. As it slowed down, the gunner zeroed in on his head and the commander read him out telling him only God kept him from "pulling the string on him." Then he thanked him.

He'll never know if King found Wemple, but he does know that every time the Col. said "Let's go find Wemple," he got scared.

He had recurring dreams about the 147th reorganizing before he learned of the Association. Joined in 1983 and attended the Winston Salem reunion. There, happily, he found 22 of his buddies, and you guessed it, Col. Wemple. After 38 years, he was home again.

## FRANCIS C. HARRIS

Inducted March, 1944; trained in Camp Fannin, Texas. Went overseas August, 1944 and was put in Co. A. 23 Battalion Armored Infantry of the 7th Armored Division. Fought through France, Belgium, Holland and Germany. Called out of Northern Holland and went into the center of the Bulge at St. Vith and held for three days when it was thought that they could not hold for one day. Only seven of the company made it back to the rear where they met the 87th Recon and fought their way out of the Bulge. Was wounded when they started to build line in depth to clear the Germans out of the area. Discovered had Trench Foot and was shipped to England, then to the States where discharged.

## BRUCE W. HARRISON

Born December 28, 1916, in Henry County, Alabama. Enlisted in Headquarters Battery, 1st Bn., 83rd Field Artillery at Ft. Benning, Georgia on January 9, 1934. Was appointed to the Armored Officer Candidate School, Ft. Knox, Kentucky, in July, 1942, by the CG, 77th Inf. Div. on the recommendation of Lt. Col. George B. Peploe, Div. G-3 (formerly G-3, 3rd Armored Div., Camp Polk, Louisiana). Graduated on October 24, 1942 from the 12th class, 1st Co. and appointed 2nd Lt., Infantry (Armor) on the same date. After ten days leave, was assigned to the 7th Armored Division, 31st Armored Regiment, 2nd Bn., and on

Bruce W. Harrison

reporting was released to Hq. 1st Bn. The division was in the field on LA maneuvers and he met the unit in the NEW Camp Polk. Returned to Ft. Knox in January, 1943, to attend Officer Communication Course #8. Upon completion, he rejoined the 7th AD at Camp Coxcomb, California, and was assigned to Hq., 3rd Bn., 31st AR as Communications Officer. When the 3rd Bn. was redesignated the 17th Tank Bn., he was assigned duties of Communications Officer and S-3 for Air. He held this position until August 3, 1945, when he departed the unit for duties in the UK. Returned to the U.S. November, 1945, and remained on active duty. Retired August, 1958 to Myrtle Beach, North Carolina as a Lt. Col. after 24 and ½ years service having served in all ranks (except Corporal) from Pvt. to Lt. Col.

## HAROLD HASSEBROCK

Born August 5, 1917, at Eagle River, Wisconsin. His parents moved to central Illinois, where he grew up. Drafted on January 26, 1942 and arrived at Camp Grant, Illinois. His brother, Loren, was drafted the same day, and they requested to stay together. They were sent to Camp Polk, Louisiana.

Harold Hassebrock

Loren and he ended up in Co. B, 23 AIB. Due to an order that two from the same family could not stay together, he was pulled out and sent to the Medical Detachment. He was put in Hq. Co. of 38, as he spent his free time with the men of his previous company. Was wounded in both legs trying to help men who were wounded crossing the Seine River on the 23rd of August, and spent the next fifteen months in Cardiff, and in the Army hospital at Springfield, Missouri.

Discharged the day before Thanksgiving in 1945, and got married on January 15, 1946 to a sweet little gal he went to school with. They have seven children and fourteen grandchildren. Retired from International Harvester Company in August of 1979.

## ROBERT W. HEINTZLEMAN

Born March 6, 1916 in Tower City, Pennsylvania and died June 14, 1985. Lived in Tremont, Pennsylvania as a young man. He enlisted in Regular Army as an infantryman and was assigned to Hawaii. Following the attack on Pearl Harbor, he returned to the United States and attended Officers Candidate School. Having been commissioned, he trained in the United States and re-entered the war in Germany as Infantry Reconnaissance Officer.

Robert W. Heintzleman

He received the European-African-Middle Eastern Campaign Medal with 4 bronze stars, American Campaign Medal, World War II Victory Medal, Army of Occupation Medal (Germany), Armed Forces Reserve Medal, National Defense Service Medal, Asiatic-Pacific Campaign Medal with a bronze star, Silver Star Medal, Bronze Star Medal, and Croix de Guerre with silver star, Army Commendation Medal.

From 1949 to 1952, he was assigned to Germany as an Intelligence Officer, returned to Ft. Benning, Georgia and later was reassigned to Japan as Advisor of Military Tactics in Army and Infantry to the Japanese Army. Retired August 31, 1962.

He married Virginia Scott. Their children are Mrs. Michael Weaver (Susan), and Jeffrey whom they adopted in Germany. Later married Helen Russel Frew. His step children are: Mrs. David Mayer (Georgina), Mrs. Leonard Miller (Helen), George Frew, Mrs. Robert Butensky (Luana), Jo Lynne Frew, Mrs. Chester Hubler (Donna).

## J.G. (JACK) HENDERSON

Born March 25, 1914, in Kansas City, Kansas. Moved to Houston, Texas in 1937 and married a Texas girl. Volunteered at Ft. Sam Houston, Texas, January 24, 1944. Basic training at Camp Fannin, Texas and shipped to Europe, August 17, 1944 as an Infantry Rifle Squad, A Company, 23 Battalion, at Metz, Germany. After the engagement in Holland, he became a Staff Sergeant and squad leader. Continued through campaigns of Northern France, Ardennes,

J.G. (Jack) Henderson

Rhineland and Central Europe. After hostilities, as one of the remaining platoons survivors, he was given an R & R furlough to the United Kingdom, which he financed by the sale of liberated Lugers to the rear echelon troops. Discharged at Camp Robinson, Arkansas, October 31, 1945.

After employment as branch manager for several finance companies, he entered banking and retired as Senior Vice President of Houston National Bank, now known as Republic Bank Houston.

## JOHN W. HENDERSON

John W. Henderson, Battery A, 440th Armored Field Artillery. Born October 1, 1915, Fulton County, Illinois. Was inducted into the Army in January, 1942 at Camp Grant, Illinois and was sent to Camp Polk, Louisiana for basic training. Was part of the cadre that made up the Lucky 7th. Was discharged at Ft. Sheridan, Illinois in October, 1945 with five major battle stars and a Presidential Unit Citation.

John W. Henderson

Boarded the S.S. Alexander to come home on his birthday. On February 14, 1946 was married to Martha Stiarwalt and they are the parents of one son, John R. Henderson and have one grandson. Was a foreman for Illinois Power Company, Havana (IL) Station for 32 years and is now retired and lives on a small farm at Maquon, Knox County, Illinois.

## CARL H. HOENGE

Born March 4, 1920, Shrewsbury, New Jersey. Was inducted into the Army at Ft.

Carl H. Hoenge

Dix, New Jersey, May, 1942. Left there for basic training at Ft. Knox, Kentucky. Left there in August, 1942, for Camp Polk, Louisiana. Became a halftrack driver for all the three years he was with the 7th Armored Division. Was in 440th, F.A. Bn. Hqs. Married and had three children: Raymond, Frances, and their late daughter Marilyn who passed away March, 1973. Has four grandchildren.

Engaged in battles and campaigns of Northern France, Ardennes, Rhineland, and Central Europe. Became a union mason when left the service in 1945. 1960, broke his back in three places and was out for two years. Then became self-employed after that. Hobbies are whittling and visiting several of his old buddies. He had five brothers and sisters, one died several years ago.

## VASEL HOMZA

Born in Larksville, Pennsylvania, February 8, 1919, and graduated from Larksville High School in June, 1937. At age 14, started working in a country grocery store and went with A&P as a meat cutter after graduation. Was inducted into the Army at New Cumberland, Pennsylvania, and sworn in on his birthday in 1942. Sent to Camp Polk, Louisiana with the 3rd Armored Division, 54th Field Artillery. Later assigned to the 7th Armored Division, 434th Field Artillery. Went to

Vasel Homza

cook's school while at Camp Polk and then on maneuvers in Louisiana, Texas and California. From the desert, went to Ft. Benning, Georgia, where assigned to Hq. Co. of the 23rd Armored Infantry Bn. Left Camp Shanks on the Queen Mary on D-Day for Scotland. In England, was "loaned" to the rear echelon and cooked for the replacement troops until the war ended. Sent back to the 23rd Hq. Co. Served with the 7th Armored from the Beaches to the Baltic Sea. Returned to the States and was discharged from Indiantown Gap, Pennsylvania, October 23, 1945.

In 1946, sustained a fractured hip and was in and out of the Veterans' Hospital in Lebanon, Pennsylvania for three years. Also attended Lebanon Business College. Married in 1949 to Marion Rosser, a nurse. They have two children, Stephen and Jean, and one grandchild. Worked for Grand Union Supermarkets as a meat supervisor for 29 years and retired in 1982. Has lived in Alexandria, Virginia since 1952.

## HERMAN "HY" HOROWITZ
## HQ /129

It all began on a small farm in the not-too-famous village of Swan Lake in upstate New York. A late spring blizzard was no deterrent and the stork managed to deliver me on April 9, 1920. Spent my formative years enjoying the monochromatic routines of an average small-town lad — school, fishing, routine farm chores, chasing small-town girls, playing ball and trying to fit the mold of most kids of that era. The lure of city lights and the charm and magnetism of a gal named Sally; and my course changed. After school I went to work in New York City.

Herman "Hy" Horowitz HQ /129

Did fine until Uncle Sam's letter arrived and shortly thereafter discovered that there really was a place called Louisiana and in its bowels a spot called Camp Polk. Was assigned to the 3rd Armored Division and accepted their invitation to enroll in a program of jogging, aerobics, law maintenance, culinary procedures and a special course in bathroom cleanliness. the Nazis in November, 1942. From January 1, 1943 to August,

To further my army career, I moved on to the "LUCKY SEVENTH" and an introduction to chiggers, 25 mile marathons, overnight camping and a host of other unexpected luxuries. Married Sally and soon after boarded the Queen Mary for a leisurely cruise to the "Big One" in Europe. No need to elaborate on the events which followed since each of you recalls them indelibly. Another ocean voyage back to the U.S.A.; this time as a veteran. New family, new friends, and a brand new career.

Discovered the Association in time to attend the 17th reunion and "Become involved". Served as President for 3 terms and tried awfully hard to follow in the footsteps of those who served before me. I tried my very best to, and feel I succeeded in providing the 7th Armored Division Association with my dedicated professionalism. I take great pride in knowing that my many contributions to the Association were appreciated and acknowledged. Would have liked to do more but the wall in my den was running out of space for any additional plaques and awards.

Must say my greatest moments came from organizing and conducting the two memorable trips to Europe; with their unforgettable retracing of the legendary WORKSHOP ROUTE. I thank each of you who enjoyed the thrill of "Going Back", for your kind letters of thanks and appreciation.

Sally and I cherish our many rewards of this long affiliation; as well as our honors, awards and lasting friendships — more than ample repayment for efforts that provided us with so many pleasures while performing these pleasant tasks.

## CLIFTON (CLIFF) HUNDLEY

Born February 3, 1916, in Salem, Virginia. Was drafted April 4, 1942 and took basic training at Ft. Knox, Kentucky. Was assigned to the 7th Armored Division and went to Camp Polk, Louisiana. Maneuvers, then spent five months on maneuvers in California desert. Given advance training at Ft. Benning, Georgia, before being sent overseas, June 6, 1944, D-Day. Arrived in Scotland. On the Queen Mary June 13, 1944. From England to France August 10, 1944. Finished the war as a T-5-C/129 Ordnance

Clifton (Cliff) Hundley

7th Armored Division. Returned to the States and was discharged October 15, 1945.

Worked for Western Electric Company in Baltimore, Maryland until he retired in 1976. Then he moved back to his home town, in Virginia, where he and his wife Ruth live at 956 Emerald Drive, Vinton, Virginia.

## MARTIN P. JACKSON

Born January 25, 1909 in Smithville, Arkansas. Moved away from there shortly after and grew up in and around Monette, Arkansas. Schooling: nearly none in the public school, in fact his last public schooling was in 1920. Got his schooling in the Army through correspondence schools, two of them American schools in Chicago and I.C.S. Pennsylvania.

Martin P. Jackson

Joined the Army (14th Cavalry) on April 29, 1930 at Ft. Demonis, Iowa and was sent from there to Ft. Crook, Nebraska for three enlistments. Then went to Ft. Ord, California in 1940, then Camp Roberts, California, then Camp Adair, Oregon. From there, went to Camp Shelby, Missouri, then overseas and joined the 7th Armored in 1944. Fought with the 7th until November 30 then asked for a transfer to the 84th Division. A 2nd Lt. told him he had been reduced to Pvt. from T/Sgt. He found out too late he was wrong and spent the rest of the time with the 84th that way. He did a total of 9 months of front-line combat without a scratch for which he thanks God who was the only one looking out for him. Received four battle stars. Did a total of 15 months overseas and was sent home November 30, 1945 with $27 for transportation by train to Portland, Oregon.

Was married April 4, 1943 to Ovene Garroutte from Grand Rond, Oregon. They're still together. They have one married daughter, Patricia who has a nine year old son, Cyrus Victor that his grandparents love very much. Retired Sgt./1st Class Jackson has been living in Lacey, Washington for 30 years, has lived in the same home for 20 years which is paid for along with a new Olds car and a G.M.C. pickup truck. He has worked ten years at the Madgan Hospital, the largest hospital in northwest Washington. He is retired from civil service and a member of the 7th Armored Division association.

## MORPHIS A. JAMIEL

Born in Warren, Rhode Island on December 19, 1921. Third oldest of thirteen children. Education includes B.S. Chemical Engineering, University of Rhode Island, J.D. Boston University Law School. Enlisted in U.S. Army as private on June 4, 1942. Commissioned 2nd Lieutenant on August 16, 1944. Served with Co. B, 38th AIB, 7th AD during WW II and with 43rd Infantry Division during Korean Conflict.

Morphis A. Jamiel

Completed branch qualification courses in seven U.S. Army branch schools, C & GS College and ICAF. Awards include Legion of Merit, Bronze Star with 2 oak leaf clusters for valor, Purple Heart, Meritorious Service Medal, and Combat Infantryman's Badge. Retired February 12, 1978 as Major General, R.I. Army National Guard, having completed 35 years combined active and reserve duty.

Served 13 years as Probate Judge, four years in R.I. Senate, and eight years in R.I. House of Representatives. Active in many Masonic bodies. Past M.I.G.M. of the Grand Council of R.I.

Occupation includes Lawyer (38 years), real estate and insurance agent, and auctioneer.

## THOMAS JENKINS

Born February 8, 1920 in Cincinnati, Ohio. Entered the U.S. Army February 9,

Thomas Jenkins

1942, Cincinnati, Ohio and was sent to the 3rd Armored Division, Camp Polk, Louisiana with the 147th Armored Signal Company of the 7th Armored Division.

Went overseas in June, 1944, and was a radio operator with G4 at Division Headquarters and also with a half track radio car at CCR in Holland.

After the war, he returned to the United States and was discharged from the Army at Indiantown Gap, Pennsylvania. He worked as a railroad brakeman on the NYC Railroad in 1941 and resumed that occupation until retirement in 1982. He is married and has three children and one grandchild.

## MACK J. JORDAN

Born December 17, 1916 in Adrian, Michigan. Inducted in March, 1941. Received basic training at the CRTC, Ft. Riley, Kansas and assigned to the 12th Cavalry at Ft. Bliss, Texas. Commissioned at Ft. Riley in June, 1942 and assigned to the 95th Infantry Division Reconnaissance Troop. Injured in a training accident at the Armored School and placed on limited duty. Shipped overseas as C.O. of a replacement company in July, 1944. Once in the ETO, requested full duty and was assigned as S-2, Hq. 87 in January, 1945 when the 7th Armored recaptured St. Vith. In late February, was assigned as C.O. of B Troop 87. They outposted the Rhine at Bad Godesburg and then moved into the Ruhr area. On March 26, he commanded a task force which, supporting task forces Brown and Griffin, participated in the attack that secured Giessen. On April 11, while on a route reconnaissance near Neider Marpe, he was ambushed and wounded. Bill Knowlton then assumed command of B Troop. After hospitalization in England, he returned to the States and was discharged with the rank of Major in 1946.

Mack J. Jordan

As a civilian, he was a member of the Administrative Staff at Drew University until retirement with his wife Nancy in Naples, Florida.

## HANS G. KAUERMANN

Born April 25, 1917 in Essen, Germany. He came to America at 10 years of age in 1927. He was inducted into the U.S. Army on March 23, 1943 at New Cumberland, Pennsylvania and was sent to the 8th Armored Division at Camp Polk, Louisiana for basic training. While there, he was in Service Company and attended Anti-Tank Gunnery School. He joined the 7th Armored Division in Verdun, France on August 31, 1944. He became Sergeant and was a Mortar Squad Leader, and later Headquarters Squad Leader and was an interpreter during campaigns of Northern France, Holland, Ardennes, Rhineland and central Europe. He was seriously wounded by a sniper on March 29, 1945 in Kirchhain, Germany approximately 90 miles from his place of birth. He was hospitalized in Southampton, England when the war ended. He returned to the States May 11, 1945 and was discharged from Hospital Center, Camp Pickett, Virginia on August 2, 1945. Returned to his former occupation and became Foreman over 52 men and machines at Apex Hosiery Company. He is married and they have two children and two grandchildren.

Hans G. Kauermann

## WALTER P. KEELY, SR.

Born and raised in Philadelphia, Pennsylvania. Enlisted in the Army on December 9, 1941. Reported for active duty at Camp Lee, Virginia on March 3, 1942 and was assigned to Co. F, 48th Armored Infantry Regiment, 3rd Armored Division. He was later assigned to the newly formed 7th Armored Division, again with F Co., 48th Armored Infantry Regiment which became C Co., 23rd Armored Infantry Battalion.

Served with C Co., 23rd Armored Infantry Bn. as S/Sgt. in charge of the 3rd Platoon machine gun squad. Additional duties included instructor in 30 and 50 caliber machine guns, martial arts, and as chemical NCO. Participated in the Louisiana maneuvers, desert training in California, and while stationed in Georgia at Ft. Benning, guarded German prisoners at Americus, and participated in hand to hand combat in night exercises with airborne troops in Columbus. Embarked from New York in June of 1944 for England and final preparation for the European Theater.

In August, arrived on the continent and participated in the division's early combat operations until wounded in Melun, France on August 24, 1944. Spent the next 10 months in various hospitals and was discharged from the convalescence hospital at Camp Pickett, Virginia.

He is presently self-employed as a realtor in Philadelphia, Pennsylvania. Has been active in several civic and fraternal organizations which include Shriners, Sons of the American Revolution, and past president of Roxborough Lion's Club.

## JAMES A. KEGIR

Born March 14, 1911, in Winston Salem, North Carolina, in Forsyth County. Inducted into the service March 11, 1942. Basic training at Ft. Polk, Louisiana, then went on maneuvers in Louisiana, Texas, and the Mojave Desert in California. Was with B Co. which went to France, Belgium, and Holland. Was in hospital, then discharged February 26, 1945.

James A. Kegir

Is retired from Food Fair Company as meat manager. Married and has two daughters and three grandsons.

Walter P. Keely, Sr.

## THOMAS J. KELLY

Born 9 September, 1923, Brooklyn, New York. Graduated Bushwick High School, 1941. In 1942, rejected three times by USMC then inducted in the Army January, 1943. Basic training in the Medical Corps at Camp Pickett, Virginia. Left for Scotland on 6 June, 1944 aboard the Queen Mary attached to the 122nd General Hospital. Left 122nd for Infantry and joined the 7th Armored Division in Belgium. Assigned as Aid Man to 1st Platoon, Co. C, 48th AIB. On 5 April, 1945, at Almert, Germany (Rhur Picket), two platoons of Co. C came under direct tank and machine gun fire inflicting heavy casualties. When the survivors were ordered to withdraw, Thomas pulled seven blinded men into a human chain and led them off the hill. Spotting other wounded on the way down, he made ten more trips up and down rescuing ten more wounded. He was recommended for the Medal of Honor by Capt. Harrison Forrester and received the same from President Truman at the White House on 12 October, 1945. Discharged December, 1945.

Thomas J. Kelly

Graduated from Fordham University, 1956 and 1962 with a B.S. and J.D. respectively. Retired from the U.S. Office of Personnel Management in 1979 with 36 years of service. Admitted to the New York Bar.

## GEORGE W. (BILL) KIDWILER

Born November 16, 1924, in Brunswick, Maryland. Graduated from Brunswick High School in 1942. Was hired by the Baltimore and Ohio Railroad, October 8, 1942. Enlisted in the Army March 18, 1943. Was sent to Camp Polk, Louisiana, in Co. C, 18th Tank Bn. Stayed with the 8th Armored Division until March, 1944. was put in a replacement depot and went overseas May 30, 1944, landing in Scotland on D-Day, June 6, 1944. Joined the 7th Armored Division, Co. B, 17th Tank Bn., in August 1944, just outside Melun. Stayed with the Company until the war ended, serving in Northern France, Ardennes, Rhineland and Central Europe. Returned to the States and was discharged December 31, 1945.

Went back to his railroading job and finished out 42 years of service and retired February 1, 1985, as a crew dispatcher. Bowled professional duckpins for about ten years until he had a heart attack. Still bowls in leagues and smaller tournaments. Is married, has one daughter and two granddaughters.

## ROY B. KILLION

Roy B. Killion

## KENNETH E. KNUTSEN

Born August 3, 1919 in Brooklyn, New York. Grew up and graduated from John Adams High School in Queens County, New York. Was drafted on February 11, 1942 and was assigned to the Third Armored Division. Following his reassignment to the Seventh Armored Division, he attended schools for Radio Operator and Radio Maintenance and was designated as a Radio Operator with Battalion Headquarters, 32nd Armored Regiment. After a series of advancements in rank, he became a Tech. Sgt. as Battalion Communication Chief with the 31st Tank Battalion while the Division was at Camp Coxcomb, California. Continued as Comm. Chief with the 31st throughout its combat period and was discharged at Ft. Dix on September 22, 1945.

Attended a school for television servicing and upon completion of the course, he obtained employment with the RCA Service Company as a field repairman and bench technician. He became the Branch Service Manager in 1951 and remained in that capacity in various branches in the New York Metropolitan area until his retirement in May, 1980. He is married, has two children, three grandchildren and enjoys his retirement playing golf, bowling, traveling and club activities.

## LOUIS F. KRESS

Born January 20, 1919 in Chicago, Illinois. Inducted November 17, 1942 at Camp Grant, Illinois. Departed from here on November 17, 1942 for Camp Polk, Louisiana. Arrived November 20, 1942. Was assigned to I Co., 48th Armored Infantry Regiment, 7th Armored Division where basic training began. Left Camp Polk and went to California to Cox Comb Camp, Desert Training Center, for maneuvers. Left for Ft. Benning, Georgia. Here the regiment was changed to a battalion. Left here May 15, 1944 for Camp Miles Standish, N.Y. Arrived May 18, 1944. Missed the boat, so they went to Camp Shankis, N.Y. Arrived June 6, 1944. June 7, 1944 boarded the Queen Mary and landed in Scotland. Went to Tidworth Barracks, England, July 1, 1944, crossed the Channel for France. Campaigns in N. France, Rhineland, Ardennes and Central Europe. Captured October 29, 1944 in Holland. Sent to Stalag 2. Liberated by Russians in May, 1945. Discharged from Ft. Sheridan in June, 1945.

George W. (Bill) Kidwiler

Kenneth E. Knutsen

Louis F. Kress

## ALBERT W. LEASURE, SR.

Born June 5, 1923, in New Castle, Pennsylvania. Was inducted into the Army on March 13, 1943, and was sent to Camp Polk for basic training. After 14 months with the 49th A.I. Bn., 8th Armored Division, was sent to Tidworth Barracks in England, where he was assigned to B Co., 38th A.I. Bn., 7th Armored Division. Took part in battles at Chartres, Melun, Reims, Verdun, and Metz. Was promoted to Sergeant in Holland, and was a squad leader through battles in Meijel, Overloon, Aachen, and others. Was captured at St. Vith during the Battle of the Bulge. After four months of walking, they were freed when the 2nd A.D. came through. Due to the lack of medical care, he went from 185 pounds to 85 pounds. Was discharged on November 2, 1945.

Albert W. Leasure, Sr.

Married his childhood sweetheart, Vivian, and they became the parents of three boys. Enlisted in the Army Reserve and was called into active duty during the Korean War, but was later discharged due to hardship at home. He and his wife raised five boys and one girl. Is now retired but keeps very active.

## LOLAR C. (BUCK) LEFTWICH

Born February 19, 1913 in Clinchco, Virginia. Inducted into the Army on March 7, 1942 at Camp Lee, Virginia and went at once to Camp Polk, Louisiana and basic training with the 3rd Armored Division. Became a member of the 31st Tank Bn. and when the 7th A.D. was activated. When the division reformed at Ft. Benning, was assigned to Troop D, 87th Rcn. Served as radio operator and gunner on armored car until his capture during the defense of St. Vith in the Battle of the Bulge. Liberated April, 1945, and returned to the States for recuperation and discharge October, 1945.

Served as commander and was active in V.F.W. Post 8979 in Clintwood, Virginia until his untimely death October 14, 1971. Was married and had three children.

Lolar C. (Buck) Leftwich

## RUSSELL M. LINHART

Born August 7, 1917, in Avalon, Pennsylvania. Inducted into the Army on March 10, 1942, New Cumberland, Pennsylvania. Had basic training at Camp Polk, Louisiana, with the 3rd Armored Division. Was also married on base there by an Army chaplain (in a little white church that is still there) September 6, 1942. Transferred to the 7th Armored Division. Made T-4th grade and was a member of the 129th Ordnance Maintenance Battalion, Co. A. Went on desert maneuvers. Overseas, drove the company truck for water. Returned to the United States October, 1945.

Went back to his job as radio announcer for West View Park Amusement Company and also did the broadcasts for the "Big Band Era" from there. Came to California 1953. Retired from International Harvester 1974 and moved to Shingletown, California. He and his wife collect war memorabilia from all wars.

Russell M. Linhart

One of their treasures is a recording of President Franklin D. Roosevelt declaring war on Germany and Japan, made December 8, 1941.

## PETER L. LISEWSKI

Born September 11, 1916 in Whately, Ma. Attended Whately Grammar, Smith Vocational School and Deerfield High School. He entered the service at Camp Devens, Massachusetts on March 18, 1942, basic training at Ft. Knox, Kentucky, with the 3rd Army Division. Transferred to the 7th Armored on cadre, at Camp Polk, Louisiana. They maneuvered in and around Louisiana and Texas, then moved to the desert of California and trained for desert warfare. Several months later, while at Ft. Benning, Georgia, a group of them were sent to Barnwell, South Carolina. There they took charge of the first German prisoners that were captured in Africa and shipped here. Back at Benning just in time to be leaving for Fort Miles Standish. After a short stay, they were railed up to Camp Shanks, New York. On June 6th, they boarded the Queen Mary and landed in Greenock, Scotland. From there on rail they crossed the Channel and engaged German troops in combat all over France, Holland, Belgium, and Germany. His most tragic memory of the war is the Battle of the Bulge, in and around St. Vith. The most exciting and dramatic experience was when B Troop, 87th Cavalry Rcn. was called upon to contact the Russians beyond the Elbe River. Discharged as S. Sgt. at Camp Devens on October 115th, 1945.

Peter L. Lisewski

Bought and operated a night club for better than ten years. Worked at the University of Massachusetts Housing Services as manager for 25 years. Retired in September, 1982. Married the former Jean F. Boyden on October 12, 1954. Has a daughter, Callie Jean Bagdon, a son, Gary Peter, and a granddaughter and a grandson Seth. He enjoys all sports, and plays a great deal of golf, some tennis and fly fishing. Also does some bowling and cross country skiing in the winter season.

## MAURICE LONSWAY

Maurice Lonsway

Born February 24, 1925, graduated from high school in 1941. Attended Holy Cross College and St. Louis University before enlisting in the Reserve Corp in 1943. Took basic training at Camp Roberts, California and went overseas as a replacement rifleman, August, 1955. Joined C Company, 23 Armored Infantry Battalion, 7th Armored Division, September, 1944, at the Moselle River. Wounded once as an infantryman, volunteered to become Aidman due to a shortage of same and after 30 minutes of intensive instruction, all the while under artillery fire, having left C Company as a rifleman rejoined it as an Aidman. Lost leg at Meijel, Holland, October 16, 1944. Discharged August, 1945.

Finished college, graduated Washington University Medical School, 1950. In practice of Pediatrics in St. Louis since 1954. Married. Has five children, two grandchildren.

## EDWARD G. MANTHEY

Edward G. Manthey

## ANTHONY J. MANZO

Born January 25, 1915 in the downtown area of Detroit, Michigan. President Roosevelt greeted him to a draft in 1941. With December 7, 1941 attack at Pearl Harbor, his induction arrived on February 3, 1942. Ft. Custer, Michigan was his first stop. Then on to Camp Polk, Louisiana for basic training with the 3rd Armored Division, 33 Armored Regiment. After basic, he was part of a cadre to form the 7th Armored Division being assigned to the 40th Armored Regiment. General Sylvester's wishes were for a Division Band and Orchestra. Anthony's civilian background as a musician qualified him as a member of the band, playing the clarinet, and playing the violin in the orchestra as well as leading it. His duties were KP, guard, maneuvers in Louisiana, desert training at Camp Coxcomb in the Mojave Desert in California. This followed for bazooka, mortar squad training plus preparations for overseas duties. He departed June 6, 1944 (D-Day) from New York harbor on the Queen Mary and landing in Scotland (Firth of Clyde). Thence to Salisbury to the Kings Barracks and then assigned to

Anthony J. Manzo

General George Patton's 3rd Army. Honorably discharged October of 1945.

Post war merchant for 12 years, graduate of the University of Michigan in 1958. Entered his current profession, real estate, in 1957. Married, father of two sons, life time member of the 7th Armored Division Association since its inception plus a life time member of the Battle of the Bulge Association. ROLL OUT THE BARREL...

## HUBERT R. MARTIN

Born October 3, 1918 in Alabama. Drafted into the Army March 9, 1942 at Ft. McPherson, Georgia and sent to Camp Polk, Louisiana. Was in the 48th AIB. Was on Louisiana and California maneuvers, then went to Ft. Benning, Georgia, and then to guard German prisoners in Moultrie, Georgia. Sailed on June 7, 1944, on the Queen Mary from New York to Scotland. Stationed at Tidworth Barracks in England. In August, 1944, crossed the Channel and went into combat where he became the jeep driver for 1st Lt. Joe Reddy. Went through parts of France that were real battleground, most of all around Metz. Arrived in Overloon, Holland October 1, 1944 where he lost his right foot to a "Screaming Mimi". Was sent by hospital boat to Charleston, South Carolina and from there was sent to McCloskey General Hospital, Temple, Texas.

Hubert R. Martin

Discharged July 21, 1945, with 40% disability. After discharge, worked as motion picture operator and retired February 1, 1981. He and his wife, Elsie, have three daughters, one son, two granddaughters, and six grandsons.

## DOMINIC MARTORELLI

Inducted into the Army from Philadelphia, Pennsylvania, his birthplace, and sworn in at Ft. Maryland on February 21, 1942 just two months before his 24th birthday. Two days after arriving at Camp Polk, Louisiana, was assigned to the 67th Armored F.A. Bn., 3rd Armored Division. Upon completion of basic training was transferred to the 440th F.A., 7th Armored Division. Left Camp

Dominic Martorelli

Polk for Artillery Mechanics School at Ft. Sill, Oklahoma, November 1942, and after graduation, rejoined the Division at Camp Cox Comb, California, March, 1943. Remained with B Btry., 440th FA Bn. throughout his stateside training and eventually shipped out to the E.T.O. on June 6, 1944 aboard the Queen Mary. Continued with the 440th through all its campaigns in Europe until some months after "V.E." Day, when he was transferred to the 183rd FA Bn. and came back to the States with them in October, 1945. Discharged from Indiantown Gap, November, 1945.

Retired in 1982 from Sperry Univac, where he worked as an electro-mechanic designer. Has been married for 40 years and has three children and six grandchildren.

## ROBERT D. MASK

When he wasn't assisting Forward Observer, was acting F.O. with the Infantry. This letter is written in tribute to the 48th, 24th, and 38th Armored Infantry. He witnessed their performance and it was superb in unbelievable hazardous conditions. He went on special assignment for special mission with First Rangers and also the 82nd Airborne. It turned out that neither compared in danger with everyday combat with the Armored Infantry. He acted as Forward Observer for eleven days with A Co., 48th Armored Infantry just before Capt. Madden was killed. In the nine months spent mostly on the front with the Infantry, he never served with anyone he thought his equal as a combat officer. However, all Seventh Armored officers rated near his equal in Robert's estimation. Robert was

Robert D. Mask

also associated with the 40th and 17th Tank Battalion and they did a great job.

It is a privilege and honor to be a part of such a fine combat division.

## MARTIN L. MAXWELL

Born June 10, 1921, in Robbinsville, North Carolina. Volunteered into the Army, March 9, 1942, and joined the 7th Armored at Camp Polk. On being placed in B Company of the 48th Armored Infantry Regiment (later B-38) he was assigned the duty of half-track driver, and remained in the role, and in the same company, until the war's end. In combat, he drove First Rifle Squad of First Rifle Platoon and he remembers that they were the first to serve as the Division Commander's personal guard during the Division's initial fighting in and around Chartres. There he observed first-hand the courage of General Sylvester. As one squad member later remarked, "He damn near got us all killed." At Melun, German machine-gun fire got Maxwell's radiator, forcing abandonment of the vehicle (later recovered). He crossed the Seine in the sunshine, the Moselle in the rain, the Salm in the snow, and the Rhine in the dark.

Martin L. Maxwell

Following the surrender, he was assigned as driver of a staff officer at Occupation Headquarters, until being returned home for discharge. He wears the Bronze Star Medal for Valor, with one oak leaf cluster.

He now resides in the place of his birth with his wife, Mary and their son, Marty. He treasures the memory of the officers and men of the 7th Armored Division.

## CARBIN O. MAYNARD

Born May 9, 1915, in Pickett County in Tennessee. Was called into the Army, July 11, 1941. Basic training at Ft. Benning, Georgia, then went to Camp Polk, Louisiana around December, 1941. He went to school at Ft. Knox, Wheel Vehicle and Motorcycle, and went back to Camp Polk and made cavalry with the 7th Armored Division. He helped train them and by May, 1943 he went to Ft. Benning and on to Boston in September.

Carbin O. Maynard

In October, he was in New York where he caught the Queen Mary to England in June, 1944. By August, he was in Scotland. He crossed the English Channel to France and went on to the Front Line. He moved in with the Division to Holland to join the British Second Army. The Germans were trying to split the Brest and Normandy Peninsulas and they fought through the hedgerows to Chartres, Verdun and Mentz.

In late October, 1944 he was captured by the Germans in Holland. By then there were only seven of their group of soldiers left. They were taken to Dusburg, Germany. They were held prisoners for 193 days at Rostock. When the war was over, they were let go. They had to walk 80 miles to reach their American friends and to be sent home.

He returned home on June, 1945, to Baxter, Tennessee. He met and married Myrtle Whittaker, December, 1945. They moved back to Pickett County where they now reside. They had four children and have four grandchildren and one great grandchild. Today, he is a retired mechanic.

## WILLIAM E. McQUISTON, JR.

Born Youngstown, Ohio, June 15, 1923, son of William E. and Emma Woodall McQuiston. Father served in the U.S. Marine Corps 1913-1917 and the A.E.F. 1917-1918, both at Verdun, 1918 in 1944. Inducted March, 1943, landed Ireland April, 1944, to England and joined Co. B., 38th Armored Infantry Battalion, 7th Armored Division for Northern France Campaign, the Rhineland Campaign in Holland and Germany and wounded in the Ardennes Cam-

William E. McQuiston, Jr.

paign. Carrying a B.A.R. across a field between St. Vith and Wallerode, wounded by sniper on Thursday, January 25, 1945, shattering right forearm resulting in 50% disability. Discharged at Nichols General Hospital, Louisville, Kentucky, September 20, 1945.

On April 3, 1948, married Mary Ruth Jordan, one son William E. III, three daughters, Kathleen, Maureen and Janet (born on his birthday, 1960). Grandchildren William E. IV and Jessica Ann Russo. Retired from U.S. Post Office after 30 years service.

Among 14 medals, awards and citations are the Purple Heart, Combat Infantry Badge and the Belgian Fourragere (Croix De Guerre with palm) and the Presidential Unit Citation for the Ardennes Campaign.

## EARL J. MEIERS

Earl reports that everything is fine in Pittsburgh now that he is retired and on free time. In 1945, he took over a beverage store in Sheraden, Pennsylvania, a small part of Pittsburgh. He worked it until 1970, then went to work for J & L Steel as a recorder in the cold mill then the hot mill at the same job. They closed the mill in 1981 and that was all for him at working at Pittsburgh.

Earl J. Meiers

He lost his wife, Grace, in September, 1972. They both ice skated and had a cottage in Harmony, Pennsylvania. He sold the cottage and moved to Cleveland, Ohio. He has an apartment and has lived there since 1981. He enjoys ice skating and golf which keep him busy in Cleveland.

He has three daughters and two sons and seven grandchildren. He says he has been very lucky and all are well.

## ARCHIE LEE MENDENHALL

Born December 26, 1923 at Cameron, Oklahoma. Married Nettie Mae Phillips. Had six children. Entered service November 17, 1943 at Ft. Sill, Oklahoma. Departed overseas September 18, 1944. Captured December 23, 1944 during the Battle of the Bulge when 88 shell exploded, blowing him up against his tank, knocking him out and wounding him in the side. His buddies carried him part of the way on forced march to prison camp. He was hospitalized and a prisoner and his doctor helped him to escape camp. He was captured by the Russians and had to escape from them too. His doctor gave him his hospital records and told him to keep them as he would need them someday. Received WW II Victory Medal, European African Middle Eastern Ribbon with 3 stars, American Theatre Ribbon, Combat Infantryman Badge, Purple Heart.

Archie Lee Mendenhall

After war became a plumber (Journeyman) before disabled and unable to work. Three open heart operations. Member DAV.

## HOMER I. MITCHELL

Born January 28, 1917, and was raised near Mechanicsville, Iowa. Went to a country school and Tipton High School. Married Ruby B. Schroeder, December 19, 1937. Had two children, Richard (born 1939) and Sandra (born 1941). They farmed near Mechanicsville from March 1939 to December 1943, then they moved to Davenport, Iowa. Homer entered service June 14, 1944, from Des Moines. They sent him to Ft. McClellan,

Homer I. Mitchell

Alabama, for basic. He came home for the last time November, 1944 on leave before going to Ft. George G. Meade, Maryland, and to Bostin, Massachusetts, then left for overseas December 8, 1944. He arrived in Liverpool, England, December 18, 1944 and was sent through France to Belgium January 3, 1945. The last letter was written January 18, 1945 in Belgium. At that time he had not been called into action. He died of wounds received January 26, 1945, in Belgium (2nd Battle of the Bulge). He liked to walk on his hands when playing around.

This biography was submitted in memory and in honor of her father by Mrs. Sandra M. Pennington.

## JOHN J. MOLCHANY

Born February 6, 1920 and raised in Catasauqua, Pennsylvania. Inducted at Ft. Meade, Maryland, on February 2, 1942. Received basic training at Camp Polk, Louisiana with the 3rd Armored Division. In cadre to form the 7th Armored Division.

John J. Molchany

Trained at Camp Polk, the California desert and Ft. Benning, Georgia. Sailed with the 7th on the Queen Mary from New York on June 7, 1944. After training at Tidworth, England, he crossed the English Channel on L.S.T. with tanks and crews into France. They went through France and up to the Baltic Sea. They were later sent to Camp Lucky Strike to board the ship to Boston, Massachusetts, then shipped from there to Indiantown Gap. Discharged October 31, 1945.

Attended his first reunion in Harrisburg, Pennsylvania on September 1, 1986, with his wife Betty. He is the proud father of five children, Josette, John, Marie, Anthony, Paul and a grandfather of eight grandchildren.

## KONRAAD S. MOLENAAR

Born December 11, 1922 in Hoorn, The Netherlands. Attended Naval School in Amsterdam until this establishment was closed by the Nazis in November, 1942. From January 1, 1943 to August, 1944, was employed as a land

Konraad S. Molenaar

surveyor in Weert, The Netherlands. During the period he was rendering aid to members of the American and British Air Forces, who were evading capture in enemy occupied Holland and for which activities, he was awarded the U.S. Medal of Freedom. He joined the Dutch Army after the liberation of Weert, September 22, 1944 and was attached to the U.S. Seventh Armored Division on October 1944, where he acted as interpreter for General Lindsay Silvester. Was transferred to the 507th Counter Intelligence Corps Detachment, G.2, Division HQ as from November 1944. He served in the Peel Marshes, Ardennes, Rhineland and Central Europe. V.E. Day found him in Ludwigslust, Mecklenburg near the Baltic Sea. Early June, 1945, the 507th C.I.C. team was detached from the Seventh Armored Division and remained in Germany for occupational duties. He was discharged November 8, 1945.

Joined the Telecommunications Department of K.L.M. Royal Dutch Airlines, assisted in the foundation of an International Aeronautical Telecommunications Organization, which he joined in 1951, at its Paris Head office. Became Executive Vice-President and retired in December 1982.

## GEORGE W. MONAGHAN

Born January 2, 1917 in Philadelphia, Pennsylvania. Was inducted in May, 1941 and sent to Ft. Meade, Maryland. Was sent to the 4th Armored Division at Pine Camp, New York. In June, 1941, went to O.C.S. at Ft. Knox and was commissioned in September, and assigned to the 7th Armored at Camp Polk. Was assigned to A Co., 40th Armored Regiment. Was on desert training in 1943 and went to Ft. Benning, where he was assigned to the Recon Troop of the 40th Regiment. Was then assigned to E Troop, 87th Recon Squadron. Was in combat in France up to Metz, then to Holland, where his reconnaissance platoon was overrun and he was captured on October 27, 1944. After surviving a death march along the Baltic Coast of Poland, he was separated from the Army in December, 1945.

Graduated from the University of Pennsylvania after the war and worked as a salesman and sales manager in Philadelphia and Dallas, Texas. Moved to California in 1956 and is now retired from General Telephone Company. Now lives in Manhattan Beach with his wife, Shirley, and his son, George.

George W. Monaghan

## HARRISON W. MORGAN

Born August 19, 1922 in Monson, Massachusettes. He was inducted into the Army on September 17, 1942, shipped to Ft. Devens, Massachusetts, then to Ft. Eustis, Virginia for antiaircraft training. After he finished there, he was shipped to Camp Maxie, Texas for infantry training. From there to Ft. Meade, Maryland, Camp Kilmer, New Jersey and overseas in August, 1944.

Harrison W. Morgan

Joined the 7th Armored in September, 1944. First combat, Overloon, where he was wounded. Was only out of action for four days. Stayed with A Company, 38th, 1st Platoon until they hit the Battle of the Bulge in St. Vith. During the night of December 21, 1944 and the morning of December 22, walking all night to get out of enemy territory, about twenty five of them were captured at daybreak in a building. Were liberated by the 9th Armored Division on April 17, 1945. Most of them made it through.

He now runs a small business in the material handling field, (storage systems, conveyors, etc.) under the name of Morgan Material Handling Company. He enjoys his business and has no plans to retire. He is married and has five children and seven grandchildren. He sends his very best to all 7th Armored personnel. He's been a member of the 7th Association since 1948.

## MARVIN A. MOSER

Born in Hickman, Nebraska, October 17, 1919. Answered Uncle Sam's call on December 19, 1942, received his discharge on October 19, 1945. Pretty darn good birthday present. Assigned to the 2nd Platoon, Rcn. Co 814th Battalion in Camp Bowie. After basic training, they all went on to Camp Hood, after more training on to Camp Polk. Got together with the 7th Armored Division in France in August, 1944. As a driver for their platoon leader, he was lead vehicle of their column in the mad rush across France for several days. They were very joyously welcomed by the French citizens with flowers and fruit. and of course returned the favors with chocolate and cigarettes. He remembers one time near Rambouillet, France, while being lead vehicle, they came around a corner in the road with about a 10 feet high limestone wall on their left, an open field to their right, a railroad running parallel to the road they were on, about 250 yards away, and a knocked-out jeep about 100 yards ahead of them still smoking. As they were getting closer to it, Marvin told the Lt., "If we are going to get it, we should be getting it any damn time now." No sooner said than done. The M-8 right behind them got an A.P. shell through the left fron tire. They didn't bother to turn around, backed out of there faster than they came in. The M-8 driver had a heck of a time backing up, so Marvin bypassed them on their right side. The gunner had his 37 MM aimed to the right and as they went by, he was just ready to fire when he saw them in his sight. Needless to say they have been very good friends since (Calvin Boykin, of Texas). The Germans fired about six rounds all together, he guesses, and missed every time.

Marvin A. Moser

He retired from the water well drilling business over two years ago, but his two sons are continuing in the business. He and his wife enjoy about four or five months of winter in Tucson, Arizona. There is now a chapter of the 7th Armored Division there called The Desert Chapter. It meets on the 2nd Wednesday of the first month of each quarter. The 814th also meets in Savannah, Missouri, the last week-end in June, every year and invites anyone to drop in if in the vicinity. He and his wife have two grand little grandsons and a grand little granddaughter. His wife and he will celebrate their 40th year of happy marriage in May of this year.

## RALPH L. MOWERY

Born in Salisbury, North Carolina, January 17, 1920 and attended Rowan County Schools. Worked in textile mills before being inducted into the Army at Ft. Bragg, North Carolina, March 10, 1942. Was sent to Camp Polk, Louisiana where he was put in the 3rd Armored Division and later transferred to the 7th Armored Division, Co B, 38th A.I.B. After desert training in California, was shipped to Ft. Benning, Georgia. From there, was sent to Camp Miles Standish, Massachusetts and later to Camp Shanks, New York. Sailed from New York on the Queen Mary, June 6, 1944, D-Day. In Camp at Tidworth Barracks, Wiltshire, England before going to France. Was wounded by sniper southwest of Melun, August 22, 1945, and was sent to the hospital in England. Rejoined the 7th Armored Division in September, but was captured by the Germans just before Christmas during the Battle of the Bulge. With the help of a German guard who had lived in the U.S. before the war, he and two other Americans escaped April 24, 1945. Arrived in the U.S. June 7, 1945. Was discharged through the Transportation Corp October 29, 1945, at Ft. DuPont, Delaware.

Was married to Fern Brown on September 2, 1942 at DeRidder, Louisiana. Has one son. Had heart by-pass surgery November, 1979 and retired from Apex Corporation due to disability February, 1982.

## FRANK J. MULA

Born February 14, 1920 in Elm Grove, West Virginia. After Pennsylvania, and New York, he graduated from Jamestown High School in 1938. After factory work, he attended the University of Illinois to study art. In 1942 he was drafted and from Ft. Niagara and was sent to Camp Polk, Louisiana. Here, in the 3rd Armored, he served as cadre to form the 7th Armored. He was a Tech. Sergeant in the 48th Armored Infantry. After desert training, the division left on the Queen Mary to Scotland, then England. In charge of an infantry platoon, his outfit crossed the channel into combat in Normandy. The division ended in Patton's 3rd Army. After Verdun, Metz, St. Vith, Holland, and the Battle of the Bulge, he was wounded. He received the Purple Heart with cluster and the Bronze Star. After recuperation in an English hospital, he was reassigned to guard German prisoners in Marseille, France.

Frank J. Mula

Then homeward, and back to the University of Illinois, where he received his Masters degree in art education. He married Helen Schaefer and they have four children. With 38 years of teaching in high school, Frank will retire in May, 1987. He and family are living in Monticello, Illinois.

## ROBERT F. (BOB) MURPHY

Born January 5, 1918 in Schenectady, New York. Graduated from St. Columba's Academy, Schenectady, New York in 1937. Enlisted in the Army at Albany, New York on February 9, 1942 and was sent to Ft. Dix, New Jersey. After three or four days at Ft. Dix, was sent to Camp Polk, Louisiana, and assigned to HQ's Co, 48th Infantry Battalion, 3rd Armored Division. Took basic training

Robert F. (Bob) Murphy

with the 3rd. Participated in the Louisiana maneuvers while at Camp Polk. Was picked as one of the cadre to form the 7th Armored Division and was assigned to the 38th Infantry Battalion. Left Camp Polk with the 7th for desert maneuvers in California. During the California maneuvers, he was assigned to a reconnaissance platoon. After maneuvers, he left with the 7th for Ft. Benning, Georgia where he was reassigned to a rifle squad in Co A, 38th Infantry Battalion. Requested this reassignment. Left Ft. Benning with the 7th for Camp Miles Standish, Massachusetts and later was shipped to Camp Shanks, New Jersey. This was the last stop for the 7th before going overseas. Boarded the Queen Mary at the New York P.O.E. on June 6, 1944. The entire 7th was loaded aboard the Queen Mary and sailed for Scotland. He stayed with the 7th until he was wounded during the Battle of Melun. Was flown back to England on a hospital plane (C-47) to recuperate at the 121st Station Hospital, Braintree, England. After wounds healed, he was sent back across the Channel for the second time. Joined the 29th Infantry Regiment on December 16, 1944 and fought with them during the Battle of the Bulge. Remained with the 29th until after the war. Left the 29th and was shipped back to Ft. Dix, New Jersey where he was discharged October 21, 1945.

Passed the civil service examination and went to work at the Scenectady Army Depot, New York. The Depot shipped supplies to the military all over the world. He was promoted to traffic manager and January, 1967 was transferred to the New Cumberland Army Depot, Pennsylvania. Retired in 1976 with 33 years of government service. Was married for 37 years. His wife died in January, 1983. He has a son and daughter and one grandchild.

## JAMES L. NABORS

Born January 24, 1919, in Wildwood, Georgia. He was raised in Georgia until his teens when his family moved to Arizona, where he graduated from Phoenix High School. Jim entered the service in February, 1942, in Cleveland, Ohio, took

Ralph L. Mowery

James L. Nabors

his basic training at Camp Polk in Louisiana, and spent five months in maneuvers in the Mojave Desert, finishing his training at Ft. Benning in Georgia. He was sent overseas on the Queen Mary, arriving in Scotland and then moving on to England. Jim was a reconnaissance man under the command of Capt. Britton in France, Central Europe, and Germany until he lost his leg in the winter of 1944. He was discharged with honors while recovering in the VA hospital in Battlecreek, Michigan.

He returned to Cleveland to the Art Gravure Corporation where he was a newspaper pressman for 43 years, serving as Union Chairman for 15 of those years. Jim passed away on January 15, 1987. He is survived by his wife, Jayne, daughters Pamela and Stayce, and son Jim the II. He resided in Brooklyn, Ohio for 40 years and was active in the VFW, Brooklyn Athletic Boosters, Brooklyn Players, Brooklyn Recreation Club, Caballeros Jr. Drum and Bugle Corp, Indiana Guides, and numerous other youth and community groups.

### EARL W. NALL

Born March 7, 1918 in Chandlerville, Illinois. Entered the Army, July, 1941 at Ft. Sheridan, Illinois. From there to Camp Polk, Louisiana with the 3rd Armored Division. He was on a cadre to the 7th Armored Division. Was on maneuvers in Louisiana, Texas and the California desert. Went overseas. Arrived in Scotland, and went to England by train. Crossed the English Channel to France. Engaged in battles and campaigns of Northern France, Ardennes, Rhineland, and Central Europe. Met the Russians at Wismar, Germany. He was a T/Sgt. with the 129th Maintenance Battalion. Was discharged October, 1945.

Went into business for himself until he retired. Is married and has one girl and one boy and four grandchildren.

Earl W. Nall

### GERALD NELSON

He left Two Rivers, Wisconsin for the Army at age 18 in June of 1943 and took basic at Ft. Knox. Left the U.S.A. as a replacement in April, 1944, and arrived in France July, 1944. Joined C Co., 40th Tank Battalion in September at Metz as that company's first replacement. Shortly after that he became a gunner in a Sherman and stayed with the company until VE Day.

Gerald Nelson

He became a barber in 1949 and has done that ever since in a nice shop in his home town. He is married, has two kids, two boats, two buildings and an extremely contented life. He enjoys bowling, fishing and WW II history. He is corresponding with his old CO somewhat and even a historian and a Belgium friend who sent him pictures from 1945 and then some in 1986.

He retired a few months ago, partially, as his son now works in his shop and he goes in quite often. He would really like to hear from old C Co. friends from 40 years ago. Anybody listening?

### WESLEY W. NEWCOME

Born September 11, 1915, in Moweaqua, Illinois. Has made his home in Illinois except while in the military service. Graduated from Decatur High School, Decatur, Illinois. Was inducted into service January 1942 at Camp Grant, Illinois and assigned for training to the 3rd Armored Division at Camp Polk, Louisiana and re-assigned to the 7th Armored Division, Co A, 33rd

Wesley W. Newcome

Armored Engineer Bn. Except for 12 weeks at Engineer Mechanical Equipment School, Ft. Belvoir, Virginia, he stayed with the same company until VE Day. Returned for discharge October 19, 1945 at Indiantown Gap, Pennsylvania.

Joined the Reserves, 1949, 815th Army Postal Unit, and was called to active duty September, 1950. Served as postal specialist at APO 676, Rio de Janeiro, Brazil, June 1951 through May 1953. Served one year at Atlanta General Depot, Atlanta, Georgia and was discharged May 1954.

From December 1945 through September 1976, was a postal employee at Decatur, Illinois and retired as postmaster from Beardstown, Illinois. He has spent 8 and ½ years working for the State of Illinois Tax Revenue Department. Retired again in February, 1986.

December 1943, he married Violet Preston, a T-5 in the Womans' Army Corps. They are still enjoying their life together.

### STANLEY F. NOVAK

Born December 16, 1916. Raised in Stuyvesant Falls, New York and inducted in the Army February 11, 1942 at Camp Upton, New York. Received basic training at Camp Polk, Louisiana, being assigned to Hq. Co., 31st Tank Battalion, 7th Armored Division, activated on March 1, 1942. Maneuvers were at Camp Polk, Mojave Desert in California and Ft. Benning, Georgia. Next came Camp Miles Standish, Camp Shanks, New York P.O.E. Sailed on the Queen Mary June 6, 1944 to Tidworth Barracks, England. Sailed from Southampton to Omaha Beach, France, where he joined

Stanley F. Novak

Patton's 3rd Army. They fought in Northern France, the Rhineland, Central Europe, (Verdun, Chartres, Melum, Chateau Thierry, Reims and Metz.) Also Holland, Ardennes-Alsace, for the Battle of the Bulge at St. Vith, Belgium. Their division was at the Baltic Sea when the war ended. Returned home on the S.S. Alexandria. Discharged from Camp Kilmer, New Jersey on September 22, 1945 as Tec. 5.

Married Evelyn Oldrich on December 25, 1943 and they have three daughters, Joan, Janis, and Julie. Also three grandchildren, Robert Jr., Nicholas, and Rachel. Retired from Fort Orange Paper Company. Active in VFW, Post 9593, serving as Quartermaster a number of years and also Commander. He and his wife reside at Stuyvesant Falls, New York.

## I. OBERDAN

Joined the 7th October, 1944 in Holland. Major Dailey assigned him to Co B, 17th Tank. Told the Major he hadn't been in a tank for over a year and he brightly replied "Your M.O.S. Number says you're a platoon leader and that's what we need." My equally brilliant reply was "Yes, sir." as I saluted and left. On October 27th, they knocked out a Tiger tank. (They all looked like Tigers to him.) The next day, an 88 knocked out their tank. John Eckerman was badly hurt with a fractured pelvis. Things were quiet for a while until December 1st when they went to help the 102nd Division (Ozark) take Linnich, Germany. Lt. Hummel was killed and their captain got hurt. Oberdan became company commander for less than 24 hours, as artillery fire hit him in the thigh the next day. He was awarded the Silver Star and Purple Heart. Spent four months in a hospital in England (two months in bed) and was then assigned to limited duty.

I. Oberdan

Became a civilian, a manufactures representative and the father of five children. Attended his first reunion in 1985 and had a great time seeing his old buddies.

## REV. RAPHAEL C. O'BRIEN

Born August 13, 1906 in Reading, Pennsylvania, the eighth of twelve children. Graduated from St. Joseph's High School in 1923. Entered St. Charles' Seminary in 1924 and was ordained May 26, 1934. Was first appointed to St. Mary's parish in Coaldale, Pennsylvania. Was then sent to St. Ann's in Phoenixville, and Holy Family in Manayunk, Philadelphia. Was commissioned as a chaplain in the US Army in September, 1941, and was first attached to the 51st AT&T Signal Battalion at Wadesboro, North Carolina. On December 2nd, went to Camp Lee as Chaplain to OCS and the hospital. On May 2nd, 1942, became chaplain to the 7th Armored Division. After living with the Seventh Armored from its inception to its end at Camp Pactrick Henry, was discharged from the army at Indian Town Gap and went back to St. Hugh's in Philadelphia. After a year and a half was given a four month leave to be treated for stomach ulcers. Spent the next eleven years at Nativity in Philadelphia. In 1958, was made pastor of St. Teresa of Avila, in Valley Forge. Retired from St. Teresa's in 1970 and became a resident of Villa St. Joseph, where presently resides, in 1981.

Rev. Raphael C. O'Brien

## CARLETON W. PEEVER

Born August 17, 1918. Joined the Army in June, 1941. Stationed at Camp Polk, Louisiana for basic training in the 3rd Armored Division. Cadre to 7th Armored maneuvers in the California desert, then back to Ft. Benning, Georgia, then to Miles Standish to overseas. Landed in France and remained in Europe with the 7th until the end of the war. Released from duty in 1945.

Called back to active duty and was in Korea for a year. Retired from the reserves after 22 years as M/Sgt. Was a carpenter in the Niles, Mi. area until he retired in 1980. Married and has two children and three grandchildren.

## HARTLEY B. PETERSON

Born in Brooklyn, New York on November 2, 1918 and has lived there with the exception of his military duty for the following 40 years. He received his early schooling at the local schools and later attended the American Institute of Banking and also the City College of New York. Spent 20 years with Chase Manhattan Bank of New York and after moving into California, worked another 10 years with the State of California. Married to his wife Ebba in 1950 and she has been his constant companion these 37 happy years. Their only daughter, Sandra, is in nursing at the Eisenhower Medical Center, Ranch Mirage, California, a place not too many miles from the desert training center and environs where they all received their training.

In the words of the Broadway hit musical "Ah yes, I remember it well": Hartley remembers that day in '42 when he startd his Army career and almost concluded it, all in the same day; a casualty of the war

Hartley B. Peterson

Carleton W. Peever

without ever hearing a shot fired. It happened in this fashion. They boarded the troop train one shivering February day bound for Camp Polk and although he lived only a few miles away, he was never so happy to see the train pull out from Camp Upton, Long Island for parts then unknown. They had barely pulled out of the station when he became a KP "volunteer," and was told to report to the mess sergeant in the kitchen car. It was a converted freight car with 2x4's stretched across the huge door openings to serve as barricades. In the center of the floor was an improvised wood-burning cooking stove surrounded by a mountain of logs. Hartley was assigned to the cocoa detail and when his 30 quart bucket was reasonably full, he courageously took off to do his duty (with trepidation). Bucket in hand, he passed the huge door opening just as the train hit a curve. Someone had forgotten to put up the 2x4 barricades, so as the bucket and he moved out of the door, he felt a strong hand grab his coveralls by the shoulders, and another, the seat of his pants and pull him to safety. A man overboard at sea would have had a better chance of being rescued than an unknown private who fell to the tracks from a speeding Long Island Railroad train. Would he have been carried the next day on the Morning Report as "missing in action?"

Hartley says most war heroes are made in the bars and clubrooms of the VFW and Legion across the country so he won't bore you with his military exploits. They are for the most part like yours. Like you, he simply did his duty.

## LAWRENCE E. PHILBIN

Born June 30, 1924 and grew up in Almonesson, New Jersey. Attended Woodbury High School, then worked at USMC Quartermaster, Philadelphia, prior to induction in April, 1943. Basic at Ft. Eustis, Virginia, then to Ft. Bliss, Texas for Paratrooper training and assigned to 652 AA, Airborne Bn. Went overseas in August, 1944 aboard USS Bienville. Disembarked in Glasgow and immediately entered training for Southampton. Crossed the channel and was assigned as replacement to HQ Co, 23 A.I. Bn at Metz. Was a Pfc assigned to a heavy weapons section near St. Vith when he

Lawrence E. Philbin

took 12 bullets in the left arm and chest, December 23, 1944. Taken to the 15th General Hospital, Ciege, then flown to Newton Abbott Hospital in England and then via USS Bienville (again) to New York in April, 1945. Assigned to Thomas England General Hospital, Atlantic City, until discharge May 2, 1946.

Returned to USMC Quartermaster May 6, 1944 as a guard in Security Department. Married June 17, 1950. Have three sons, three grandchnildren. Retired as guard Lieutenant June 30, 1976 to a farm in Washington Twp, Gloucester County, New Jersey. He is a life member of the 7th Armored Division Association, VFW and DAV.

## FRANK PIETRASZKO

Inducted into the U.S. Army February 7, 1942 at Camp Polk, Louisiana. Yes, a new adventure had opened in their lives as young men. A new life began with the 3rd Armored which was already activated. The cadre for the 7th began to form. Many men were transferred to the 7th Division. Later it was maneuvers in Louisiana, then to California, the Mojave Desert. Excitement ran rampant and the men saw the desert where early settlers crossed for a new life. Many men cussed the heat during hot desert training. When the company commander said passes to L.A. and Hollywood, what a thrill to see movieland. Back to Ft. Benning, Georgia, then to Camp Shanks and the Big Lady, Queen Mary waiting for the 7th Division to board her. To Scotland, Southhampton, the English Channel to Omaha Beach.

Frank Pietraszko

## GENE K. POSEY

Born February 17, 1915 at Dunkerton, Iowa. Enlisted from 1932 to 1938 as Machine Gunner and Bugler, Co. D, 133

Gene K. Posey

Infantry and Co. H, 168th Infantry, I.N.G. Enlisted in the army July, 1942, Des Moines, Iowa. Completed officers training Camp Perry, Ohio and was assigned to the 11th Armored Division. Transferred to the 129th Ordnance Maintenance Battalion, 7th Armored Division, Camp Polk, Louisiana, January, 1943. Participated in technical training and field exercises at Camp Polk, Louisiana, Desert maneuvers, Camp Coxcomb on the California desert and to Ft. Benning, Georgia for extensive technical training, Division reorganization and exhaustive field training exercises in preparation for overseas movement.

Departed Ft. Benning, Georgia with advanced detachment under General Thompson for England, March 1944, aboard troop ship Nieuw Amsterdam. Assigned as Ordnance Combat Liaison Officer, worked closely with 17th Tank Bn and supporting units through campaigns of Northern France, Rhineland and Central Europe and was wounded during the Battle of Metz. At completion of hostilities, served with 1st Armored Division, 80th Ordnance Bn and Stuttgart Military Post Ordnance Office. Reverted to inactive reserve status and returned to the States in June 1948.

Returned to active duty February, 1951, and served at Rock Island Arsenal, MAAG, Taiwan, USARPAC Hq, Hawaii, Hq USARJ, Japan and ARADCOM units as Ordnance Special Weapons, and Guided Missile Staff Officer in Texas, Oklahoma, Florida, Georgia, New Mexico, and California. Reitred from Ft. Baker, California, June, 1968, as Lieutenant Colonel with over 30 years of military service.

## MORRIS W. POWELL

Inducted into the Army in February, 1944 at Camp Wolters, Texas. From there he was sent to Camp Polk, Louisiana where he joined the 7th Armored. After basic training, he worked for a while as a special service driver. Later he was assigned to a halftrack and became the driver for the S-Z section of C.C.A. Headquarters. A few words cannot tell all of the human interest stories, but he was proud to have been a part of a great orga-

Morris W. Powell

nization as the "Lucky Seventh" and he feels they were blessed with some of the finest men and officers the Army could produce. They lost a few of those fine officers and men in that frozen Hell they called The Bulge and he will always remember them as some of the finest.

After returning to the states, Morris was married and has two daughters and one grandson. His home is in Waxahachie, Texas. He worked 30 years for a refrigeration company, retired and now works at a part-time job. There has been a lot of water under the bridge since those days and occasionally he thinks back of the good and the bad of them. He believes he knows now what General Patton meant in his speech to the soldiers before they crossed the channel. He said: "Some of these days when your grandson sits on your knee and says, "Pappy, where were you in the war?" you will not have to tell him you were in Louisiana scooping s--- with a shovel."

## WILLIAM W. POWER

Born October 27, 1908 in Winnetka, Illinois. Graduated from the University of Wisconsin, 1931. Drafted June 16, 1941 in Chicago, Illinois and assigned to HQ 1st Bn 36th Armored Infantry Regiment, 3rd A.D., Camp Polk, Louisiana. Promoted to Corporal, Sergeant, Staff Sergeant, and Bn Sergeant Major. Graduated from Armored OCS, Ft. Knox, August 22, 1942 and assigned to 2nd Bn, 40th Armored Regiment, Camp Polk, Louisiana. Promoted 1st Lt. and appointed Co Commander of E Co and promoted to Capt. May, 1943. Under the reorganization of the Armored Divisions, he was appointed Co Commander of B Co, 40th Tank Bn 7th A.D. In April of 1944 was appointed S-2 40th Tank Bn and served in that capacity to the end of the war. Was awarded stars for the four European campaigns as well as a Silver Star and a Bronze Star. Was discharged at Ft. Sheridan, Illinois, November 1945 and remained in the reserves until April, 1954, when he resigned his commission with the rank of Major.

Went into business with his brother until April 1954 when he joined the staff of the Vice President of Sales, Signode Strapping Company, Chicago, Illinois. Moved to Wayne, Pennsylvania in 1958, where presently resides, and became Eastern Sales Manager for Signode Steel Strapping Co., retiring in 1974.

Worked for a judge of the Court of Common Pleas in West Chester, Pennsylvania, retiring in 1979. Married and has one daughter who is married to an Englishman who is Vice President of an English owned Company. They have two boys, ages six and eight, and live one mile from the Powers.

## STANLEY C. PRATT

Born March 3, 1922 in Dansville, New York. Reared in Dayton, Ohio. Inducted into the Army, October, 1942, and sent to the 89th Division 340th Field Artillery at Camp Carson, Colorado. Trained as a "105" gunner. Went overseas as a replacement in the 2nd Armored Division as a Tank Gunner. Was wounded and after leaving hospital joined the 7th Armored Division in Holland as a replacement in the 38th Infantry Battalion, Co. B as a gunner. January 28, 1945, was flown to England Hospital where he remained until April, 1945. Then home to USA via the Queen Mary. Was given a medical discharge from Wakeman Hospital, Camp Atteberry, Indiana, September, 1945. Resumed civilian life as an apprentice toolmaker. Married Madelyn Ruble in May, 1947. Has one son and two daughters. Retired from General Motors, Delco-Moraine Division in 1980 as a Tool Room Supervisor with 30 years service.

William W. Power

Stanley C. Pratt

## JAMES P. RAFFERTY

Jim joined the C. Co 33rd Armored Engineer Battalion 7th Armored Division as a replacement at Nancy, France, about the 1st of September, 1944. They regrouped during the week, went in convoy to the Netherlands to support the British 2nd Army. They stopped overnight at Weert, Holland. the following days after that were at the front lines. They were clearing mine fields. Their lieutenant, Karesh, was disarming a mine when it discharged, blowing Lt. Karesh's arm off and he fell onto another mine which took his leg. Jim went into the minefield to carry him out and when returning, stepped on a mine, blowing his own right leg off. He called the other men from the truck to bring rope, put it around Lt. Karesh, and they pulled him out. They then returned to pull Jim out. This all occurred on the 21st of October, 1944. Capt. Darden checked on the lieutenant and Jim the next day in the field hospital. They were doing as well as could be expected. That same day, Jim was transferred to 15th General Hospital in Liege, Belgium. He was then transferred through a chain of hospitals, finally ending up back in the U.S. He was sent to Walter Reed Hospital in Washington D.C. where he spent 21 months recovering. He was awarded the Silver Star, Purple Heart, and three battle stars.

James P. Rafferty

## THOMAS P. RAGONE

Born November 19, 1919, in Albany, New York. Enlisted October, 1940, assigned to Company D, 106th Infantry. Was discharged October, 1941 from Ft. McClellen, Alabama. Recalled January, 1942 to Camp Upton, New York and was sent to Niagara Falls as an M.P. In March, 1942, he enlisted in the Paratroopers, took basic training at Ft. Benning, Georgia. After training, left the Paratroopers and joined the newly formed Seventh Armored Division, Camp Polk, Louisiana; followed by desert maneuvers in California. Thence to Ft. Benning, Georgia, was given advanced training as a Tank Commander. He was then sent overseas as part of the 40th Tank Battalion, 7th Armored

Thomas P. Ragone

Division. Was engaged in battles and campaigns of Northern France, Ardennes, Rhineland and Central Europe. Was discharged October, 1945 at Ft. Dix, New Jersey.

He is married 43 years this year, has three children, and five grandchildren. Worked as a printer for 40 years retired, but presently is helping his son, Tom in his own printing business.

In conclusion, he wants to say he is happy to be one of the Lucky Seventh to return home.

## JAMES H. RIDDLE

Born March 5, 1918 in Oneonta, Alabama. Inducted into the Army March 9, 1942, at Camp Shelby, Mississippi. Was sent to the 3rd Armored Division at Camp Polk, Louisiana for basic training. He became part of a cadre forming the 7th Armored Division. Acting Squad Leader with Co B, 23 Infantry Battalion. Later transferred to the Co Motor Pool as Truck Driver. Spent five months on maneuvers in the California desert. Returned August 11, 1944 to Ft. Benning, Georgia for advanced training. Was assigned to Guard Duty. Worked German prisoners harvesting peanuts in Georgia. On April 20th, left Ft. Benning for POE Port of Embarkation. June 6th sailed on the Queen Mary, arriving in Scotland. On to England where they picked up their equipment. On August 11, he landed on Utah Beach. Was in the campaigns of Northern France. Was wounded September 29, 1944 crossing the Moselle River. Arrived back in the States December 30, 1944. Sent to Welch Convalescent Hospital at Daytona Beach, Florida on July 20, 1945. Was reassigned to the 1493 Station Compliment, MP duty until December 18. Sent to Camp Blanding Florida Separation Center. Was discharged.

Worked for the City of Daytona Beach as a carpenter until retirement in 1983. Married with four children and eight grandchildren.

## BARRON C. RILEY

Born February 7, 1919 in Columbus, Ohio. He was inducted into the army on February 4, 1942 at Ft. Hayes Barracks. Was first assigned to the 3rd Armored Division at Camp Polk, Louisiana for basic training. Later was transferred to the 7th Armored Division after completing a course in water purification at Ft. Belvoir, Virginia. He was assigned as a sergeant to the 334rd AR. Engineers, Co. C. Spent five months on manuevers in the Mojave Desert before being sent to Ft. Benning, Georgia. From there, he went to Camp Shanks in New York, for embarkation. Sailed June 7, 1944, on the Queen Mary for Scotland, then to England, France, Holland, Belgium and Germany. Was discharged at Indiantown Gap, Pennsylvania on December 5, 1945 and inducted in the Army February 11, 1942 at Camp Upton, New York. After the war he attended electronic classes at Franklin University in Columbus, Ohio. Since 1952 he has owned and operated his own television business. His wife Irene and he have a son and a daughter and three grandsons. As he left Columbus, Ohio on the train for Camp Polk back in 1942, he met Albert, Midge, Orris (Cpl 33rd AR. Engineers, Co. C) from Brownsville, Pennsylvania. Not only was Midge his army buddy, but he, with his family, has been there lifelong friend. Midge passed away August 21, 1978.

## ROBERT E. RING

Born May 18, 1919 and raised in Claypool, Indiana. Graduated from Claypool, Indiana High School. Entered the Army on May 19, 1942 at Toledo, Ohio and was sent to Ft. Knox, Kentucky for basic training. After basic training was sent to Camp Polk, Louisiana — joining there the 7th Armored Division, 147th Armored Signal Company, Division Signal Supply. Discharged September 22, 1945 at Camp Atterbury, Indiana.

Robert E. Ring

Returned to Warsaw, Indiana and spent several years farming. Later he entered the church furniture business, first as Installation Foreman, then Sales Representative. In 1977, they moved to Glendale, Arizona and he is now a sales representative for Imperial Woodworks, Inc. out of Waco, Texas.

Several years ago, he and his wife toured Europe, attending the Passion Play in Oberammergau. During their tour of Europe, he was able to see some of the territory, especially going down the Rhine River, where the 7th Armored Division had fought during World War II.

He has been married 45 years, has two children, Tom Ring of Glendale, Arizona and LeEtta Bartlett of Houston, Texas. Two grandchildren, Julie and Matthew Ring.

## EARL D. ROTHERHAM

Born October 11, 1915, in New Orleans, Louisiana. Entered the Army on February 5, 1942, at Camp Beauregard, Louisiana and was sent to 3rd Armored Division at Camp Polk, Louisiana for basic training. Later assigned to HQ 489th Armored Field Artillery Battalion of the 7th Armored Division. Spent five months on maneuvers in the California desert. Also given advanced training at Ft. Benning, Georgia before being sent

James H. Riddle

Barron C. Riley

Earl D. Rotherham

overseas. Embarked for Europe from Boston, Massachusetts, February, 1944 aboard HMS Queen Mary and arrived Glasgow, Scotland. Then went to England. Departed Southampton, England for France aboard an LST. Landed on Utah Beach June 7, 1944. Engaged in battles and campaigns of Northern France, Ardennes-Alsace, Rhineland and Central Europe. Wounded in Battle of the Bulge and on January 1, 1945 was awarded the Purple Heart. Remained with the "Lucky Seventh" (from the beaches to the Baltic) until the end of the war in Europe. Departed France aboard HMS Queen Elizabeth for the U.S.

Arrived Camp Kilmer, New York, September 15, 1945 and discharged at Camp Shelby, Mississippi, September 28, 1945. Returned to railroad employment until his retirement. Was married and had two children and four grandchildren. Lived in Chalmette, Louisiana until his death in December, 1985.

## EDMUND R. RUSCHKEWICZ

Born May 5, 1918 in Ludington, Michigan. He was inducted on June 12, 1941, at Ft. Custer, Battle Creek, Michigan. Took basic training at Ft. Custer and later transferred to Camp Polk, Louisiana. Was assigned to Company B, 83rd Reconnaissance Battalion, 3rd Armored Division. After maneuvers in Louisiana, entered the newly formed 87th Cavalry Reconnaissance Battalion of the 7th Armored Division. From there he went on maneuvers in the California desert and was given nine months advance training at Ft. Benning, Georgia before being sent overseas. He left Ft. Benning in April, 1944 in France. He was engaged in battles at Northern France, Ardennes, Rhineland and Central Europe. After the war, he received orders to go to Berlin to report to the USA motor pool. After seven months in Berlin, returned to the States, arriving November 26, 1945. Was discharged from Indiantown Gap, Pennsylvania as a Staff Sergeant.

He returned to Ludington, Michigan and started work February 14, 1946 for the C&O-B&O railroad in the mechanical department, retiring June, 1984. He is married and has two sons and daughter-in-laws and six grandchildren.

Edmund R. Ruschkewicz

## WALTER C. RYAN, JR.

Born, raised and educated in Detroit, Michigan. Inducted at Camp Custer, Michigan on February 3, 1942. Received basic training at Camp Polk, Louisiana with the 3rd Armored Division. Participated in maneuvers in Louisiana, California and Ft. Benning, Georgia. After the reorganization at Ft. Benning, Georgia, Co. H., 31st Armored Regiment became Co. B, 17th Tank Battalion, 7th Armored Division.

Walter C. Ryan, Jr.

Boarded the Queen Mary on June 6, 1944 and sailed the next day for Scotland. After debarkation, travelled by rail to Tidworth Barracks, near Salisbury, England. Two months later, left for France via LST and landed on Omaha Beach about August 11, 1944.

Was promoted from Cpl. Gunner to Sgt. in November, 1944. First action as a Tank Commander was in the Ardennes in December, 1944. Walked across the Rhine River on a "Baily" Bridge at Remagen, then on through the Ruhr Pocket and up to the Baltic Sea.

Married Fay Spitz in 1974, has a son Wally and a daughter Nancy by a previous marriage, a step-daughter Susan and five grandchildren. Retired from U.S. Immigration Service in October, 1982 as a Supervising Inspector. Lives with wife in Port Charlotte, Florida and has been a member of the 7th Armored Division Association since 1949 and has attended 37 of the 40 annual reunions.

## JOSEPH SAFER

1936: Graduated University of Florida; commissioned 2nd Lt., Artillery, USAR. 1941: Called to active duty 14th FA Bn., 2nd Armored Division. Cadred to 3rd Armored Division at Camp Polk. Married to former Loretto Ludlam two weeks after Pearl Harbor.

Joseph Safer

Detailed with American Tank Detachment (Egypt/Lybia). Upon return from Middle East, transferred to 8th Armored Division at Ft. Knox, and then to Artillery School (Department of Tactics). Joined 7th Armored Division at Ft. Benning, in April, 1944. Served throughout Europe, first as Div Arty S3, later as Div Arty Executive. Volunteered, with Lt. Gene Sheehan, to serve with division against Japan. Depressed as we watched thousands (from division and others) pass through on way home. After Japan's surrender, returned to US where, due to certain family complications, he got out of active Army.

Recalled in Korean conflict, stayed in Army until retirement. Post WWII service highlights: Instructor Artillery School, 8th Army (Korea), AFFE/8th Army (Japan).

Attended California State University at Fresno receiving MBA required for next occupation — Junior College Instructor. Instructed at Fresno City College until 1985 retirement. Reside in Fresno. Enjoying retirement with wife and doing some travelling. Both very active, and hope to remain so.

## WARREN L. SCHOECK

Born in Waterbury, Connecticut and graduated from Leavenworth High School in 1933. Inducted on February 11, 1942, and sent to Camp Polk in Louisiana where served with the 3rd Armored Division until the 7th Armored was formed. Stayed with Service Co of the 7th Tank Bn to the end of the war. Was

Warren L. Schoeck

assigned to be a truck driver and then the wrecker driver. Discharged from Camp Chaffee, Arkansas on October 15, 1945.

After the service, became and asphalt paving contractor until his retirement in 1985.

## ROBERT J. SCHULZ, JR.

Born April 1, 1920. Raised in Trenton, New Jersey. Inducted on March 12, 1942, at Ft. Dix, New Jersey. Sent to 3rd Armored Division at Camp Polk, Louisiana for basic training. Completed radio operators course at Polk and was promoted to PFC. Became part of cadre forming the 7th Armored Division. Assigned to 31st Regiment, Maintenance Co. Assigned the duties of Regimental Maintenance Clerk. After completion of desert training, was shipped to Ft. Benning, Georgia and assigned to Service Co, 31st Tank Bn. Went to Ft. Knox, Kentucky for 14 week radio repair course. Upon completion, was promoted to Technician 4th, the rank held until discharge. Fought with CCB in Europe under the command of Lt. Col. Earlenbush. Participated in all four campaigns with the 7th Armored Division. After surrender of Germany, was sent to Rheims Replacement Depot for reassignment to CBI. The Pacific war ended prior to his reassignment. Discharged at Ft. Monmouth, New Jersey on December 14, 1945.

Entered civilian serive at Ft. Dix, New Jersey with post engineers and later transferred to the Naval Air Turbine Test Station in Trenton, New Jersey. Retired from civilian service June 30, 1972. Is married and has three children and seven grandchildren.

## WALTER SHUSTER

Born June 7, 1919, Shelton, Connecticut. Entered service February 2, 1942 (followed later by three brothers and a sister.) Was on cadre forming 7th Armored at Camp Polk, Louisiana. Stayed with the Division, as a Corporal, in the 77th Armored Battalion Medics until the Victory Ship brought us home. Worst experience: an incredibly black night, on a smokey Moselle River hill, trying to get an ambulance load of wounded down to the pontoon bridges, through a minefield path that no longer could be seen because of the smokescreen and the darkest of night. Quite a story. Close call when shrapnel fused the driver's door shut on the ambulance from a close hit near Metz while checking mines near rear wheels. Coldest at St. Vith, taking a litter squad between lines (dressed in O.D.'s) to pick up treeburst victims in the snow while Germans and G.I.'s in white camouflage suits watched us with our little Red Cross brassards walk between the lines of foxholes.

Walter Shuster

Usually in charge of ambulance squad, hospital tent and latrine erection, corporal of the guard, also company barber. Discharged, Ft. Devens, Massachusetts, October 14, 1945 — 30 pounds skinnier.

Took tool and diemaking under the G.I. Bill. Married Ruth C. Hinman on furlough December 12, 1942. Has five children: Daniel, Donald, Cynthia, Vernon, and Patricia, and has five grandchildren to date. His wife died of cancer in 1970. Still working, at 67, toward a future retirement.

## JAMES D. SKROUPA

Born August 2, 1925. Raised in Apollo and Jeannette, Pennsylvania. Graduated

James D. Skroupa

from Jeannette High School in 1943 and entered the service. Trained at Camp Blanding, Florida, and additional training in Camp Rucker, Alabama and Ft. Meade, Maryland. Joined C Co, 48th Armored Infantry Battalion in France.

At Meijel, Holland on the morning of October 29, 1944, was captured by elements of the 9th and the 15th Panzer Grenadier Divisions. They held their position as ordered for three days despite the lack of artillery, air or tank support. After capture, moved through northern Germany from Dusseldorf to Berlin. Survived forced marches, locked in box cars for days, strafed and bombed by allied planes, and forced to work on the bombed railway. While working near Berlin was liberated by the Russians and fought together with front line troops back to the allied lines on May 10, 1945. The Hell Boxcar rides and Hell Marches were over.

Returned to civilian life and received a Bachelor of Science in Engineering and also obtained a registered professional engineering license from the state of Maryland. He and wife, Margarete have two sons, James and Mark.

## THOMAS P. SNELLINGS

Born November 6, 1922, in Richmond, Virginia. Graduated from Chester High School, Chester, Virginia, in

Thomas P. Snellings

Robert J. Schulz, Jr.

1941. On October 8, 1942, was inducted into the Air Force. Took basic training at Duncan Field, San Antonio (now Lackland Air Force Base). Went to two administration schools and was assigned to the 34th Bomb Group a month before going to England on April 13, 1944. Left the Air Force January 15, 1945 for the Infantry. After advanced combat training at Tidworth Barracks, was assigned to the 23 AIB Co A, Jan's squad, last of February, 1945. The division was at that time in the Ruhr area. Came home with the 7th Armored Division and was discharged from the service on October 17, 1945.

Worked for an RCA distributor for about six years, then went with a maintenance chemical company for a few years. After that he went to a sales representative job with a chemical company from Chesapeake, Virginia. Retired in September, 1983.

## ANTHONY S. SNIPAS

Enlisted in the Army March 7, 1942. Sent to Camp Polk, Louisiana for basic training in Co. C, 36 Armored Infantry, 3rd Armored Division. Sent to Ft. Knox, Kentucky to Wheeled Vehicle School in May. Promoted to T/5 mechanic in July and served as mechanic in Motor Pool, Co C, 48th Armored Infantry, 7th Armored Division. Received T/4 rating in Holland, September, 1944. Hospitalized October, 1944 to January, 1945, 4106 U.S. Army Hospital, Bristol, England. Many men were from Co. C at this hospital, wounded near Metz. Assigned to 210 Ordnance MAM Co. from January to May, 1945. Rehospitalized another month. Assigned to Co. E, 346 Engineers, G.S. Regiment. Became Motor Sgt. of Motor Pool. Discharged December 12, 1945.

Anthony S. Snipas

Married Frances La Conic (Co. C maintenance vehicle was named after her). Has four children and six grandchildren. Frances passed away after 40 years of happy married life.

Returned to old job in refrigeration field, became foreman. Applied for position with Tobyhanna Army Depot, Pennsylvania in 1956. Worked until retired with disability in 1976. Attained position of Supervisor. At present, his health isn't too bad. Can no longer hear and wears hearing aid.

## MORRIS E. SORENSON

Born in Ephraim, Utah on June 13, 1913, graduated from Ehpraim High School, Snow College and then served as a missionary for the LSS Church in Sweden 1934-37. Received B.S. degree from BYU in 1939 and a Master's Degree from the University of Utah in 1940 and was elected to Phi Kappa Phi. Employed by the US Department of Justice. Took military leave and enlisted in the Army for one year. Commissioned as a 2nd Lt. at Ft. Benning and assigned to the newly activated Seventh Armored Division at Camp Polk, Louisiana. Served in Hqs 48th A.I. Regt., 39th A.I. Bn., Ass't Div G-2, S-2 CCA and finally G-2 until the Division was deactivated. Assigned to the Office of Military Government in Germany for two years and then transferred to the Staff and Faculty at Ft. Benning, Georgia. Graduated from the Command and General College at Ft. Leavenworth in 1949; assigned to Staff and Faculty at Ft. Knox.

Morris E. Sorenson

In the Korean conflict was a member of Special Intelligence Branch on General MacArthur's staff and later was sent to Korea as a member of the UN Truce Delegation. For his work with the UN Truce Delegation, was given a special citation and promotion to Lt. Col. Subsequently served as ExO, CCA, 1st Armored Division at Ft. Hood and later assignments included Staff and Faculty at Marine Corps Schools, Army Intelligence School, Oberammergau, Germany and Logistic Services at Mannheim. Retired from the army at Ft. Irwin, California while serving as Headquarters Commandant and CO of Special Troops.

Received further graduate training at the University of Utah and thereafter worked for the Utah State Office of Education as an Administrator for 19 years. Since retirement from the latter position, has travelled extensively in Europe and South America. He is a charter member of Utah Friendship Force and has participated in group exchanges with Venezuela, Berlin and Brazil. Life member of Retired Officers Association and Sons of the Utah Pioneers; Program Chairman and President-elect of Ephraim Rotary Club. Active in church and civic affairs; special interests include hunting, fishing, photography and travel. He is married to Lucile Armstrong and they have three daughters, three sons, 12 grandchildren and six great grandchildren.

## ALBERT SPINAZZOLA

The dashing young G.I. has lost some of his wavy hair and added some weight. The awkward teenager has become a handsome woman and mother. He met Alberte (Betty) Freymann in the village of Theux, Belgium in the home of her parents. He found warmth, friendship and a place to rest before moving on to continue battle into Germany with the 31st Tank Bn.

Betty Freymann and Albert Spinazzola

Many years later, after settling in Columbus, Ohio, he saw a story in the WORKSHOP NEWS that a plaque honoring the division had been hung in the city of Spa. The story mentioned an Alex Freymann as the First Alderman of Spa. He wrote to the mayor of Spa to see if Alex was related to the Freymanns he had known during the war. Answer came from Betty, now Mrs. Roland Bergers of Liege. Her brother Alex was the First Alderman of Spa, but had died in 1972. Her parents had died in 1968. Betty and her two sisters were alive and all lived in Belgium.

Albert and his wife returned to Belgium in 1976 and were greeted by the three sisters and their families as well as Alex's widow and children. Their friendship continues.

## HERMAN M. (SZCZEPANIAK) STEVENSON, SR.

Born November 18, 1923 in Baltimore, Maryland. Graduated from St. Stanislaus and Maryland Institute of Mechanical Arts. Inducted into the army March, 1944, Ft. George G. Meade, Maryland under the Polish name Szczepaniak. Basic training, Camp Blanding, Florida, 17 weeks in Heavy Weapons, sent to P.O.E. New York, thence over-

Herman M. (Szczepaniak) Stevenson, Sr.

seas to a replacement depot in Europe. Assigned to Troop B, 87th Recon. Squadron, 7th Armored Division as a scout and machine-gunner in northern France. Engaged in the Battle of the Bulge at St. Vith, Belgium, wounded and captured in December. Imprisoned and marched to various camps and stalags in Gerolstein, Ulm, Limburg 12A, XIB in Fallingbostel, Germany for five months. Liberated and hospitalized from Frankfurt, Germany to the 91st General Hospital, England. Returned to the States at Newport News, Virginia. Discharged at Ft. George Meade, Maryland, December, 1945.

Surname changed by court order for sake of children's schooling. Currently employed as acting supervisor, Baltimore City Government Mechanical Shop Division. Happily married over 40 years, has a lovely daughters, two sons, grandfather of five grandchildren. Member of the Maryland Ex-POW's and also the 7th Armored Division organizations.

## JOSEPH STRAVITSCH

Born in Brooklyn, New York, March 15, 1918 and educated in N.Y.C. school system. In 1935, joined the N.Y. National Guard, Co. C, 106th Inf. Reg., 27th Div. and spent the summers camping at Camp Smith, N.Y. July, 1935, was spent with the CMTC at Camp Dix, N.J. (now Ft. Dix). 1942 to 1945 the U.S. Army occupied his time. Inducted at Ft. Jay, Governors Island, N.Y., then on to Camp Upton, N.Y. Basic training at Ft. Knox, Kentucky and then assigned to 7th Armored Division, Camp Polk, Louisiana, Hq. Co. 40th Tank Reg. Participated in Texas-Louisiana maneuvers in the

Joseph Stravitsch

fall of 1942 and then the 1943 Desert maneuvers at Camp Coxcomb, Mojave Desert, California. Reorganized at Ft. Benning, Georgia and assigned to Hq. Co., 40th Tank Bn. Camp Miles Standish, Camp Shanks and then aboard the Queen Mary to Scotland. On to Tidworth Barracks, south to Southampton, loaded on LST and sailed to Omaha Beach. Joined Patton's 3rd Army in the race through France (Chartres, Chateau Thiery, Verdun and Metz). Moved north through Belgium, Luxembourg to Weert and Overloon, Holland. December 16, 1944 found them at St. Vith in the Battle of the Bulge. Crossed the Rhine at Remagan Bridge, through the heartland of Germany to shake hands with the Russians at the Baltic Sea. Received 4 battle stars, the Belgium Fourragere and the Bronze star for Heroic Service. After VE Day, was reassigned to the 40th Amph. Tractor Bn. and trained in the North Sea for the invasion of Japan. VJ Day ended our training. Returned home on the SS "SOB" — this must have been the name of the ship because everyone said "When is the 'SOB' going to stop rocking?" etc. Landed at Boston, Camp Miles Standish, then went to Camp Dix, N.J. Separated from service November 24, 1945. Fondest memory was at the liberation of a POW Camp in Germany. A British soldier came over with tears in his eye, shook my hand and said, "Thanks, Yank, it's been a long time."

Employed by Con Edison in 1937 and retired in 1979 as Superintendent after 42 years of service. Received a degree from State University of N.Y. He and Clara married in 1941 and have always enjoyed traveling through the years they've seen most of the beautiful sights in 50 states, visited over 50 countries. After retirement, moved to Dunedin, Florida and acquired a motor home. Family consists of a son in Texas and a daughter in New Jersey and six grandchildren. Thankful for good health and a very interesting life.

## JOHN STRINCOSKY

Born on June 26, 1917, and attended Rivesville High School, West Virginia. Married Sara Louise Candid, 1939. She passed away on December 3, 1986. He is the father of one daughter, Mrs. Norman (Rosalind) Clinton, and the grandfather of two girls, Denise Marie Minger and Norma Jean Clinton.

Joined the Army in 1942 with the 13th Armored Division and was sent overseas as a replacement with the B-87 7th Armored Division in April, 1944. Was captured by the Germans in the Battle of the Bulge on December 22, 1944 and released in April 1945.

He returned to work for Bethlehem Steel as a machine operator, and after 43 and ¾ years, retired in 1979. His hobbies

John Strincosky

are fishing, hunting, reading and chores around the house.

He is a member of the Immaculate Conception Church, a life member of the Veterans of Foreign Wars Post 7048, a life member of the Seventh Armored Division, a life member of the Ex-POW's, a member of the American Legion, and a member of UMWA Local 4071.

## ALFRED I. STROBEL

Born in Middleville, New York. Entered the Army in February, 1942, at Ft. Niagara, New York. Being a cold winter day, he welcomed the news that he would be sent to Camp Polk, Louisiana where he received basic training with the 32nd Recon. of the 3rd Armored Division. When the 7th Armored Division was formed, he joined the 31st Arm. Reg. Band under M/S Joe Strong. He's glad he didn't miss that part of his life. Sailed from New York aboard the Queen Mary on June 6, 1944, D-Day.

Alfred I. Strobel

He remained with the band until the end of the war serving with Division Trains throughout the four campaigns in Europe, guarding prisoners, handling ammo and supplies and also M.P. traffic duty. He also had the privilege of playing with the 7th Armored Division Orchestra under S/Sgt. Depasquale from Ft. Benning until the War's end. Eventually, he was transferred to the 2nd Armored Division, serving in Berlin as Security Guard during the Potsdam Conference, seeing Truman, Churchill and Stalin on a number of occasions.

Returning to the U.S. aboard the A.P. Hill from Antwerp in 1945, he was discharged from Ft. Dix in December, 1945.

He returned to his hometown where he has been ever since. He married a cute little gal in 1944 and has two sons and one daughter and three grandchildren. Retired from the Remington Arms Co. in 1982. They attended his first reunion with the 7th Armored Division on their big 40th in Harrisburg. A wonderful experience!

## LEONARD I. SUDENFIELD

Born May 26, 1925, in Boston, Massachusetts. Inducted August 18, 1943, at Ft. Devens, Massachusetts. Received basic training at Ft. McClellan Alabama Infantry Training Center. Joined B Co. 38th Armored Infantry Battalion at Ft. Benning, Georgia and went overseas on the Queen Mary in June, 1944.

Leonard I. Sudenfield

Participated in the battles of France, Belgium, and Holland. Was wounded in France and spent some time in the 91st General Hospital in Oxford, England. Returned to the United States with the 9th Air Force in November, 1945. At the end of November, 1945, was discharged with the Purple Heart, Bronze Star, and Combat Infantryman's Badge. Is life member of the Seventh Armored Division Association the Order of the Purple Heart, and the DAV.

For the past 37 years, has been doing research and teaching at Massachusetts Institute of Technology.

## PETER F. SUNICH

Born in the upper peninsula of Calumet, Michigan. This area was known as the world's greatest copper mining town. After the Depression of 1933, he moved to Detroit and was employed at the General Motors Chevrolet Division. When he was inducted into the service, he had

Peter F. Sunich

his basic training at Camp Polk, Louisiana, with the 3rd Armored Division. When the 7th was formed, he was transferred into what was later known as the "Lucky Seventy." His service time with Troop A, 87th Recon covered areas in France, Holland, Belgium and Germany. They were in four major campaigns and he was awarded the Bronze Star. Upon his return, he went back to work for General Motors Corporation and retired in 1975. He now resides in Sterling Heights, Michigan.

## DENVER P. SUTHERLAND

Born June 4, 1919, near Nora Virginia. Inducted into the Army March 7, 1942 at Camp Lee, Virginia. Went immediately to Camp Polk, Louisiana and basic training with the 3rd Armored Division. When the 7th was activated, he became a member of Troop B, 87th Rcn. and remained there until after the war ended in Europe. Served as an armored car driver throughout the campaign. Drove the CO after the Battle of the Bulge and was driving for Bill Knowlton on the mission to contact the Russians.

Denver P. Sutherland

Probably the most memorable incident would be the jubilant French people as their towns would be liberated and the near the end of the war, the jubilant American prisoners of war as prison camps were overrun.

Married and has a daughter and two grandchildren, Gredel and Cassa Baker.

## STAN SZUDAREK

Born January 2, 1920 in Cleveland, Ohio. Interested in baseball in his youth; played sandlot ball in Class A. Got into professional ball in 1941 for the West Palm Beach Indians. Got drafted February 3, 1942 and went to Camp Polk, Louisiana with the 3rd Armored Division. After training was put on cadre for the 7th Armored Division, Co C, 23rd Armored Infantry Bn. Got involved playing ball with the division team. He was the only non-com on the team and was the regular catcher. Went on Louisiana maneuvers then to New York and then on the Queen Mary overseas. When retaking St. Vith under Gen. Patton, was wounded in left knee, January 22, 1945, putting the end to his baseball career. Discharged from hospital February 13, 1946.

Stan Szudarek

Worked for Mobil Oil Company for 38 years and retired in 1978. Left knee joint removed at V.A. hospital and now has a plaster knee joint. Married in 1947 to Jean Gos and has three sons and five grandsons.

## GEORGE K. TANHAM

After leaving the Army in March, 1946, he went to graduate school at Stanford University. A year and a half later he became an instructor at the California Institute of Technology and did not finish his PhD until 1951. He taught, among other things, a course in military history, and was Master of Student Houses, that is, in charge of all the men's dormitories — great fun. In 1955 he joined the Rand Corporation as a researcher, became

Deputy Vice President in 1960, and Vice President and Trustee of the Rand Corporation in 1970. Twice during that period he left Rand for government service, a tour with AID as Associate Director of USOM in Saigon, and from 1968 to 1970 as Special Assistant to the U.S. Ambassador to Thailand for Counter-Insurgency, holding the rank of Minister. In 1982, he retired from Rand but has remained active in research for Rand and some other companies in the Washington area. He has traveled many times to Southeast Asia and Europe and occasionally in the Middle East. He has published four books and numerous articles, most of them on counter-insurgency in Southeast Asia.

He has a farm in the Shenandoah Valley in Virginia which is a real joy, and hopes to spend more time there in the future. He has served on the Board of Trustees of schools and on the boards of a couple of corporations. He has spent lots of time traveling, researching, and most happily, on his farm and garden. He is separated from his wife, but has seven wonderful children and seven grandchildren.

## EDWARD O. TAYLOR

Montclair, New Jersey was his birthplace in the year 1918. He attended the Montclair Public Schools and Trenton, (N.J.) State College. He graduated in 1940 as an industrial arts teacher. Taught in Camden, New Jersey for one year and received his "Greetings." Sent to Camp Polk in the 3rd Armored Division for basic training. Was selected for the cadre which formed the 7th Armored Division. Louisiana maneuvers were followed by a stay at Camp Coxcomb, California. This was followed by a move to Ft. Benning which was in turn followed by a move to Camp Shanks, New York. On D-Day, they sailed on the Queen Mary to Grenoch, Scotland and from there to Tidworth Barracks. They crossed the English Channel and landed at Omaha Beach. From there he travelled across France, Holland, Belgium, and Germany. Served as a chief computer in the fire direction center of the 434 with the rank of Staff Sergeant. Was separated from the 434th at Mudau, Germany, having acquired sufficient points to be sent home for discharge.

Was discharged at Ft. Dix on November 1, 1945. He and Kay were married soon thereafter. Returned to teaching and taught for 37 years in various school systems in New Jersey. The last 17 years were at Hawthorne, New Jersey where he retired in 1982.

Edward O. Taylor

## HENRY R. TAYLOR

Joined the 7th Armored Division at Ft. Benning, Georgia, Went with the 7th from Georgia to Overloon, Holland, where he was wounded seriously. Stayed in hospitals for nine months before he was discharged.

Henry R. Taylor

## JAMES E. "ED" THOMPSON

His association with the 7th Armored Division began as one of many urgently needed replacements during the Battle of the Bulge.

James E. "Ed" Thompson

Born May 25, 1921, in Lineville, Alabama and was inducted in the service in June 1944. After basic training was completed at Camp Wheeler, Georgia, he was shipped overseas on the Dutch ship "Volendam" and traveled across France and into Belgium in a "40 & 8" boxcar. Was assigned to HQ/38th located near Verviers, Belgium on January 1, 1945. Played a small role in recapturing the territory around St. Vith during one of the coldest winters in Europe in 50 years. Experienced some of his closest calls in this area, along with frost-bitten feet. Alternating between combat zones and rest areas, they pushed their way to the Rhine, across Central Germany, the Ruhr Pocket and north to the Baltic. He was fortunate in surviving those war experiences without injury. So many were not. At the close of the war, he was stationed in Schroenburg, then Dessau on the Elbe and next in Leibenstadt. In August, 1945, he became Battalion Communications Chief in Sennfeld. When the 7th Armored Division returned to the States, transferred to the 14th A.I.B. of the 1st Armored Division and shipped home in March, 1946.

Retired January 1, 1983 as District Marketing Supervisor for Alabama Power Company after 43 years of service. He and wife of 45 years, Tommie, reside in Jasper, Alabama. They have one daughter, Carol Savage, and two grandchildren, Wesley and Mary Ben, both enrolled in Auburn University. In 1985 he completed a journal of his army days as a legacy for his family.

## GEORGE K. THORNHILL

Born November 16, 1918 and raised in Rossburg, Ohio. Inducted February 9, 1942, Ft. Campbell, Kentucky. Basic training at Camp Polk, Louisiana. Received wheel vehicle and tank mechanic training at Ft. Knox, Kentucky in 1942 and 1943. Sailed on the Queen Mary June 7, 1944 and arrived at Glasgow, Scotland, June 13, 1944 then to England and on to Omaha Beach, arriving on August 13, 1944. Went with Patton's army up through France. Knew his brother, Nelson, was somewhere in Verdun, France. They were reunited and spent the afternoon drinking Cognac and trying to repair a German Tiger tank. Injured in Holland, October 24, 1944 and was transferred to four overseas hospitals. Had bone graft on left femur in March, 1945, at Crile General Hospital, Cleveland, Ohio. Was discharged on his birthday, November 16, 1945.

George K. Thornhill

Returned to Rossburg and is engaged in farming and supervision at a small hometown manufacturing plant. He and his wife, Mary, have five children and nine grandsons, the latest of which is named after his Granddad.

## JAMES TOTONI

Born August 3, 1921, in Chicago, Illinois. Married July 5, 1942 and inducted into the Army November 1, 1942 at Camp Grant, Illinois. Sent to Camp Polk, Louisiana, where he joined the 7th Armored, Hq 38th as machine gunner. Went to California for maneuvers then to Swainsboro, Georgia to guard German prisoners. From there went to Ft. Benning for further training. Shipped overseas on the Queen Mary on June 5, 1944, arriving in England June 4, 1944.

James Totoni

Wounded in Selignia, and after spending one month in the field hospital, rejoined Hq 38th in Holland. Was captured by the Germans, December 23, 1944 at St. Vith. Marched all through Germany as a P.O.W. and was liberated by the Americans near Lubeck on April 12, 1945. Arrived in the States May 15, 1945, and was discharged from the service on October 13, 1945 at Ft. Wadsworth, New York.

Owned and operated a truck stop, "Fanny and Jim's," with his mother-in-law from 1946 to 1966. He then went to work for his father's trucking company, "Nick Totoni & Sons" where he still is employed. Lives in Chicago, still married and has three daughters and nine grandchildren.

## JACK TRAMBLEY

Born August 23, 1919 in Duluth, Minnesota. He graduated from high school in 1938 and attended the University of Minnesota. Moved to California in 1941 and entered the University of California, Berkeley. He enlisted in the service February 13, 1941 at San Leandro, California and was sent to Ft. Snelling, Minnesota, then to Ft. Sill, Oklahoma Administration School. After completion, was sent to Camp Polk, Louisiana as part of the cadre to form the 814th TD Bn. Served as HQ. Co. Supply Sergeant. The battalion was shipped to Birmingham, England, then to the Portsmouth area assisting in the operation of the invasion camps. After landing in Normandy, they were later attached to the 7th Armored Division. He remained with the 7th and the 814th for the duration, returned to the states, was discharged at Camp Beale AFB, California, November 24, 1945.

He returned to school, later worked as an accountant then an electrician. In 1951, he joined the Coca-Cola Bottling Company of California as a route salesman and retired as District Manager after 31 years of service. Today, he enjoys his retirement as a wholesale distributor of sporting goods, an interesting and enjoyable business. He is married with four children and five grandchildren.

Jack Trambley

## DANIEL J. WALKER, JR.

Born November 27, 1915 in Scotland County, North Carolina. Graduated from University of North Carolina, A.B., 1936, Law, J.D., 1948. Entered Army, February, 1942, Ft. Jackson, South Carolina; thence to Camp Chaffee, Arkansas, Sixth Armored Division, October 1942 to Ft. Knox, Kentucky, O.C.S., graduated as 2nd Lt., February 1943, them to Service Co 40th Tank Bn, Camp Polk, Louisiana, remaining in that company until the end of the war.

Daniel J. Walker, Jr.

Participated in campaigns of Northern France, Ardennes, Rhineland and Central Europe. During that time promoted to 1st Lt. and awarded the Bronze Star. At the end of the war, along with much personnel of the 40th Tank Bn, transferred to the 40th Amphibious Tractor Bn and moved to the Scheldt Estuary in Holland to train for landings in the Pacific. Became Co Commander of the Headquarters and service Co of that battalion. Separated from service at Ft. Bragg, North Carolina in December, 1945, receiving promotion to Captain then.

Practiced law in Burlington and Graham, North Carolina, since 1948. Held several public offices including Clerk of the Superior Court, County Attorney and County Manager. Married to the former Sarah Nicholson in 1941. Presently partner, Allen and Walker, Burlington. Presbyterian elder; Kiwanian past president, Burlington Club. Home, Graham, North Carolina.

## J. MITCHELL WELLS

Born May 1, 1920 in Morgan County, Kentucky, 90 miles southeast of Lexington, Kentucky. Went to school at Cannel City, Kentucky. Entered the Army in May of 1942. Had basic training in Camp Croft, South Carolina, before joining Hq. Co. 129th Ord. 7th Armored Division in Camp Polk, Louisiana. Was sent to school at Ft. Knox, Kentucky after maneuvers in Louisiana. After school, joined his outfit in Camp Coxcomb, California. After desert training, went to Ft. Benning, Georgia. Was married in February of 1943 while in school at Ft. Knox, Kentucky. During time spent overseas was a driver for Lt. Col. George E. Hughes and did messenger work. Was with the 129th Ord. until after the war and then was transferred to the 5th Armored Division to return to the United States. Was discharged October, 1945.

J. Mitchell Wells

In November, started driving a tanker for Ashland Oil Inc. Worked at this for 32 years. Then in 1980, had to take a disability retirement. Over the years he and his first wife had three daughters. In 1977, she died of cancer. He married again to Frankie Frazier and they with their daughter Lori, moved to Okeechobee, Florida. His wife and he do a lot of fishing on Lake Okeechobee.

## WESLEY H. WERTH

Born April 3, 1923, near Minden, Nebraska and lived there for 18 years. Worked in Lincoln, Nebraska until inducted into the Army in September, 1943. Basic training at Camp Fannin, Texas; joined Co A. 23 Armored Infantry, 7th Armored Division at Ft. Benning. Sailed to England on the Queen

Wesley H. Werth

Mary. Trained at Tidworth Barracks before the Normandy Landing.

With General Patton's 3rd Army, moved through La Haye du Puits, Coutances, Avranches, Lavel, LeMans. Entered combat near Chartes. Went through Dreux. Continued through Melun and Nagis. Wounded near Provins, when a 75mm anti-tank shell hit his half-track. Taken to Orleans to a MASH type unit, then to Braintree, England to a hospital for recovery. Five months later returned to Compiegne, France on limited duty until after VE Day.

Returned to USA, August, 1945, to Army Hospital, Okmulgee, Oklahoma, where he met his wife, Roberta. Received medical discharge, December 1945, Camp Carson, Colorado. Returned to work, Lincoln, Nebraska and in September, 1946, enrolled in Oklahoma State University. Received an engineering degree in 1950. Joined the Boeing Company in Wichita, Kansas and have been employed there for 36 and ½ years. They have three children and five grandchildren. He has been a member of the American Legion since 1947.

## OSCAR R. "WACKEY" WICKIZER, JR.

Born September 7, 1920, in Valparaiso, Indiana and graduated from Valparaiso High School. Enlisted in the Army on March 30, 1942 at Ft. Benjamin Harrison, Indiana and was sent to Ft. Knox, Kentucky for basic training, then to Camp Polk Louisiana, to join the 7th Armored Division for advanced training. From there, he went to maneuvers in the California desert and then to Ft. Ben-

ning, Georgia. Sent overseas and landed on Omaha Beach. Was a half track driver and was engaged in battles and campaigns in Northern France, the Ardennes, Rhineland, and Central Europe. Finished the War at the Baltic Sea and returned to the United States and was discharged at Camp Ataberry, Indiana on December 2, 1945.

Retired from Carlton Caterpillar Company in September, 1985. He and his wife Mae have one son and two grandchildren.

## JOSEPH J. WILHELM

Born and raised in St. Marys, Pennsylvania and has made his home there. Was employed at the Stackpole Corporation for 47 and ½ years until his retirement in 1980. Enjoys reading World War II books. Is married to the former Leanna Hess, and is the father of five children: Joseph H., Donald, Barbara, Debra and a son Gary deceased in infancy. He is also the proud grandfather of five grandchildren.

Joseph J. Wilhelm

## DALE WILLIAMS

Born in Hamilton County in southern Illinois October 28, 1918. Married in 1941 and was drafted into the Army in January, 1942 at Camp Grant, Illinois. Arrived in Camp Polk, February 1st. Took basic training with E Co of the 36th Infantry Regiment of the 3rd Armored Division. Transferred to D Co of the 48th Infantry Regiment of the 7th Armored Division, and later to the 23rd Infantry Battalion of the 7th.

Dale Williams

Had training at Camp Polk, Louisiana, Camp Coxcomb, California and Ft. Benning, Georgia. Left the states from Camp Shanks on the Queen Mary and landed in Glasgow, Scotland. Left England for the beachhead at Omaha Beach.

Back to the states to Camp Sheridan Illinois and discharged October 24, 1945. Worked as a truck driver until 1965 and was employed with civil service in the Transportation Department. Was forced to retire in 1980 by a heart attack. Moved to the Ozark Mountains in Arkansas where he is enjoying the good weather and mild winters.

## CECIL G. WILSON

Served with the 7th Armored, 48th Infantry. Three major operations in Battle of St. Vith, Belgium and European section. Crossed the Rhine between Coholan, Germany to the Baltic Sea.

Cecil G. Wilson

## CHARLES C. WILSON

Charles C. Wilson

Oscar R. "Wackey" Wickizer, Jr.

## RAYMOND J. "SQUEKY" WOLAN

Raymond J. "Squeky" Wolan

Born May 21, 1942 and raised in Chicago, Illinois. Entered the Army in October of 1942 and joined the 7th Armored Division at Camp Polk, Louisiana. Took basic training there with Co. I, 48th Armored Infantry Regiment. After basic, he remained with I Co and then went to California on desert maneuvers for five months. The regiment was then split up into battalions and he stayed with C-48. From there, he proceeded to Georgia to become a radio operator and held this position until they went to England. When they hit the beach in France, he became Communications Chief. Later, he became a jeep driver and a radio operator for Cpt. Forrester. He was with the 7th Armored until the Battle of the Bulge where he was wounded on December 2, 1944. Upon exiting the hospital in May, 1945, he rejoined the 7th Armored at the Elb River. Then, in mid-October, he was sent back to the U.S. and was then discharged.

Upon returning to Chicago, he resumed his job at Joanna Western Mills as a machine operator and then as a supervisor for the past 16 years. He retired in February, 1986, and now enjoys working and relaxing at his home in Lockport, Illinois.

## ROBERT MORSE WOOD

Born October 9, 1920. Graduated from the United States Military Academy in January 1943, and after attending the Engineer School at Ft. Belvoir, joined the 33 Armored Engineers. When the fighting ended in Europe he was transferred to the First Armored Division for eventual reassignment to the Orient but peace came before the reassignment. Next were assignments to 7th Army Headquarters, then 3rd Army Headquarters and, finally, the United States Constabulary. Returning to the United States, he was assigned to the New York

Robert Morse Wood

District Corps of Engineers working on construction projects in and around New York City. From there, he left the service.

After a position in finance with a utility holding company and a two year tour of duty back in the Army during the Korean War, he joined a New York Stock Exchange member firm and spent the rest of his career on Wall Street as an officer and partner in the investment banking and corporate finance division. Now retired from Wall Street, he has started a securities firm in Annapolis, Maryland and is now Chairman and Chief Executive Officer.

## WALTER B. WRIGHT

Drafted in the spring of '44 at the age of 30 after eight years of directing high school bands in Wisconsin. Completed basic, then shipped over to join the 7th Armored Division Band in Heerlen, Holland — just in time for the Battle of the Bulge. In a small detachment of the band, he went to Poteau with CCA where that combat command held until December 23rd when the withdrawal through Vielsalm took place.

Walter B. Wright

Rejoining the band in reserve near Spa, he looked for a few days of R & R at this great resort of European kings and aristocracy. Instead, he made the mistake of scratching his ear when the band's first sergeant asked who could drive a car. So they gave him a jeep and it was back into action as a liaison driver until V.E. Day. Since he was a replacement without enough points to go home. He had to stay over for another eight months and fight the "battles of Delitsch, Heidelberg and Bremerhaven."

Returned to direct high school bands in Wisconsin for a total of 42 years. Retired with Ruth at 124 Broadway, Sheboygan Falls, Wisconsin 53085. (Five daughters, seven grandchildren, two great grandsons) Write to me!

General Hasbrouck's farewell to the Seventh Armored Division.

The reprinting of Volume I and Volume II of <u>The Lucky Seventh</u> would not have been possible without the use of the original editions belonging to:

Donald William Ketchem

The 7th Armored Division Association would like to express their gratitude for his generous contribution to preserving the history of the division. The Association would also like to recognize his service to his country and the 7th Armored Division with the following biographical sketch.

Donald William Ketchem joined the U.S. Army at the end of March 1943. He trained at Fort Polk, LA for 14 months with 8th Armored Division. He was sent to the United Kingdom to join with the 7th Armored Division in September 1944. With the 7th Armored Division he assisted in the liberation of France. Upon conflict at Metz, he was seconded to C Company of the 23rd Armored Division Battalion of the 7th AD. Following combat in Holland, he served in the support in Operation Market Garden. At the start of the Battle of the Bulge, he and his men were rushed 60 miles overnight to St. Vith to engage in combat with Nazi German forces. He crossed the Rhine to the Baltic Sea. He served with the U.S. Army of Occupation and assisted with the hunt for Nazi-German war criminals. He is the recipient of the Combat Infantry Badge, the Presidential Unit Citation, the Bronze Star, the Good Conduct Medal, the American Campaign Medal, the European Theater of Operations Medal with 4 Battle Stars, the World War II Victory Medal and the U.S. Army of Occupation Medal. Later he served as President of the U.S. Army 7th Armored Division Association from 1997 through 1999. His family has been highly supportive of the association.

From left to right: General William A. Knowlton,
Colonel Neil Chapin, Staff Sergeant Donald W. Ketchem

www.ingramcontent.com/pod-product-compliance
Lightning Source LLC
Chambersburg PA
CBHW080545170426
43195CB00016B/2682